Freedom Summer

CARTER G. WOODSON INSTITUTE
SERIES IN BLACK STUDIES
Armstead L. Robinson, General Editor

Freedom Summer

SALLY BELFRAGE

With a Foreword by Robert P. Moses

University Press of Virginia
Charlottesville and London

THE UNIVERSITY PRESS OF VIRGINIA
Copyright © 1965 by Sally Belfrage

First published in 1965 by The Viking Press, Inc.
First University Press of Virginia printing 1990

The lines quoted on page 205 from *The Wild Palms* by William Faulkner are
used by permission of Random House, Inc. Copyright 1939 by William Faulkn

Quotations from various songs of the freedom movement are from *We Shall
Overcome*, compiled and edited by Guy and Candie Carawan. Copyright 1963
by Oak Publications, Inc. and used by their permission.

Library of Congress Cataloging-in-Publication Data

Belfrage, Sally
    Freedom summer / Sally Belfrage ; with a foreword by Robert P.
Moses.
        p.   cm.
    Reprint, with new foreword & pref. Originally published: New York
: Viking Press, 1965.
    Includes bibliographical references.
    ISBN 0-8139-1299-7 (pbk.)
    1. Afro-Americans—Civil rights—Mississippi.   2. Mississippi—
Race relations.   3. Belfrage, Sally.   4. Civil rights
workers—Mississippi—Biography.   5. Civil rights movements—
Mississippi—History—20th century.   I. Title.
E185.93.M6B4   1965b
305.896'0730762—dc20   90-12454
                                                           CIP

Printed in the United States of America

For my father and mother

Contents

Foreword

There is a lot of poetry in Sally's book.

Poetry about the volunteers and their arrival at orientation:

All one Sunday in June they arrived at the college in
Ohio.
And then they were sent singly down the hall to have
their picture taken—two poses each, holding numbers under their chins.
They formed in haphazard circles around the guitars
. . . as they sang the words they scarcely knew.

Then . . . a woman whose badge read "Mrs. Fannie
Lou Hamer" was suddenly leading them, molding
their noise into music.

Here was clearly someone with force enough for all
of them, who knew the meaning of "Oh Freedom"
and "We Shall Not Be Moved" in her flesh and spirit
as they never would.

Poetry about the volunteers' struggle with good and evil;
courage and fear; society and personal responsibility:

The music had begun—the music that . . . would
somehow have to come to mean enough to drive off
fear.

They had come from all ends of the country, having
developed in as many vacuums, and were astonished
to discover one another. . . , ludicrous in their unfashionable idealism. . . , complicated heroes who

could acknowledge the world's evil in themselves,
confront it, and speak the words that everyone else
was gagging on: "I am responsible."

Poetry about the black people of Mississippi all dressed in colors and in song.

Mrs. Hamer led the first chorus:

Go tell it on the mountain,
Over the hills and everywhere,
Go tell it on the mountain
To let my people go.

When the verses came, they clapped.

Who's that yonder dressed in black?
Let my people go.

Poetry about the heart of a SNCC worker:

A gaunt, fierce-eyed young man raised his hand and
was recognized. When he began to speak it was in
waves approaching hysteria. "It's hell in Mississippi!"
he said, his voice breaking. "And you've got to realize that nobody *cares*. We care. . . . They say that
democracy exists in America. But it's an idea. It
doesn't function. You have got to make it function in
Mississippi, so that it can function in the rest of the
country, and in the world."

Poetry about freedom and struggle, silence and song:

He finished, stood there, then walked out the door.
The silence which followed him was absolute. It
lasted a minute, two; no one moved. They knew,

now, what could not be applauded. Suddenly, a
beautiful voice from the back of the room pierced the
quiet.

They say that freedom is a constant struggle.
They say that freedom is a constant struggle.
They say that freedom is a constant struggle.
Oh, Lord, we've struggled so long,
We must be free, we must be free.

It was a new song to me and to the others. But I
knew it, and all the voices in the room joined in as
though the song came from the deepest part of themselves, and they had always known it.

Poetry about a young SNCC field secretary.

One day Samuel T. Mills came to the library. He said
he was eight, or nine, or seven, and he wrote his
name on everything. He didn't know his address or
what the "T" stood for, though the other children
called him just that. . . .

Samuel was smooth dark brown with skin the texture
of a plum and a stomach the shape of one when he
ate. . . . He wore nothing but some crusty blue jeans
riding precariously on his hips and dragging in the
dust. . . .

He had a deep gravelly lisping voice
which laughed with love for his friends.
Eli asked him,
"What are you going to be when you grow up,
Sammy?"
and he answered,
"A Nick fiel thectay."

"When you're in Mississippi the rest of the country isn't real. And when you're in the rest of the country, Mississippi isn't real."

Thanks, Sally, for your book,

Bob Moses
(Nick fiel thectay)

Preface to the Virginia Edition

When I wrote *Freedom Summer* after returning from Mississippi in 1964, the experience was all too fresh to fit into any of the perspectives that historians, fabulists, and various popularizers go in for. In some ways, an advantage: this is what happened— around me, at any rate, and in the (not atypical) town of Greenwood. Later interpretations of these events have, as could be expected, tried to fit them into an idea more or less remote from the way it was. On one side the Mississippi Freedom Summer is often now overromanticized into an exercise in pure democracy and people's power and viewed with a kind of wistful envy by contemporary young people almost as if it were our generation's Spanish Civil War. On the other, it has been relegated to a minor role in something larger than itself: launching pad for the political and social activism of the sixties.

As for the romance, there is some very minor validity in it, though I can only leave the question for the book to answer. The launching-pad proposition has perhaps more in support. A thousand young people, fairly wet behind the ears, learned lessons in Mississippi that gave them a fine-tuned sensitivity to injustice, as well as the elementary tools to fight it. Most of SNCC's recruits had started out as theoretically liberal, comfortably white, unextraordinary college students. To some it was a lark, an action against various clichés that turned out not to be clichés and also to be very dangerous. Some were incredibly courageous, some just reckless; most didn't know yet who they were. They found out. An extreme situation is a quick education. They learned to treat skeptically, if not with outright cynicism, the anthems and credos of their country that had so recently been drilled into them at school. They became usefully contemptuous of the threat of red-baiting and attuned to hypocrisy in the gov-

ernmental power they had, only that spring, by and large un-
questioningly respected. They gained a whole new image not
only of themselves but of the possibilities for social change. Controversy and rebellion got to be considered not just virtuous but
hip. A movement to secure equal rights for black people ended
up spawning other minority struggles as well as the women's and
antiwar movements, and student activism in general. By the late
sixties its influence even reached Northern Ireland, where a
civil rights movement modeled directly on the one in the U.S.
South ultimately ignited the troubles that after more than twenty
years show no sign of abating.[1]

Of course, there is everything to be said for finding patterns in
events, searching for causes and effects, viewing history in a
broad sweep rather than a series of isolated occurrences. But
somehow something vital has been lost here, and one might be
pardoned for wondering why, as usual, some valuable scholar-
ship as well as fanciful mythmaking have obscured what the summer was all about—the empowerment of American black people.

The corollary, and the other thing it was about, was racism,
and the possibility that white Americans could confront themselves on the issue. As longtime activist Rev. C. T. Vivian has
put it: "What happened in the Sixties was that this entire country took just a few beginning steps toward admitting it had been
wrong on race. And the result was an explosion of creativity and
humanity in all directions. We moved temporarily toward becoming a more humane society for everyone."[2] In the last
months of his life, Martin Luther King went further. "America is
deeply racist," he said in an interview, "and its democracy is
flawed both economically and socially. . . . The black revolution
is much more than a struggle for the rights of Negroes. It is forcing America to face all its interrelated flaws—racism, poverty,
militarism, and materialism. It is exposing evils that are rooted
deeply in the whole structure of our society. It reveals systemic
rather than superficial flaws and suggests that radical reconstruction of society itself is the real issue to be faced."[3]

While veterans of that summer in Mississippi would have

little trouble relating to these words, you would never know anything of the kind was going on from a popularization like the film *Mississippi Burning*—where the gung-ho G-man ("Hoover boy" to the local rednecks, as if J. Edgar were not every bit as racist as they themselves) goes all-out to bring to justice the murderers of Schwerner, Chaney, and Goodman by, for instance, dragging the rivers and swamps without somehow turning up any of the nameless black bodies in fact found at the time, and eventually nabbing the malefactors by the combined use of the underhand and the strong arm. Why spoil the plot by showing that far from beavering away in their hundreds, FBI agents refused even to act within their legal authority and did nothing more aggressive than witness atrocities and stand around taking notes? More mysteriously, nobody in *that* 1964 Mississippi sang freedom songs, only the odd hymn—appropriate to a characterization of the huddled mass of pious, patient, passive, and most of all anonymous darkies awaiting the beneficent attentions of some renegade representatives of the oppressor. For no black in the film has a name, much less any responsibility in the shattering events of the summer of 1964 that, as part of decades of creative struggle, they organized and led and suffered for.

There is one possible plus in the hoopla of such a media event. From being seen as yesterday's news, the summer is on the map again—if only as part of that strange landmass, Mythical America. But in the popular adventure, any caviling about historical accuracy is for spoilsports: the heroes are brave to no particular purpose, the villains shift according to the vogue, and a man's gotta do, etc. One must cultivate detachment, considering the summer as the mere stuff of legend, so it can turn into a neat—with any luck, anomalous—story having a beginning, middle, and end. Especially an end. That way people don't have to give thought to why, after the initial gains of the sixties, so many U.S. schools are again effectively segregated; or why black men two decades later earned an average of $13,218 to the whites' $23,032; or why the black infant mortality rate remains twice as high as the white.

To the extent that these questions are addressed at all, they tend to attract theories about the inherent inequality of blacks that are as racist as the real reasons for the questions. The fashion is to blame the victim—usually to heap scorn on the black family—and to disdain to take responsibility for the real cause: the economic, social, and political apartheid of the U.S.A.

*

I have never been back to Mississippi. Theoretically, a lot of us are still on the books for skipping bail. Mississippi must have made a fortune out of bail. There have been changes. With 31 percent of its registered voters black, the state now has more elected black officials than any other state, including a black congressman, as well as the only black Democratic state chairman. But in 1989 this was also still a place where a DA, in successfully pursuing a death sentence for a black man before an all-white jury, could say both in court and on television that his guiding philosophy was to "get rid of as many blacks as possible."[4]

*

Looked at twenty-five years later, it is clear that three matters received rather short shrift in this book: food, sex, and violence. There were different reasons for each.

Nothing special stopped me writing about food except subscription to the common belief that food was an issue too trivially domestic to be taken seriously (a stance less likely on an empty stomach), as well as the fear of offending the local people whose tasty but deficient meals I mostly shared. This was not, of course, their fault; nor was the standard snack-and-soda nourishment of civil rights workers anybody's responsibility but their own. But when I returned home I was underweight, colored gray, and spotted from back to front with pimples. More important, I lacked energy. At the time I failed to recognize the wider implications of this. In the ensuing years, witnessing the impaired diet of the poor all over the world—those who can eat at all—I wondered how those in condition most likely to rebel could summon the simple energy to do it.

There is a nutritional imperialism in operation everywhere. Photo-features on our own domestic third world no longer show even a family resemblance to the work of Walker Evans or Dorothea Lange: the skin-thin refugees from the thirties' Dust Bowl have become the bloated victims of junk food. At least they are alive. In much of the Third World they starve. Is it a coincidence that the hungry are African, or Middle Eastern, or Latin American? It is hard to believe that the white world cares if such children die. If that is not true, why is it still happening?

I didn't write about this issue because I failed to see it. Similarly, sex. While volunteers were asked at their pre-Mississippi orientation to refrain from notching up their "summer Negro," there has been latter-day smoke indicating *some* sort of fire—specifically charges by feminist academics that "the roots of feminism rested in the 'victimization' of white women by black men."[5] Feminism's roots need no such adjectives as "white" and "black." While it is almost certainly true that the modern American feminist movement owes its origins to that Mississippi summer, this had to do with women volunteers taking a new vocabulary of oppression back home with them in September, more than with this alleged victimization—in my experience, at any rate, which can't have been too unusual. Even if anybody had ever offered to victimize me, there was simply no time or space; my single most plaintive wish was just once to be alone.

Violence. At the end of the summer, pushed beyond their endurance, some people in the movement wanted to react to the violence confronting them with more than the other cheek. There was talk about guns. "If you write about the guns, we'll kill you!" someone said to me with furious and frightening heat. I couldn't write about them in any case, because I had no information. A massive debate was starting up about ends and means; no one yet knew what the guns meant, what could be done with them, or even who had any. No one knew where anything was going, which direction the movement would next take. Separatism and black power were ultimately the direction, providing more of a target than ever—if such were needed—for the FBI's Cointelpro operation designed to combat the liberation struggle.

In a memo dated March 4, 1968, and later released under the Freedom of Information Act, Hoover specifically listed the program's goals (whose implementation had in fact begun long before):

1. Prevent the *coalition* of militant black nationalist groups. In unity there is strength; a truism that is no less valid for all its triteness. An effective coalition of black nationalist groups might be the first step toward . . . the beginning of a true black revolution.

2. Prevent the *rise of a "messiah"* who could unify, and electrify, the militant black nationalist movement. . . . [There follows a series of potential candidates for this post, including Stokely Carmichael, who "has the necessary charisma to be a real threat."]

3. Prevent *violence* on the part of black nationalist groups. . . . Through counterintelligence it should be possible to pinpoint potential troublemakers and neutralize them before they exercise their potential for violence.

4. Prevent militant black nationalist groups and leaders from gaining *respectability,* by discrediting them to . . . the responsible Negro community . . . , the white community, both the responsible community and to "liberals" who have vestiges of sympathy for militant black nationalist [*sic*] simply because they are Negroes . . . [and] Negro radicals, the followers of the movement. . . .

5. A final goal should be to prevent the long-range
growth of militant black nationalist organizations, especially among youth.[6]

The results of these policies (successfully employed in the developing world, so why not at home?) were clear only later.
Phony letters, either of the poison-pen genre or from ostensible
well-wishers, were sent out to try to discredit the movement or
break its spirit. Activitists received spurious—but convincing—
threats. Splits were engineered by infiltrators and violence initiated by provocateurs. Those leaders who couldn't be preempted
or co-opted or absorbed or corrupted happened to be assassi-
nated. There were the exceptions such as Bob Moses, who like
Stokely Carmichael dropped out of domestic movement politics
and went to Africa, then used his considerable talents and ener-
gies elsewhere. But no pattern was apparent then, and people
chose to see each repressive incident in an isolated way; our
minds were unable fully to encompass the horror of what was
happening. (The mainstream media still seems unready for this.)
    Thus were the blacks dealt with. As for the whites, with the
spirit of protest and of community now part of their lives, the
student volunteers fanned out over the country to their cam-
puses and took up other struggles. They were changed for good;
they had come to see how naked were their kings. But they, unlike what Julian Bond has called the "industry of reminiscence
and revision,"[7] know well that while many groups have styled
themselves The Movement, this one really moved—with its
own motor, under its own steam. It wasn't part of anything except itself: one of the great—unfinished—revolutions in American history.

*

A final observation about the title, both of this book and of the
summer. For years after *Freedom Summer* was first published,

people would say to me something about "your book *Mississippi Summer.*" This got so tedious that I realized it obviously should have been called what everybody seemed to think it was called (rubbed in by an Englishman complaining that "'Freedom' has such dreadful sort of CIA connotations."). Having grown to consider mine the most inapt of titles, I was flattered, annoyed, and surprised to find that in 1988 another author had borrowed it for his book, too, and also by extension for the summer itself. Throughout his text he refers to what was going on by that name and gets others doing it too, though at the time nobody called it anything but "the summer project"—a name as unpretentious as the day-to-day happenings of those hot weeks, so full of love and hate, when people had all they could do putting one foot ahead of another and doing their job.

Sally Belfrage

Notes

1. Subject of a later book of mine, *Living with War: A Belfast Year* (New York and London: Penguin, 1988).

2. Quoted by Anne Braden in (N.Y.) *Guardian*, July 5, 1989.

3. David J. Garrow, *The FBI and Martin Luther King, Jr.* (New York: W. W. Norton, 1981).

4. Letter in (Manchester) *Guardian Weekly*, Aug. 6, 1989, from Clive A. Stafford Smith, Southern Prisoners' Defense Committee, quoting District Attorney Ed Peters.

5. Quoted by Joanne Grant in *New Directions for Women*, Jan.–Feb. 1989.

6. FBI document reproduced (in differently censored versions) in Garrow, *The FBI and Martin Luther King, Jr.*, and in Nelson Blackstock, *The FBI's Secret War on Political Freedom* (New York: Pathfinder, 1988).

7. From Keynote Address given at "New Directions in Civil Rights" Conference, Charlottesville, Va., May 4, 1988.

Freedom Summer

1. Basic Training

All one Sunday in June they arrived at the college in Ohio. Their cars pulled in past the sign crayoned ORIENTATION, down the grassy drive to a cluster of dormitories and administration buildings. The atmosphere of campus, brick and ivy, matched them nearly perfectly: their ages fit, their haircuts, dress, and choice of words, and their baggage, books, guitars. It might have been the start of summer school.

They left the stuff in the cars or in heaps on the lawn and went inside to register. Their names were taken; meal tickets, mimeographed literature, name badges, and room assignments distributed; powers of attorney signed; and then they were sent singly down the hall to have their pictures taken—two poses each, holding numbers under their chins. Out on the lawn again afterwards, they formed in haphazard circles around the guitars, looking at each other self-consciously as they sang the words they scarcely knew.

Then there was a change: a woman whose badge read "Mrs. Fannie Lou Hamer" was suddenly leading them, molding their noise into music.

> If you miss me from the back of the bus,
> You can't find me nowhere,
> Come on up to the front of the bus,
> I'll be ridin' up there. . . .

Her voice gave everything she had, and her circle soon incorporated the others, expanding first in size and in volume and then something else—it gained passion. Few of them knew who she was, and in her plump, perspiring face many could probably see something of the woman who cleaned their mothers' floors at home. But here was clearly someone with force enough for all of them, who knew the meaning of "Oh Freedom" and "We Shall Not Be Moved" in her flesh and spirit as they never would. They lost their shyness and began to sing the choruses with abandon, though their voices all together dimmed beside hers.

3

> Paul and Silas, bound in jail,
> Had no money for to go their bail,
> Keep your eyes on the prize,
> Hold on, hold on.

"Hold on," they bellowed back, "Hold o-o-on. Keep your eyes on the prize, hold on."

The music had begun—the music that would have to take the place for them, all summer, of swimming, solitude, sex, movies, walking, drinking, driving, or any of the releases they had ever grown to need; and would somehow have to come to mean enough to drive off fear.

It was the second of two training periods for six hundred student volunteers en route to Mississippi, at the Western College for Women in Oxford, southwest Ohio. The teachers—SNCC field secretaries, guest speakers, some native Mississippi movement workers, and "resource people"—had a week in which to give the volunteers, eighty-five per cent white, one hundred per cent middle-class, some introduction to the foreign land which they were going to try to change.

SNCC, pronounced "Snick," is the Student Nonviolent Coordinating Committee. From informal, decentralized beginnings four years before, it had grown into an organization, with hundreds of full-time fieldworkers in all the Southern states, hundreds of thousands of adherents, and support from Northern fund-raisers. For the 1964 Mississippi Summer Project, SNCC was the spine of COFO, the Council of Federated Organizations, whose other member groups included the Congress of Racial Equality, Martin Luther King's Southern Christian Leadership Conference, and Mississippi state branches of the National Association for the Advancement of Colored People.

On the paths to the dining room, the volunteers greeted each other and smiled as though they had met and were already friends. They had come from all ends of the country, having developed in as many vacuums, and were astonished to discover one another. There was the predictable vague division between the radically inclined, sandaled sophisticates from New York and California, and what one of them called "the girls from Wichita who have very straight teeth and say 'nifty,' 'grisly,' and 'neat.'" But they had more in common than not—on one level, three hundred indestructible innocents, apostles of Dr. Pangloss, ludicrous in their unfashionable idealism; on another, complicated heroes who could acknowledge the world's evil in themselves, confront it, and speak the words that everyone else was gagging on: "I am responsible." Few could explain what it was, in the middle of their generation's apathy, that had made them care, but the fact that they did seemed a phenomenon of as much hope for America as the Negro revolution they were coming to join.

They left possessions carelessly around, concerned with something else besides the theft of their cameras, and joined the cafeteria line. Conversation began without introductions—about what the work would be, where the places were, how the system worked.

"I wanted to do voter registration, but my parents said they wouldn't let me go and I'm not twenty-one yet."

"They're not taking any more girls for voter registration anyway. I wanted that too."

"What are you going to do?"

"Teach. I taught in Harlem last year and I guess I was pretty good at it, so I'll have to do it again."

"What's the matter with that?"

"I hate teaching."

"But it's important."

"I know. But what we really have to do is get people registered."

"It isn't going to be that easy to get people registered. Have you seen the test? It depends completely on some registrar's interpretation—you couldn't pass it with a Ph.D. if the guy says no. And then the people who try lose their jobs and get shot at—"

"Are you scared?"

"Sure I'm scared. You'd have to be out of your mind not to be scared."

Then a new voice, a Negro in CORE T-shirt: "You talk about fear —it's like the heat down there, it's continually oppressive. You think they're rational. But, you know, you suddenly realize they want to *kill* you."

Giggles (nervous).

"And the thing is, it's not funny. That's why I'm laughing."

We collected trayfuls of meatballs and cake; I found a seat at a table with a long pale Englishman, three very earnest young girls, and a Mississippi preacher who introduced himself as the Reverend Russell from Holmes County. The distinctions among the various counties of Mississippi were not yet clear—or how much could be conveyed about a situation's relative tension or progress, liberality or danger, by giving it a county name. Reverend Russell was a chamber of commerce for Holmes: in his opinion it was absurd to sign up for anywhere else. "Things is just *fine* in our county," he said. "We got us a co-op, we owns seventy-three per cent of the land. We got the *power*."

While two of the girls, not yet acclimatized to the accent, asked each other what he was saying, the third questioned him further. He didn't understand her either. Everyone spoke very distinctly, and he went on. "Holmes is the best they is. We ain't had but one bombin'. Ain't no other counties with the colored in our position. When we calls a boycott, we gets a *boycott*. They close down one store we boycotted." He laughed, adding conspiratorially, "Now they got them a law 'gainst boycotts and passin' out boycott leaflets, so we says 'selective buyin'.' And if they finds out that's the name we use, we can find us another name."

"And how do you get it organized now, if you can't pass out literature?" one girl asked.

"Oh, that's easy," he said. "We jus' announce it in the churches."

A staff member turned on a microphone at the back of the room and announced an optional meeting after dinner to discuss the topic: Why are we going to Mississippi? When I turned back to Reverend Russell, he was saying, "I sees people, not colors. My father always say to me, 'Don't matter how big a man is, if you can beat him thinkin'. . . .'"

The college was built for the academic year and was not equipped for heat waves. Volunteers who came to the "optional" meeting— every one of the three hundred—sat in packed liquid rows in paralyzing heat. They were welcomed by Bruce Hanson on behalf of the National Council of Churches—sponsor of the orientation—with the words: "Any of you who don't want to go to Mississippi can leave."

"Is this meeting about why *aren't* we going?" said someone behind me.

Vincent Harding, a compact, squarely built Negro Mennonite, who was to lead the discussion, rearranged the question: the "Why?"

that would keep being asked throughout the week. No one was being seduced into Mississippi; the slimmest private doubts were encouraged, and Bruce Hanson's welcome began each day like the pledge of allegiance.

"Are you going," Vincent Harding started, "as 'In' members of the society to pull the 'Outs' in with you? Or are we all 'Outs'? Are you going to bring the Negroes of Mississippi into the doubtful pleasures of middle-class existence, or to seek to build a new kind of existence in which words like 'middle-class' may no longer be relevant? Are we trying to make liberal readjustments or basic change?" The floor took over.

White boy: "For me there is only one race, the human race. It's one nation. Mississippi is our back yard as much as Harlem. I've had it good for a long time. But I've seen too many people hungry for too long."

Negro boy: "We have to try to change the South so that the people of the North will want to do better. The South is a battle-field: the North is in a stalemate. For us, it's all intolerable. But we have to work where the situation is flexible enough for change. Open hate is preferable to hypocrisy—it can be moved."

White girl: "There's not enough justice and not enough liberty. There's not enough truth and there's not enough beauty. Who will work to make these things? It's everyone's job."

Southern white boy: "I'm involved in this for my own freedom. We have to build a new South, a South ruled by law, democracy, and humanity. I couldn't not have come."

White boy: "I'm going because the worst thing after burning churches and murdering children is keeping silent."

Mrs. Hamer stood, reducing the audience to intense silence. "We need you," she said. "Help us communicate with white people. Regardless of what they act like, there's some good there. How can we say we love God, and hate our brothers and sisters? We got to reach them; if only the people comin' down can help us reach them."

A Negro girl with a Northern accent spoke then from another source. "It's been part of our education to distrust white people," she began quietly, "and no matter how hard we try, we can't get rid of the remnants of suspicion." Then, fiercely: *"You're going to have to make your position very clear if you're going to cross the line."*

Vincent Harding tried to draw these poles together. "There is an

ambiguous feeling. . . . The Negroes would like you to know what
it's like to be a Negro. They want it to be well with you; but at the
same time they want something to happen to you." He didn't mean
white deaths and mutilations, he meant white comprehension. A
feeling had persisted in the group that had preceded us in Ohio, and
had left the day before for Mississippi, that they were being sent as
sacrificial victims. Although they recognized that publicity and federal involvement could be achieved only if the victims were white—
in a state where the beating and murder of Negroes was endemic
and a matter of no national interest—there was resentment. "We
think all these problems must be aired now, before they explode on
us in Mississippi." That was part of what the week was for.

All were left with more questions than had ever occurred to them
before. But there were still songs. Mrs. Hamer led the first chorus:

> Go tell it on the mountain,
> Over the hills and everywhere,
> Go tell it on the mountain
> To let my people go.

When the verses came, they clapped.

> Who's that yonder dressed in black?
> Let my people go.
> Must be the hypocrites turnin' back.
> Let my people go.

Then:

> Who's that yonder dressed in red?
> Let my people go.
> Look like the children Bob Moses led. . . .

They didn't know about Bob Moses yet.

A general meeting the next morning established the routine for
the week. Volunteers had continued to arrive through the night;
now the full complement was assembled in the auditorium, expect-
ant and prompt, clipboards in their laps and pencils sharpened.
Their listening, questioning, and note-taking habits were those of college students, and helped one forget that the lessons were not altogether removed from experience. "I." appeared on the top of innumerable sheets of paper; "(a), (b), (c)." The first a, b, and c

were for the areas of work, outlined by the staff members in charge:

Community centers: ten or fifteen were planned, with facilities for arts and crafts, recreation, libraries, literacy classes for adults, health, and day care.

Freedom Schools: to supplement and complement the regular schools, there would be a general academic curriculum with remedial work, but also emphasis on Negro history and current events.

The political program: a major voter registration drive in all the projects, with a parallel organization of the Mississippi Freedom Democratic Party, working toward a challenge to the seating of the regular Mississippi Democrats at the national party convention in Atlantic City in late August.

Then Bob Moses, the Director of the Summer Project, came to the front of the floor. He didn't introduce himself, but somehow one knew who he was. Everyone had heard a little—that he was twenty-nine, began in Harlem, had a Master's degree in philosophy from Harvard, and that he had given up teaching in New York to go South after the first sit-ins. He had been in Mississippi for three years, and he wore its uniform: a T-shirt and denim overalls, in the bib of which he propped his hands. He began as though in the middle of a thought. "When Mrs. Hamer sang, 'If you miss me from the freedom fight, you can't find me nowhere; Come on over to the graveyard, I'll be buried over there. . . .' That's true."

Moving up to the stage, he drew a map of Mississippi on a blackboard and patiently, from the beginning, outlined the state's areas and attitudes. The top left segment became the Delta: industry was cotton; power in the Citizens' Councils; and opposition to the movement systematic and calculated, aimed at the leadership (including Moses himself—in 1963, the SNCC worker beside him, Jimmy Travis, was shot in the neck and the shoulder as they rode together in a car outside Greenwood), and at decreasing the Negro population by the expedient of automating the cotton fields, thereby "getting it down to a livable ratio." The segment beneath the Delta was the hill country, mostly poor white farmers who had been organizing since the March on Washington. Amite County, McComb: Klan territory, where violence was indiscriminately aimed at "keeping the nigger in his place" and no one was safe. Five Negroes had been murdered there since December. No indictments.

Mississippi gained texture and dimension on the blackboard.

Moses put down the chalk, paused, then looked out at us, his eyes reflective behind horn-rims. When he began again he seemed to be addressing each one separately, though talking to no one at all, just thinking aloud. "When you come South, you bring with you the concern of the country—because the people of the country don't identify with Negroes. The guerrilla war in Mississippi is not much different from that in Vietnam. But when we tried to see President Johnson, his secretary said that Vietnam was popping up all over his calendar and he hadn't time to talk to us." Now, he said, because of the Summer Project, because whites were involved, a crack team of FBI men was going down to Mississippi to investigate. "We have been asking for them for three years. Now the federal government is concerned; there will be more protection for us, and hopefully for the Negroes who live there."

He stood looking at his feet. "Our goals are limited. If we can go and come back alive, then that is something. If you can go into Negro homes and just sit and talk, that will be a huge job. We're not thinking of integrating the lunch counters. The Negroes in Mississippi haven't the money to eat in those places anyway. They still don't dare go into the white half of the integrated bus terminals— they must weigh that against having their houses bombed or losing their jobs."

He stopped again, and everyone waited without a sound. "Mississippi has been called 'The Closed Society.' It is closed, locked. We think the key is in the vote. Any change, any possibility for dissidence and opposition, depends first on a political breakthrough."

He frowned, then said a few words on the subject of nonviolence. No COFO workers, staff or volunteers, would be permitted to carry guns. The police could murder the armed and then claim self-defense. "We don't preach that others carry guns or refrain from carrying them. You may find some difficult, limiting situations. If you were in a house which was under attack, and the owner was shot, and there were kids there, and you could take his gun to protect them—should you? I can't answer that. I don't think anyone can answer that. . . .

"The question of arrest. In Mississippi a charge is not necessary. It can be made up later. There will be many arrests; but I think it should be avoided. The work you are going for can't be done in jail. We have a staff of volunteer lawyers who are coming during the summer. Now, among these lawyers there are some who people say are politically less desirable than others. This kind of thing bogs us down. I don't want to get caught up in a discussion of communism in the movement. It's divisive, and it's not a negotiable issue with us.

"Money. We don't have any. But where you have people and programs and the minimum materials, a lot can be done."

He stood pondering something, quite still. The next words came, almost disembodied from him. "We've had discussions all winter about race hatred." The audience had become absorbed in him, an extension of his soft voice; he no longer had color—but the words gave our flesh a tint again and opposed it to his. "There is an analogy to *The Plague,* by Camus. The country isn't willing yet to admit it has the plague, but it pervades the whole society. Everyone must come to grips with this, because it affects us all. We must discuss it openly and honestly, even with the danger that we get too analytic and tangled up. If we ignore it, it's going to blow up in our faces."

There was an interruption then at a side entrance: three or four staff members had come in and were whispering agitatedly. One of them walked over to the stage and sprang up to whisper to Moses, who bent on his knees to hear. In a moment he was alone again. Still crouched, he gazed at the floor at his feet, unconscious of us. Time passed. When he stood and spoke, he was somewhere else; it was simply that he was obliged to say something, but his voice was automatic. "Yesterday morning, three of our people left Meridian, Mississippi, to investigate a church-burning in Neshoba County. They haven't come back, and we haven't had any word from them. We spoke to John Doar in the Justice Department. He promised to order the FBI to act, but the local FBI still says they have been given no authority."

He stood, while activity burst out around him. In the audience, people asked each other who the three were; volunteers who had been at the first week of orientation remembered them. Then a thin girl in shorts was talking to us from the stage: Rita Schwerner, the wife of one of the three.

She paced as she spoke, her eyes distraught and her face quite white, but in a voice that was even and disciplined. It was suddenly clear that she, Moses, and others on the staff had been up all the night before. The three men had been arrested for speeding. Deputy

Sheriff Price of Neshoba claimed to have released them at 10 p.m. the same day. All the jails in the area had been checked, with no results. The Jackson FBI office kept saying they were not sure a federal statute had been violated.

Rita asked us to form in groups by home areas and wire our congressmen that the federal government, though begged to investigate, had refused to act, and that if the government did not act, none of us was safe. Someone in the audience asked her to spell the names. She erased most of Moses' map of Mississippi from the blackboard and, in large, square capitals, printed:

> JAMES CHANEY—CORE STAFF
> MICHAEL SCHWERNER—CORE STAFF
> ANDREW GOODMAN—SUMMER PROJECT VOLUNTEER

Underneath, she printed: NESHOBA COUNTY—DISAPPEARED.

California and New York split out the left and right doors; others formed by states inside. We composed telegrams, collected money and sent them, and tried to rub out the reality of the situation with action. No one was willing to believe that the event involved more than a disappearance. It was hard to believe even that. Somehow it seemed only a climactic object lesson, part of the morning's lecture, an anecdote to give life to the words of Bob Moses. To think of it in other terms was to be forced to identify with the three, to be prepared, irrevocably, to give one's life.

The volunteers broke up into their specialized units—Freedom School, community center, voter registration—in the afternoons, and met again in the auditorium for general lectures in the mornings. Each day began with an announcement like Vincent Harding's on Tuesday: "There has been no word of the three people in Neshoba. The staff met all night. When we sing 'We are not afraid,' we mean we are afraid. We sing 'Ain't gonna let my fear turn me round,' because many of you might want to turn around now." For three days no one cleaned the blackboard on the stage; the names were still there, over the partially erased map of Mississippi.

Tuesday was about Southerners, black and white. Harding talked of the three centuries of slavery and segregation in America—"the

great melting pot where color evidently didn't melt"—and the symptoms produced in the victims. "Some have a broken spirit—'I been
down so long that down don't bother me.'" Afraid of whites, they
seek at any cost to stay on good terms with them, "always agreeing,
never honest, therefore never human with you—and underneath it
there is a deep distrust and hatred of you because they have to behave this way."

Others become black supremacists. Harding's advice to his largely
white audience was to tackle them with: " 'Yeah, baby, I know you
think black is great. Well, I think white is great.' You got a dialogue
going there," he said, "and that's a beginning."

Still others react with sexual aggressiveness. "Some Negroes think
the only way that whites can prove they're really in the movement is
by going to bed with a Negro." Harding thought this might be a
particular problem for the white girls who were "going for 'my summer Negro.' The summer Negro is no different from the token Negro
in the school. We're going to Mississippi because men have been using other men. Using people sexually is no different from using them
politically or economically."

And finally, among the Negroes we were to meet would be the
freed: "some in their old age, some freed even from the need to
hate, to deceive. When you find them, hold them tightly."

From the other side came Charles Morgan, the white Birmingham
lawyer forced to leave his home because of his public stand on the
1963 church-bombing in which four children were killed. "In white
Mississippi," he said, "you have a little house on a little green plot in
a little town. For them, the worst thing in the world is controversy
—because, you see, they're just like the family you left behind next
door. But in the South, controversy means only one thing: being on
the wrong side of the race question. When faced with it, nice people
commit crimes in the name of a great cause. They have their own
rationality. What they're concerned with is Main Street: 'Let's keep
it just as it is.' What you're talking about is power, and they got it.
And they have a bunch of people who are going to convince you
that you are wrong—one way or another."

He dug into the volunteers, attacking the martyr instinct and any
remnants of fearlessness among them, and somehow reconstructed
the Southern white as a human being, an image long gone in most of

his audience. Once liberated from bigotry, they were unable to mind their own business, and ultimately, like Morgan, had had to leave their friends, their towns, their states. But how were Morgans made? What was the process, and how could it be encouraged?

There was no time to pursue it. A gaunt, fierce-eyed young man raised his hand and was recognized. When he began to speak it was in waves approaching hysteria. "It's hell in Mississippi!" he said, his voice breaking. "And you've got to realize that nobody *cares.* We care. We've got to change the *system.* It's hard. It's just like one person beating his head against this building to tear it down. It's impossible, but we have got to *do* it. They say that democracy exists in America. But it's an idea. It doesn't function. You have got to make it function in Mississippi, so that it can function in the rest of the country, and in the world."

There was a silence resembling fear in the room. "Who is it?" someone craned around and asked my row. "Jimmy Travis," another whispered. "The one who was shot. Didn't you see the scar on his neck?"

"The three people," Travis said. I think he was crying. "I don't know. I hurt. These people are lost. I don't know where they are. What can we do? The *system!* The system is the reason these people are missing. It's easier to know that someone is in jail, even that someone is dead, than to wait and wonder what happened."

He pointed to Chuck Morgan. "This cat is from Birmingham, Alabama. This cat knows what's going on. I'm black. You're white. If you're going down there, you're going to be treated worse than black. Because you are supposed to be free. But I say that no one is free until everyone is. And until we can show the people of Mississippi that we are willing to make the extreme sacrifice, we can't change the world.

"It's hard. So hard. But all we have is each other. When something happens to you, we care. We really *care.*"

He slumped against the door behind him, then disappeared through it. There was a second's silence, then a splattering of applause which grew, wavered, died out. A girl stood in the uncomfortable quiet that followed, Morgan still at the podium, no one looking at anyone else. "You've got to understand Jimmy," she said. She was a Mississippi Negro. "He was nearly killed. It was something he had to say. You shouldn't applaud."

The lectures and classes continued, and there was no news from Neshoba. The tension clouded us in until it was all there was to breathe. In free time we composed letters and telegrams to anyone conceivably influential enough to get the government to act: to send federal marshals and outside FBI agents to Mississippi. Moses explained, "The inside agents, Mississippians, are psychologically incapable of carrying on the necessary investigations. We need the FBI before the fact. We have them now after the fact." It wasn't a question of military occupation, as Southerners were claiming: "We're not looking for generalized chaos in which troops can come and take over. We're looking for a framework in which people can do their work—for the summer, and then afterwards, a means of extending it to the Negroes of the state."

There was one television set on the campus, and the floor around it was jammed for news broadcasts. But when the next news arrived, it was during dinner on Tuesday night. Bob Moses came in quietly, turned on the microphone and said, "The car has been found outside Philadelphia. It's badly burned. There is no news of the three boys."

That night there was a bonfire in a clearing in the woods, with beer and the Freedom Singers, a SNCC quartet. It was impossible to be with it. Groping back through the dark trees, I found myself beside another volunteer whose face and color I couldn't see until we reached the campus lights. He was white, very young, a California freshman. He had come to Ohio for the first week of orientation, he said, and stayed on to the second. I asked him about the bad press the first week had got: the New York papers had written of race tension and beatniks. "It was the most depressing week of my life," the Californian said of it. "Just the worst thing I ever went through." He couldn't explain why. "I don't know, I think I lost my mind." Pressed, he could only mutter, "I thought it would be organized, and when I got here nobody knew what they were doing."

We lost the path for a moment, and he didn't go on until the dormitories were finally in view. "All they did," he said in a rush now, "for eleven hours a day, was talk about how *prejudiced* we were. The staff wouldn't talk to us, it was like they despised us. And nothing about the work we were going for, just stuff about how all the Negroes in Mississippi will hate us whatever we do." He had decided to switch projects, from voter registration to Freedom Schools, hoping they would be less disordered. It didn't look as though he was going to Mississippi at all.

Tactics: Nonviolence was the subject of Wednesday's lecture, delivered by a Negro minister with a mystical bent. His language was full of "self-bearing goodwill," "the inner listening ear to the spirit of love," "invisible spiritual forces," "wrestling with the ultimate reality," and suggestions about discipline which involved meditation, reading the Scriptures (also the Hindu and Taoist), fasting (for inner purity), and experimentation with agape.

The sermon was greeted with a great chill. There was a small minority of missionaries among the volunteers who told the journalists that they were going to Mississippi because the Lord had sent them, and for these, nonviolence was a theological necessity; for most, it was a tactical one. A puzzled SNCC field secretary stood up and asked where all the meditation and agape fitted in when you were being shot at, and the minister was not entirely able to satisfy him.

The meeting ended early so that a more relevant lesson could be conducted. An important part of the week's work had developed around a single sheet among our mimeographed materials headed "Possible Role-Playing Situations": scenarios for acting out in classrooms.

1. *The Cell* (four persons, white, same sex): A white civil rights worker is thrown into a cell with three ardent segregationists. As the jailer opens the cell, he identifies the civil rights worker to the inmates—"Got some company for you fellas, one of those Northern nigger-loving agitators. Now you treat him nice."

2. *Police Harassment* (seven persons, white and Negro, male and female): Two state troopers stop a carload of five civil rights workers for speeding on a little-used highway.

3. *The Guest* (seven persons, white and Negro, male and female): A white civil rights worker who is staying with a Mississippi Negro family receives an anonymous note or phone call warning him that unless he clears out of town by midnight the family will be attacked and the house burned to the ground.

4. *Canvassing* (five persons, white and Negro, male and female): An integrated team of civil rights workers visits a Negro home to try to persuade the adults of the family to register to vote. (Variation: While the team is talking with the family, the plantation owner arrives on the scene with a shotgun.)

Now there were larger, more physical situations to be played out. The press was particularly fond of these sessions. Television cameras were poised around the lawns, still photographers climbed the walls to get the angles, reporters from Chicago, London, even Tangier nudged each other out of the way. In the center of a huge circle of volunteers, one toughened SNCC worker was saying to another, "Some o' these cats don't even know if they supposed to make up the bed in the morning." "Some o' them," returned the other, "don't even know how." "*Dig*, man!" said the first again, wheeling violently on his friend, who just as quickly doubled up and fell to the grass.

The idea was immediately to assume a fetal position: "Cover your head, roll up in a knot, hit the ground," one of them instructed as he delivered a series of violent blows and kicks to his partner, who remained intact in his knot. "Head as close to your knees as possible. Legs together." (Slam, punch.) "Girls, keep your skirt pinned under your knees if you're modest. Don't carry watches, pens, glasses, contact lenses, and never more than five or ten dollars. No sandals." (Kick, push.) "A T-shirt will save you some skin if you're being dragged on your stomach."

The cameras whirred at the pupils as they tried it out on each other, laughing tentatively. "If you're caught from behind, go limp," the SNCC man said, heaving a volunteer to the ground. To those who watched without coming to the volunteer's aid: "If your friend is getting his head beat, fall on him, man! What happens to one happens to everybody." A mound of bodies grappled with each other on the grass. "Keep your feet together. A leg out here and another out there and one stomp in the right place, you got a broken leg."

Catching a couple of girls grinning self-consciously, he whirled around on them and shouted, "*Don't laugh!*" All the element of the comic suddenly left the situation, to be replaced, for many, by panic. This was survival. A hypothetical situation was set up, assignments given. Some of us were to try to enter a courthouse with a group of registrants, others were to play the white mob outside. The little band started out toward the alley formed by the whites—who knew the words. "Two, four, six, eight, we don't want to integrate!" "Niggah lovah!" "Commie rat!" "Take that, goddamn yankee agitatah!" The epithets reached a pitch of crazed reality, bodies plunged at each other kicking, pummeling, dragging; fetal positions were held together with sheer adrenalin. In moments, friends became enemies: the animal they released so near to the surface, the curses so accessible, that one wondered how humanity had survived at all.

Later in the day there were scenes of wild agitation all over the campus, as volunteers knocked each other down, socking and punching. The madness was very real to them; but it had the unexpected effect of increasing anxiety rather than spending it. Back in the classroom, we continued under the tutelage of a white Mississippi boy who had switched extremes after the riots at Ole Miss, where he had studied. A space was cleared in the center of the room and in it he methodically brutalized us, one by one, to wear down reserve. Simulated clubs, dogs, cattle prods. A girl took a tear-gas gun disguised as a fountain pen from her purse for demonstration; he ordered her not to carry it South, but explained to us how to react to its use. The discussion continued and moved to what we should take with us on days when we could anticipate arrest. An indignant female voice objected, "But you get a chance to go *home* first, don't you? I mean before they take you to jail?" From the lack of reaction, it appeared she was not alone in her illusions.

Suddenly, in the calmness of the talk, a shot crashed through the room. Terror overcame everyone: volunteers sitting on the window ledge scrambled out on the fire escape, others screamed and stampeded to the door. In a second I thought: "Jesus, they've started already!" I grappled for my bag, realized I needed my life more, began to run, remembered instructions, fell to the floor and crawled. The door was blocked with bodies; no one could get out. Then the smell started—wild sweet-sour, filling the lungs and blocking breath like asthma, stinging the eyes. Through my tears I saw above me the Ole Miss boy. He was standing in the hall, holding the discharged tear-gas pen, disgusted. One by one the others noticed him, untangled their limbs, and when the air had cleared, sheepishly took their seats. Then they were told what they should have done.

It was quite evident how vulnerable we were, helpless. Now what? It had to be learned. The Ole Miss boy, with an imagination developed in a life of knowing the enemy, dealt out some weird hands. In the middle of an explanation about which organs needed most to be protected and how, a vague-looking girl leaned her head around the door to ask if this was the right room for the Freedom School teachers. Without a second's pause he lunged at her, upsetting her armload of books on the floor, and with authentic Southern savagery began to berate and humiliate her. It seemed to me he meant it, that he had snapped finally—perhaps had been a Klan agent all along, and now the strain had conquered—and that he was going to kill her. She clearly believed it herself. She stood there pitifully and gazed at him in supplication, tears coming to her eyes, then bent a little to ward off the words. She saw the books, and moved as if to protect them. He kicked them all over the floor. She looked up again, bewildered, whereupon he shoved her over on the floor too. Only then did his pity make him hesitate, and she realized what was happening. She collected her books and staggered out, smiling weakly, to find the Freedom School teachers.

The session ended in a desperate, prolonged free-for-all, with people either sprawled about the floor or mauling those who were. The Ole Miss boy, whom I hated as much as the enemy by now, handed me the "cattle prod," a picket sign. I held it high and was instantly hauled to the floor, while feet and fists battered at me. They tired and stopped; I peeked through my folded fingers (against the rules) to see them stomping on someone else. Hoping I was forgotten, I started to get up (aware that the first lesson was, after all, to *run*), but they saw and were at me again. This time I clenched into more of a rock than a fetus, surprised to discover that, abstractions aside, in an extremity of fear I had no desire whatever to hit anyone back, at all, ever. The next time they stopped, and feeling like SNCC's most perfect moral victim, I nonviolently fled to the door.

The fracas continued and from my distance I tried to decide what I would make of it had I arrived there innocently. It might have been a peculiar orgy except for the shrieks of "Communist bastard!" "Black bitch!" and "Professional visitin' troublemaker!" (a new epithet supplied by Governor Paul Johnson of Mississippi, reported in the paper that day). Then I noticed that the Ole Miss boy, who had been playing the most vicious role, had escaped too and was standing behind me. He shook his head, looking at them, and murmured, "My God, the mob in every man."

Bayard Rustin, the next morning's speaker, had the crowd's respect before he began—not only for his organization of the March on Washington, but for his principled nonviolence based on a pacifism tested in many jails. "All mankind is my community," he said, and: "When I say I love Eastland, it sounds preposterous—a man who brutalizes people. But *you* love him or you wouldn't be here. You're going to Mississippi to create social change—and you love Eastland in your desire to create conditions which will redeem his children. Loving your enemy is manifest in putting your arms not around the man but around the social situation, to take power from those who misuse it—at which point they can become human too."

He suggested that our difficulties in connecting with white Mississippi might not be insurmountable. "One can evaluate others in the light of one's own experience, see them in one's self, understand how one can become that bestial." He smiled and bummed a cigarette off a volunteer in the first row. "Last week I was smoking and wondering why a white Southerner can't act on what he believes. Then I took another puff. I *know* cigarettes will give me lung cancer. Well, I can understand him. In this we are one. We are both intensely stupid."

The President sent two hundred sailors to search for the missing boys. Rita Schwerner and all the staff members who could be spared were in Meridian and Philadelphia. Nothing visible was being done by the authorities to prevent the same thing from happening to anyone else. We clung to the television set.

On Thursday there was a TV special: "The Search in Mississippi." Classes were scheduled for the same time, but everyone, thinking himself alone, was in the lounge—a couple of hundred in a space meant for a third that many, crammed in the room and out through the hall. On the screen appeared the faces of the enemy, the friend, the one who sat beside us now, the one who had gone ahead reporting how it was. The program contained interviews filmed the day before in the room where we sat.

The voice was SNCC Executive-Secretary James Forman's, and he was speaking in the auditorium where we had spent half the week. The camera played around the audience, at the volunteers like us, some of them the same—staff and holdovers—and finally came to rest on a very young, dark, thin but tender face. Only when it was gone was it identified as Andrew Goodman's.

But then the face was Senator Eastland's—whose children we would redeem? "Around where I live it's seventy-five per cent colored," he was saying. "Many's the time I've slept at home with the doors unlocked. We don't have any racial fiction, uh, friction."

Aaron Henry, head of the Mississippi NAACP, and also of COFO: "Fifty-one per cent of the people in the Delta earn less than a thousand dollars a year. This is the fiftieth state economically. The reason we're fiftieth is because that's how many states there are. We used to be forty-eighth."

Senator Eastland: "There is no attempt to prevent Nigras registering. You go by what some agitator claims. They're perfectly free to go to the clerk's office to register to vote."

Mrs. Hamer: "I tried to register in 1962. I was fired the same day, after working on the plantation for eighteen years. My husband worked there thirty years. When my employer found out I'd been down to the courthouse, she said I'd have to withdraw or be fired. 'We are not ready for this in Mississippi,' she said. 'Well, I wasn't registering for you,' I told her. 'I was trying to register for myself.'"

Governor Johnson: "The hard core of this [COFO] group is your beatnik-type people. Nonconformists, hair down to their shoulder blades, some that you'd call weirdos. . . . They don't realize that they're following a group of professional agitators, many of them with criminal records, people who've been in trouble all their lives— you can see it in their face. We're not going to tolerate any group from the outside of Mississippi or from the inside of Mississippi to take the law in their own hands. We're going to see that the law is maintained, and maintained Mississippi style."

The audience in the lounge joined in the show, expressing some unequivocal opinions of the speakers. At the end, under the titles, we ourselves appeared, standing, singing "We Shall Overcome." We stood and joined our own voices:

> Black and white together now—
> Oh deep in my heart, I do believe,
> We shall overcome someday.

For a long time after the program had finished we remained there, while Mrs. Hamer led more stanzas, more songs.

There was one side still to be heard. John Doar of the Justice Department's Civil Rights Division came from Washington to speak, as he had the week before. I got to the auditorium early, after an 8 a.m. class, and found a seat near the front while volunteers drifted in. Near me a group began to sing in slow rhythm. "We need justice, Lord, come by here. Oh, Lord, come by here." An old Negro woman was weeping into her handkerchief. Behind her a white girl with high cheekbones and dark hair pulled severely back sang gravely while tears fell down her cheeks, oblivious of a movie camera on the stage poised on her face, just as it had been on Andrew Goodman's the week before.

Moses urged us to be polite to Doar, an effort at which the previous group had apparently failed. "A year ago this week Medgar Evers was buried. It was a near riot situation, and Doar was sent in to prevent worse. He has helped us." The camera buzzed behind his words. Doar arrived.

"This is a serious operation that you are involved in," he said straight off. "I wish the world were different; I don't like it any better than you do." He was tall, blue-eyed, narrow-shouldered, and his face wore a steady, concerned frown. He outlined the reasons why "there is no possible way that anyone can be completely protected from violence." Suggesting that there were many native white realists in the state, he asked us to "help them correct a problem that they must realize they want to get behind." On his own forces: "If we don't make good sound judgments and imaginative investigations, we should be criticized."

Perhaps some felt that this man and his government represented them, but in the past week many who had started out as ordinary college students with respect for all the ordinary institutions had learned about cynicism. Because of Moses' admonition, however, most of the muttering remained only that, and when Doar asked for questions just two hands were raised.

"How is it that the government can protect the Vietnamese from the Viet Cong and the same government will not accept the moral responsibility of protecting the people in Mississippi?"

"Maintaining law and order is a state responsibility," Doar said.

"But how is it"—the questioner persisted—"that the government can accept this responsibility in Vietnam?"

"I would rather confine myself to Mississippi."

Next was Staughton Lynd, a professor of history at Yale, who would run the statewide Freedom School program. "In 1890," he began, in his dry, quiet voice, "during the railroad strike, the government went into Illinois. Its right to do so was upheld by the Supreme Court. In a crisis, the President does have the established power to send a police force into a state, whether the state wants it or not. The question is, is the situation in Mississippi a crisis? What we are trying to communicate is that it *is*. . . . It's a moral question. If you have this power to act, and if you have the moral responsibility yet choose not to act, how in the world do all of you live with this responsibility?"

"I believe we are a government of law," Doar said. "I have taken a vow to uphold the law. I just try to do the best I can under law. I have no trouble living with myself. The people I know in the federal government and administration are fine people, and they have no trouble living with themselves either."

On this, the meeting adjourned. "What a lot of junk," a girl said on the walk to lunch. A few days before she had told me that her plans to join the Peace Corps had been interrupted because of the urgency of Mississippi. "I don't know who I'm fighting any more. To think that I nearly *worked* for those people. There are a lot of great words, but where is their conscience? They just want to keep the Southern vote for the Democrats. They're not going to do a damn thing they don't have to." She kicked at the ground.

"And did you get that movie camera?" she went on. "Can't you just catch it on next week's TV special? I kept seeing the guy aiming it at me and I wondered how I ought to look for my mother and father after I disappear. Smile, or look noble, or what. You know, it seems to me that the most finally horrible thing in the world is posing for your own obituary photograph."

We had to cross a stone bridge to reach the dining room. Teetering on the ledge, another newsman was whirring his camera at everyone who passed. When we reached it, the girl made a face.

They followed us into the classrooms and dormitories, around the lounges, out along the paths. They asked people to sing that song again for the American public. There was footage, yardage, mileage of every face in the place. "At the beginning it made me feel important," a boy from Utah said at lunch. "But they have a way of degrading everything they touch." "It's because we need them more than they need us," his neighbor returned, "and they know it." "It's just their job," commented a third. "Well, I feel unclean," the boy from Utah said.

We had been given our choice of job and area. I was to be a librarian in Greenwood. The library coordinator, who had a degree but no experience, said, "Some of you are going to be worrying about being black or white; I'm just worried about being green." The Freedom School teachers had received thick folders of lesson material and had discussed their approach; the voter registration workers had learned techniques of canvassing and means of gathering evidence for federal lawsuits. COFO lawyers had let us all in on some of the law's mysteries, the charges Mississippi was able to bring, how to insure one's right to appeal, when to stand mute or plead *nolo contendere*. In general sessions we had been prepared for everything, usually the worst.

On the last day, the Oxford barbershop had lines three deep for every chair, and the beards and "hair down to the shoulder blades" vanished. The students gleamed as though they had been polished. They were packed, scared, cheerful, and ready. A few had gone home. Two psychiatrists among the "resource people" had mixed with us all week and scrutinized every volunteer. Parents had been phoning hysterically; the bulletin board outside the dining room was buried in messages which had gone unanswered. At least one mother came to collect her daughter. An Oklahoma boy was forced to drop out after receiving a letter from his father saying, "If you think you're going to liberate Mississippi, I'm getting a posse and coming to liberate *you*." In the end, only ten went home. The rest gathered in the evening for a last general meeting.

Jim Forman had just arrived back from Mississippi. A large, rumpled, dark-brown man who needed a haircut, he had the good speaker's urgency, power over a mood. His volatility was the other side of Moses' pensive strength, but both earned an audience's total attention, total sympathy. He wanted to give us a little history and background. "I know Moses spoke on Monday, but he is a very shy person." Moses, crouched against the stage with his head down, smiled. It was the first time I had ever seen him smile.

Forman asked us to rise and to sing "We'll Never Turn Back," with our arms around each other, and then he repeated some of the lines very carefully:

> We have hung our head and cried
> For those like Lee who died,
> Died for you and died for me,
> Died for the cause of equality,
> But we'll never turn back—

The song was written by a young SNCC worker in memory of Herbert Lee, shot to death in Amite County, Mississippi, by a member of the Mississippi State Legislature who was never indicted. Forman went over the details of the case, how the only witness to the crime, Louis Allen, was shotgunned dead in January 1964, on the night before he was to leave the state. He named these deaths as punctuations in the life of the Mississippi movement, as was Medgar Evers', and the five newest murders in as many months. Despite these events, he said, SNCC had developed from the first sit-ins to "Moses and His Boys, the Nonviolent Guerrillas," the Delta voter registration program, and, after the Civil Rights Bill, the Summer Project.

There was danger, and work to do. "You've got to get down to the nitty gritty. You've got to be willing to sweep the floors." He smiled and his voice took on a sarcastic tone. "Of course you're *teachers,* so you're more *sophis*ticated than the voter registration workers. In fact, some of you probably signed up because you think it's safer work. But you can't start shouting, 'Hey, I'm a Freedom School teacher, I'm all right.' Because in Mississippi nobody has any rights.

"All of you should have nervousitis. If you have doubts, we'll admire you for dropping out. But I think the best thing to say is, you know, we'll be there with you, and . . . we'll never turn back."

It was Moses' turn. As he stood, he swayed slightly, then held the microphone. His head dropped, and the voice was so soft it seemed to stroke us. He wondered if any of us had read Tolkien's *The Fellowship of the Ring.* "There is a weariness . . . from constant attention to the things you are doing, the struggle of good against evil." I thought of what one of the volunteers had said that day of Moses: "He's like someone you only read about in novels. He has great currents of moral perplexity running through him."

Then Moses said, "The kids are dead."

He paused—quite without regard for dramatic effect. But long enough for it to hit us: this was the first time it had been spoken: they are dead. Up to now they had simply "disappeared." There had been no reason for us to believe anything else.

"When we heard the news at the beginning I knew they were dead. When we heard they had been arrested I knew there had been a frame-up. We didn't say this earlier because of Rita, because she was really holding out for every hope." Rita had gone to Meridian now.

"There may be more deaths." He waited, seeking the words he needed. "I justify myself because I'm taking risks myself, and I'm not asking people to do things I'm not willing to do. And the other thing is, people were being killed already, the Negroes of Mississippi, and I feel, anyway, responsible for their deaths. Herbert Lee killed, Louis Allen killed, five others killed this year. In some way you have to come to grips with that, know what it means. If you are going to do anything about it, other people are going to be killed. No privileged group in history has ever given up anything without some kind of blood sacrifice, something."

He sank into his tiredness again and the volunteers just watched him. He wasn't looking at us, but at a space between him and the floor.

"There are people who left today, went home. I was worried yesterday because no one had left and that was bad, it was unreal.

"The way some people characterize this project is that it is an attempt to get some people killed so the federal government will move into Mississippi. And the way some of us feel about it is that in our country we have some real evil, and the attempt to do something about it involves enormous effort . . . and therefore tremendous risks. If for any reason you're hesitant about what you're getting into, it's better for you to leave. Because what has got to be done has to be done in a certain way, or otherwise it won't get done.

"You have to break off a little chunk of a problem and work on it, and try to see where it leads, and concentrate on it."

His voice had faded almost to a whisper, and it was as if he were speaking out of his sleep, out of his unconscious directly into ours.

"All I can say really is . . . be patient with the kids, and with Mississippi. Because there is a distinction between being slow and being stupid. And the kids in Mississippi are very, very . . . very slow."

He finished, stood there, then walked out the door. The silence which followed him was absolute. It lasted a minute, two; no one moved. They knew, now, what could not be applauded. Suddenly, a beautiful voice from the back of the room pierced the quiet.

> They say that freedom is a constant struggle.
> They say that freedom is a constant struggle.
> They say that freedom is a constant struggle.
> Oh, Lord, we've struggled so long,
> We must be free, we must be free.

It was a new song to me and to the others. But I knew it, and all the voices in the room joined in as though the song came from the deepest part of themselves, and they had always known it.

2. Seat of Leflore

*THE OLD SOUTH! History and romance faithfully preserved.
Enchanting ante bellum homes, historic parks and battlefields and
a storied past reminiscent of hoopskirts, steamboats on Ol'
Man River and cotton plantations. This is Mississippi!*

—MISSISSIPPI NEWS AND VIEWS, June 1964

The cars, with buses added, pulled out all Saturday, June 27, just as
they had arrived the week before, but the passengers were changed.
There was an excess of motion and activity, maybe to avoid other
preoccupations. Volunteers grouped on the sunny lawns, scattered
through the campus collecting roadmaps, art supplies, knapsacks,
and books, throwing out aspirins, nail files, and address books, bun-
dling up possessions, and flinging goodbyes, some tearful, some
stubbornly casual, from windows of departing buses.

"Hell of a graduation this is." Someone tried to make a joke of his
panic, taking a last look at the Western College for Women. We finally drove away, not with all the enthusiasm we displayed to each
other. Even the car behaved as though it were connected to the
campus by a length of rubber band. But it was headed irrevocably
toward the object of all the talk, all the good intention, all the hopes
and terrors built up in a week and in a life. The old Ford in which I
rode carried three for Greenwood, one for Ruleville, stray clothes
and sleeping bags, and a mixed air of anxiety and buoyant bravado.
Heidi Dole, riding in the front with a lapful of roadmaps, broke the
silence a few miles out. "You know," she said, "that week is going
to seem pretty unreal after the next one. I have a feeling it's going to
have to last us all summer. The inspiration, I mean, the group feeling." No one said anything. "It was so marvelous," she added, "to be
in a place where no one disapproved of what you were doing." Her
family and friends back at the ranch out West thought her misled, if

not mad. She had never come across such people as she had found in Ohio. "I felt like I knew everyone before. You know, I recognized them all right away."

Regularly spaced road signs reading simply SOUTH seemed to yank us forward like connecting points of a funicular, each one forcing the destination, each one safer than the next, inevitable reminder. We pulled in at a roadside restaurant in Kentucky to find some oversize lollipops on sale for fifteen dollars each and a busload of our friends, still integrated at the tables, explosively in love with each other, grabbing at the time still left to them together. Later that night we stopped and drank a great deal of beer.

"I don't know what all the fuss is about," the owner of the car, Ed Bauer, kept reassuring someone. "It's still the United States of America." An engineering student from a California family so Republican that its latest addition had been christened "Barry G.," Ed saw no intrinsic evil in anyone, believing that white Mississippi couldn't be that bad if you approached it properly. The rest of us were behaving as warily as a band of illegally documented refugees on the Orient Express approaching a forbidden Balkan border. The night seemed peaceful enough, but the change from light to dark was becoming substantive, and everything ahead was dark. SOUTH! The signs sprang out in the black. Now and then someone hummed a few bars of a freedom song. I tried to think of any other song I had ever sung, but everything had been eclipsed by these urgent tunes. We laughed a little and spoke in past tenses.

Bret Breneman, a tanned blond boy from Honolulu whose resemblance to Albee's American Dream gave him a slightly miscast unreality, reminisced about being thrown out of England once for lack of a pound note. Ed Bauer had a throwout story too—from the Mediterranean in 1961, while in the Navy, for fighting a Negro in the streets of Villefranche. Our image in Europe. "I didn't know you couldn't fight a Negro just because you didn't like him and wanted to fight him; if you were doing that, it meant you hated Negroes." Back on the ship ready to be sent home, he was congratulated by his mates for beating up the nigger; then he understood.

All night we passed the cars and buses of the others. In Memphis, by the Mississippi border, a Volkswagen driven by a Negro with two white passengers caught up with us at a traffic light; it was due at a meeting point at which the colors would separate for the further drive. (*Avoid riding in integrated groups,* we had been taught. Or "disintegrate the cars," as someone said.) Since the Memphis public facilities were segregated, we found a Negro café in the slums for breakfast. As we entered, a procession of whites with one Negro, the people inside halted in mid-sentence, frozen, and studied us in the mirror behind the counter. The Negro with us sat in a vacant seat apart from us and seemed suddenly willing to forget the connection. The waitress, wearing the name-tag "Willa Lenoir," attended to him and ignored us—a pause long enough to register, before approaching and asking meticulously, "May I serve you?"

Our conversation sounded conspicuously loud. The two white boys from the Volkswagen had just been talking with Justice Department officials in Washington. They were destined to work in Mc-Comb, southwest Mississippi—the most dangerous part of the state —and wanted at least federal awareness, or if possible, protection. When they asked about the assignment of marshals to the area they had been told that there were only six hundred in all and that they were spread around the country. "Serving *court* orders!" one of the boys had jeered. "You don't need federal marshals for that. *I* could serve court orders!" Burke Marshall, then Assistant Attorney General for Civil Rights, had given them the impression that *they* were the ones at fault, causing all the trouble. "We aren't running a police force," was repeated like a chant. "We are an investigative, not a protective body."

The boys told us of Rita Schwerner's attempt to see Allen Dulles. He had kept her waiting for three-quarters of an hour, then given her five minutes before offering his hand and, "I extend to you my deepest sympathy; I'm sorry, but I have an appointment now," proceeding out the door. Rita had cried after him, "I don't want your sympathy! I want my husband back!"

The other patrons of the restaurant were savoring their food slowly, listening. By the time we left, there was a perceptible thaw; they almost smiled.

A sign to the right of the road read WELCOME TO MISSISSIPPI, THE MAGNOLIA STATE. It pictured a magnolia-blossoming plantation. I leaned over to push down the lock buttons. (*Lock the doors at all times,* our *Security Handbook* said, *and keep the windows wound up.*) "Oh come on," Ed Bauer complained. "It's still—"

"—the United States of America," someone finished. (Was it? A peculiar condition is induced by one's first view of the Confederate flag flying.)

Flat, endless Delta land of cotton, straight two-laned road, monotony, with only an occasional miserable shack to interrupt a landscape that was a visual forever. The wood and tarpaper shacks were unpainted, erupting from the centers of the fields, their outhouses leaning grotesquely askew nearby. A very few of them had flower gardens and a little tree, attempts at brightness, but by most the cotton grew to the door and the houses simply sagged as though about to melt into the ground. Shimmering in the heat mirage, they looked utterly insubstantial and invented. Dark men and women lazed on the tilting boards that were porches, or hacked at the dry dirt; now and then a band of cotton-choppers was bent in the sun to weed the crop. SAVE OUR REPUBLIC! said a billboard, IMPEACH EARL WARREN! alone among miles of the pale, heat-colored earth, where the little plants grew, not a foot high. Another billboard shouted KILLS 'EM FAST! KEEPS 'EM DYING! and only abreast of it could you see the smaller print above, advertising a boll weevil pesticide. At a crossroads, pointers to towns named Savage, Coldwater, Alligator.

The heat was still and dazzling, only our speed churning a little breeze through the crack in the window. The passengers observed a weird silence, which seemed to spread outward without an end. Except for brief, sudden swamps clogged with foliage, there were no trees. In the quiet, the sounds of other cars seemed loud as airplanes. Inspecting them out of the window became a quick and surreptitious habit: white or Negro? Then, as they passed (*Stay five miles below the speed limit*), checking their license plates: anything but red-on-white was a relief. Ours were conspicuously Californian. Many cars and trucks bore no tags at all. (*Cars without license plates should immediately be reported.*) Some had Confederate plates in front, Goldwater and Citizens' Council stickers in back, some carried shotguns or rifles on the seats or on racks in the rear window.

On the way to Ruleville we passed the State Penitentiary at Parchman, where Negro prisoners, barefoot and in caricature costumes of black-and-white stripes, clustered between a high electric barbed-wire fence and some dilapidated one-story barracks. Outside, a roadstand sold leather goods and souvenirs made inside. A penitentiary suggests something impregnable and stone, but Parchman seemed hardly more than a larger shack—as if to suggest that all Mississippi Negroes are in jail anyway.

We left Heidi in a crowded Ruleville living room, where a picture of a white Jesus became the Last Supper when you moved. Mrs. Hamer had not yet returned to her house among the row strung along the rutted dirt road. Down the way was a church which had been bombed three days before. There had not been much damage, luckily, Heidi's Negro hostess explained. She had the same name as my stepfather, part of whose family once settled in Virginia. For a second, a link with anyone there seemed wonderful to me, but there was no way to make the idea that we might be related wonderful to her.

A car of white men passed the house twice, looking at us and the Ford with malevolent eyes. (*Be conscious of cars which circle offices or houses.*) As we left I locked the doors again and Ed didn't say anything about the United States of America. We rolled on toward Greenwood through the infinite cotton patch.

There was nowhere that litter of neon, billboards, and gas stations, the identical sleep-and-eateries that negate distance and make American highways so much the same as each other; the country was foreign, resembling Spain or Syria or anywhere where heat and poverty combine to overwhelm attempts at the streamlined. Only at the outskirts of Greenwood did the asphalt widen, lines straighten, and ads for the Holiday Inn flash out America again. (*Know all the roads in and out of town,* the *Security Handbook* said.) GRAND BOULEVARD, the first sign announced. Tall, well-spaced oaks touched leaves above our heads and sheltered houses—porticoed, pillared, and carefully kept—on either side; it seemed the site of all the Southern legends I had ever read. Lacy verandas, colonial façades, lawns smooth as carpets, blackamoor hitching posts, tended old wealth whose owners, tucked away inside, left the street so deserted that the mind could easily populate it with belles descending surrey steps to julepy cotillions under the kindly eye of black retainers. Near the end of the street a peeling ante-bellum mansion wore a faded Confederate flag down its front like a hand-me-down dress. We were a long way from home.

Grand Boulevard finished at the Yazoo River; Front Street, the neoclassic County Courthouse, the City Hall, streets called Market,

Church, and Main, J. C. Penney's, Woolworth's, a hotel or two, some Protestant steeples—all the accouterments of an American town of twenty thousand. We studied the faces of pedestrians and police for homicidal tendencies. Then we crossed the tracks, and for a block or two the wiry, cheesy commercial atmosphere remained but as a cheap exaggeration of itself; then the pavement bellied out and sidewalks disappeared or fell away in broken pieces: Niggertown. Rows of shanties perched on stones and bricks and jammed together in precarious asymmetry were interrupted, though not often, by a spacious lawn adorned with air-conditioned ranch house and a fence. The better-off Negroes had no choice of neighbors. The only other structures with anything of the right angle housed grocery stores with Chinese names and churches. The hot, end-to-end living sent the people out into the streets, where children, watched by parents on the porches, roamed barefoot, and all the somber privateness of white Greenwood was reversed.

"The heart of the greatest long-staple cotton growing area in the world," Greenwood is built for, and sustained and surrounded by cotton. For the sake of cotton the town ends on all sides with jagged abruptness. Left of the highway to the COFO headquarters was the squalid chaotic crowd of Negro cottages; to the right, limitless fields of the leafy plant. The latter was still a money-making commodity, the former no longer; so the plant if not the man was allowed to breathe.

The town of Greenwood, seat of Leflore County, was named for the last of the Choctaw chieftains, Greenwood Le Flore, who built a river landing for cotton shippers upstream on the Yazoo in the 1830's. He was half-Indian, half-French. He became Choctaw chieftain because the tribe, "influenced" by the spirit of democracy, had chosen him in a general election rather than for his lineage; and he was the last of the Choctaw chieftains because he proceeded to surrender what remained of his people's land—about a third of present-day Mississippi—to the federal government in the Treaty of Dancing Rabbit. The Choctaws denounced him as a traitor; but Le Flore had had the foresight to arrange an amendment to the treaty guaranteeing himself government protection and an estate, on which he built a palatial pretension called Malmaison, after the Empress Josephine's house. His understandable affection for the government in

Washington nearly cost him his life during the Civil War, when he insisted on flying the Union flag, was ostracized by both the Indians and the Southern whites, and had his Malmaison set on fire by Confederates. But he survived to be buried in peacetime near the house, wrapped in the Stars and Stripes. And the white citizenry of his namesake town forgot his treachery to them, as well they might, erecting a plaque in honor of his treachery to others.

Greenwood itself, its industry devastated by the Civil War, became again a center of cotton growing, ginning, compressing, and warehousing. These operations demanded the labor of Negroes, who still constitute half the population of the town, and two-thirds of the county. The proportion is reduced annually as the cotton fields are automated and Negroes leave for Northern ghettos. In Mississippi, the Negro population has dropped from nearly 60 per cent at the turn of the century to the present 42 per cent; in Leflore County in the 1950's alone the decrease amounted to 13.8 per cent. White power encourages Negro migration, particularly in view of the probability of increasing Negro suffrage: Governor Johnson had recently boasted that "under Governor Barnett, over 260,000 Negroes fled Mississippi." Cotton-picking machinery is being introduced throughout the Delta, and chemical weed-killers promise soon to eliminate the need for hand cotton-chopping. Alternative industrial jobs are reserved almost entirely for whites. Cotton pickers are not automatically able to fill such positions, and Mississippi has refused to participate in federal retraining programs because they are integrated, pay the federal minimum wage of $1.25 an hour (more than any Negro laborer could expect from the job that would result), and because they would keep Negroes in the state. The Negro removal project, however, is not among those specified in the Leflore County *Over-all Economic Development Program* (a report required of counties seeking federal funds). While noting that nearly half the county's housing units have no running water, the report lists among the thirteen goals to be "considered first in action plans" such items as "watershed projects," "sheltered workshop for handicapped people," "preservation of the family farm," and "expand and improve more wildlife and hunting facilities."

We turned off Highway 82 near the town limits. The streets had lettered names; we sought 708 Avenue N, a brick building with two stories. It was the tallest one in view for blocks, and surrounded by cars, baggage, and the only multicolored group of people anywhere short of the next COFO project.

There was no one conspicuously in charge of anything, so we wandered upstairs and waited with the rest. The library, my future domain, spread over most of the second floor—a large, light, square room with windows on three sides, divided by waist-high partitions. Big pegboards blocked off other sections of the room, and books spilled off shelves, out of boxes, and around the floor. In operation since the spring, the library had been compacted into half its original allotment to make room for extra desks. Behind and under the people sprawled around the benches and tables were signs of expert carpentry: the floor was tiled in beige and the walls paneled in light shellacked wood, with shelves to the ceiling on all sides. On the only shelfless wall hung a poster of the Bill of Rights. Someone had penciled quotation marks around the title.

At the moment, however, there were many distractions from a library inspection—volunteers asleep on their knapsacks, oblivious of others typing, talking, and one group singing, its leader playing a guitar beneath a list of rules headed NO GUITAR PLAYING. Another rule, NO CARD PLAYING, was being unobserved by some local teen-agers playing whist on the librarian's desk. Somewhere a microphone was being tested, "One-two-three, one-two-three, can you hear me?" Three Negro girls were teasing each other's hair into bee-hives in and out of the bathroom in the back. Children of all sizes ran among prone bodies, trunks, bags, boxes, books, and knots of the newly arrived who were conducting exhausted conversations. It was incredibly hot, a sort of clinging, breezeless, final heat. (*Your metabolism will change,* they'd said in Ohio; *you'll get used to it.* Nothing noticeable had happened to my metabolism yet.)

Someone with a list was wandering around reading names. A Negro girl of twelve, named Cora Lou, asked me where I came from. She was slim, nearly as tall as I, with her hair divided into seven pigtails, and she considered me from various angles, smiling. When my name was read with the address of the home to which I'd been assigned, Cora Lou pulled me aside. "I want you to stay with *me*," she said. I hesitated. "Would it be all right with your mother?" She just smiled as though that were an idiotic question. Another name was substituted for mine on the housing list, and Cora Lou took my hand as we picked our way through the bags and bodies to the stairs.

She led me to a house nearby, explaining that "a woman with blue hair" was staying there too and that I could sleep in the same double bed, which Cora Lou normally shared with her big sister. We entered through a screen door directly into the kitchen, a crowded, cheerful room with tattered linoleum and gay curtains at the windows. Mrs. Amos (the name her husband suggested later in the summer when I wondered what to call them if I wrote about them), a kind-faced woman with a golden smile, was making bread at the stove, propping and unpropping its broken door with a length of metal pipe wedged into the floor. Behind her, the "woman with blue hair" turned out to be Lorna Smith, a Californian of sixty-seven whom I had known when I was a small child. We were entirely unprepared for the reunion, and Mrs. Amos watched with amazement. Then she welcomed me to live there.

SNCC had started working in Greenwood three years before, and civil rights workers, black and white, from North and South, had been bedding down on the sofas and floors, using the bathroom, and eating Amos grits and chicken ever since. She hadn't planned to house summer volunteers, but Cora Lou's guest immediately became to her another child. (That made six—there were already two girls and three boys, one of them working in the North.) She hugged me, fed me fried chicken and cornbread, and installed me in the back bedroom with Lorna. Other Amoses appeared gradually for dinner, which they ate separately or together, whenever they were ready. The youngest, Earl Henry, skipped around with an inexhaustible merriment like Cora Lou's, as though they each had some deadly hilarious secret that no one else could ever grasp. Gloria Jean was eighteen and very beautiful, very silent. Their double names were never abbreviated to the first, but since Gloria Jean's presented too many syllables for long-distance summonses, she was called Glori-Jean, Glo-Jean, or in the greatest of hurries what sounded like Gloji. The eldest son at home was just named Edgar. Because he had a paper route that began at 4 a.m., he spent most of the day sleeping, even when he was awake. Until he gave up the job halfway through the summer, I thought he was going through a particularly sullen form of adolescence; then it became clear that he had just been constantly exhausted. Mr. Amos, a handsome man in his forties, arrived home from work last. Apparently resigned to the results of his wife's generosity, he was quite unshaken by the announcement that his family had expanded since morning to include a fully grown blonde. They asked me no questions except whether I wanted anything, and accepted me from the first moment.

Cora Lou walked me to Wing's, the grocery store, to get some cigarettes. (*Don't go anywhere alone.*) Wing, like other Chinese, had for some baffling reason settled in Greenwood. Considered by the whites to be little better than black, the Chinese lived and went to school with Negroes. Wing spoke a Cantonese dialect to his family; his daughters had an incongruous Delta drawl. He was gracious, if not altogether friendly, to COFO workers, who did most of their shopping and check-cashing there.

We lingered in his air-conditioning as long as it took to eat some ice cream, then started back. Pointing out the brand-new high school across the way, Cora Lou announced that soon she would be attending it. She jogged along the road triumphantly, as pleased with the day as if she'd been given it for Christmas. We stopped by a yard where three very small boys whom I recognized from the chaos in the library were having a tricycle race. "Who's best?" one of them shouted. I pretended to be judge, but the one whose yard it was knew the shortcuts and easily beat the others. Cora Lou and I swung along a few steps more, then hit the gutter as a car swerved past, apparently aimed at us. A freckled redhead leaned out toward me as if to say something. He was an all-American college boy with a sweet face. My eyes followed his as the car began to recede; then he stuck his head entirely out of the window and spat. A shout echoed after him: "*Your father a nigger?*" When I turned finally, I saw Cora Lou walking on ahead, her head bent.

The volunteers gradually dispersed to their new homes, while those who had come the week before sat on benches outside the office with local Negroes in the cool (slightly less sizzling) twilight, beginning to know each other. Behind them in a small chapel some children were making *musique concrète* on an old upright piano. The conversation was gay though its subject was not: the week had been hard, not just from the tension of the three boys' disappearance, but because of harassment in Itta Bena, a town ten miles away. Three civil rights workers, two of them white, were accosted while canvassing and taken to the bus stop by four white men. They were given the alternatives of leaving town immediately or never leaving it. They had stayed, and Greenwood project members had supported them by attending an Itta Bena mass meeting which had been subsequently threatened with bombing. There was no bombing, and three of the white men had been arrested by the FBI and released on high bail: two thousand dollars for two, one thousand dollars for the third. There was hope that the FBI and Justice Department might, after all, fulfill their roles.

The local police were fulfilling theirs, in the "Mississippi style" that Governor Johnson expected of them. Lorna Smith told of taking a group of children to the park to read them some Sunday school leaflets she had brought with her; more children had accumulated until the circle was big enough to attract the attention of some policemen, who drove up in a squad car yelling at her.

"I got up," she related, "and went over to them to shake hands. They said they didn't want to shake hands, and they asked me for my name and home address. Then they wanted to know what I was doing there, and I said, 'We're having a party. Won't you join us?' Well, they ignored that, they just told me to go back where I came from and to stop foolin' with niggers. I said, 'Negroes.' He said, 'We call them niggers here.' I said, 'But I'm from California and we call them Negroes there.' 'Well,' he answered, 'you're in Mississippi now.'

"Then," she went on, "a Negro woman came over, and they turned to her and shouted, 'Get out of here, you black bitch, we don't need you here.' They wanted to know where I was staying, and I truthfully said I didn't know the address. (*Under no circumstances should you give the name or address of the local person with whom you are living.*) At the end, before they drove away, I said, 'Can't we be friends? I have a son just about your age.' One of them replied, 'I'll bet he's proud of you.' I said, 'Yes, he's very proud.'

"When they were gone I turned to the Negro woman and she was crying. I put my arm around her; she asked if I'd heard what they called her. I told her, 'Don't you worry. I intend to tell this to world-famous authors, and I hope it appears eventually in a book.' "

Part of Lorna's traveled life had been spent working for, among others, Upton Sinclair and Theodore Dreiser; she passed idle time reminiscing about them with volunteers, with Mrs. Amos, with hardened, shot-at field secretaries, and with sheriff's deputies at the courthouse. All but the latter loved her. Her blue hair had resulted from a visit to a Negro beauty parlor where a white woman's white hair was an unknown phenomenon. She fearlessly charged across town to talk sense to anyone who would listen, engaging in terrifying combat with the resistant; and shouted at aged Negro ladies standing around the office to get to work and help her clean things up. She was halfway through her month in Greenwood; in the first fortnight the work had involved emptying out the entire ground floor of the COFO building of a ceiling-high mess of books and rat corpses. Her technique with a broom handle when confronted with a rat not yet a corpse had won her a permanent place in Greenwood folklore. "But why are you here?" they kept asking her. "I saw on television that they wanted people," she answered, "and I just had to come."

For the sake of organization, COFO had divided Mississippi conveniently into its five congressional districts. SNCC ran four of them, although the Third, the most dangerous southwest, had yet to be cracked. The Fourth District, manned and financed by CORE, contained Meridian and Philadelphia, where the three boys had disappeared. The Second, Mississippi's northwest Delta country, was sixty-six per cent Negro, mostly rural, with only three large towns, Greenville, Clarksdale, and Greenwood—the last was headquarters for SNCC, as Jackson was for COFO. The Project Director for the Second District was Stokely Carmichael. A West Indian by birth— as are two other top SNCC staff members, Ivanhoe Donaldson and Courtland Cox—Stokely, an articulate graduate of the Bronx High School of Science and Howard University, was twenty-two, tall, lithe, with a black Indian's face capable of an evil white grin. He flashed it often at the volunteers assembled in the library that night for their first meeting together. They spread around, thirty of them, on benches, boxes, and floor, or arranged themselves on window sills to catch the "breeze," while Stokely sat on a table top swinging his legs and trying to master the names of the new arrivals—an effort he soon abandoned, calling everybody "Sweets."

He had just returned from Philadelphia, where a lot of the leadership had been summoned after the disappearance. "All the whites are out on the corners with their guns," he reported. "I'll bet seventy per cent of them know what happened to the boys. But if one of them says anything, he's as good as dead. Sheriff Rainey of Neshoba County got elected on his record as nigger-killer. It's certain about two; some say the number's nearer eight." Stokely's grin, oddly out of key, gave him a reckless quality of immortality in the face of insuperable dangers but the words indicated a mortal's sense of what they were. "The only reason *I* went to Philadelphia was because The Man (the white man, Mr. Charlie) gave us a twenty-four-hour armed guard. After all, I'm my mother's only second child."

He went over our various jobs, the group listening to him as intently as schoolchildren before an exam. They were a handsome, strangely assorted team. Girls in sopping summer dresses and boys with stubbly chins had a general casualness of appearance that was hardly endearing to the white community, balanced by others whose scrubbed, bright-eyed, straight-toothed, indefatigable freshness could survive any possible change in diet, climate, or attempt at self-Bohemianization. There was Bambi Brown, a still, smooth, ivory girl from Des Moines who would be doing most of the community center work; beside her, George Johnson, Yale law student, a tall, blond Peace Corps veteran fluent in Swahili; Linda Wetmore, a laughing redhead who looked like a cheerleader or a cover girl but had a will which dealt with any opposition as though it didn't exist, until it didn't; next to her Monroe Sharpe, a Negro artist from Chicago and Paris, with a smile missing two front teeth and a heavy silver medallion around his neck; at their feet, splat out on the floor, Eli Zaretsky, whose Brooklyn "dose," "ting," and eloquent humor were clung to as tightly as an uncompromised principle: a revolutionary with the temperament of a poet. There was every conceivable color combination of skin and hair, including a Japanese, and sharp, nasal, drawling, or just nervous accents reflecting the American range from Boston to Tennessee to California and beyond. Their average age could not have been more than twenty, and average condition, student. Mixed among them were a half-dozen local movement kids who, at seventeen, were toughened veterans capable of making the volunteers seem like flowers.

Freedom School teachers, Stokely was saying, should guard against developing the usual teacher-student relationship: there would be a great deal of learning on both sides. The community center people would have the job of finding a community center: the building where we now were had been originally refurbished for that purpose, but the ground floor was needed to house the SNCC national office and space upstairs had to go to Greenwood Project people. The voter registration workers, most of whom had come the week before, were already organized and covering the town to get as many local Negroes as possible down to the courthouse to attempt to register. In a parallel effort they were signing people up in the Freedom Democratic Party. The whites would be working only in town: they were too easily visible on the plantations, whose "owners have a legal right to shoot you if they catch you trespassing." It had been clear on the trip to Greenwood that there was no access to most sharecroppers' houses without trespassing, as they were placed at some distance from the road, with a long flat view.

The plantations would be covered by less conspicuous Negro workers. "SNCC policy is to work the areas where there is violence. Never get scared by violence"—because if such pressures worked, they could be applied everywhere, and the movement would be lost. "Any time they shoot one of us, ten of us go back next time. Then if they shoot ten, we take a hundred."

The unreality of this sort of talk was diluted by the expectations we had developed in Ohio, but it was still disconcerting to be casually told, not that there would be violence, but that we shouldn't fear it. The silence in the room was covered only by the whir of the fan. I tried to look around at the books on the shelves, wondering how to begin organizing them. Stokely went on methodically to list the "taboos."

The first item was religion. "I know many of you aren't religious, but you've got to understand what it means to the people here. Don't go getting into arguments about it with them; you'll only lose them. None of them has ever heard of atheism. The church is the only place that the Negroes can call their own. They would rather have a church than a house, or a Cadillac for the minister than shoes for their own children. We are doing the Lord's work. Don't forget that. The movement developed largely out of the churches, and if God can start a movement, hooray for God." We were to attend Sunday services, an effective way of meeting and influencing people; there would be an opportunity to speak and make announcements. Different churches would be assigned each week.

Then the matter of clothes. Local people were unaccustomed to girls in pants, especially male pants. No male pants.

Drinking. Mississippi is a dry state, which means there is a bootlegger per corner. The police get paid off, of course: the usual rate is a hundred dollars a month and a free bottle each, and there are even laws within laws specifying when "liquor stores," illegal in the first place, may not be open at all. Alcohol is taxed by the state authorities who prohibit it. ("It may be against God's law to drink it," one legislator has said, "but it ain't against God's law to tax it.") However, on the basis of theory, if not practice, the authorities would be looking to pick up civil rights workers on drinking charges. If arrested for drunken driving, you can be held for eight hours before being given access to a lawyer. "Anything can happen in eight hours. . . ." Stokely paused, giving us time to imagine what could. "The project is not going to take any responsibility for this, no bail, nothing, across the board. If you're arrested for being drunk, you're on your own. But besides that, if the community sees you drunk in the streets they'll want nothing to do with you." No drinking.

Interracial dating. "There is always the problem of the male going in and taking the female of the other race." Negro women were the historical victims of white men on a spree, and the community had understandable feelings on the subject. "As far as white girls with Negro boys—of course none of that on the other side of town. I don't know what our people's attitude will be. We'll have to wait and see."

No profanity. Besides offending the community, it is a Mississippi crime.

We were warned about speaking on the phone: local vigilantes were in on all the conversations. Soon COFO would be installing two-way radio systems throughout the state; though these were no more private, they might save lives, particularly on the road. When the national SNCC office moved in downstairs, two WATS lines would be installed, one national, one state. (The Wide Area Telephone Service enables a subscriber to make unlimited calls anywhere in the specified area for a large flat rate.) Codes had been established for different towns and counties in the state to avoid pinpointing those conversing, and others for use in cases of immediate danger.

Finally, again, *never leave a jail at night.* Lawrence Guyot, a SNCC field secretary, was quoted as having told a policeman about to release him: "If you don't rearrest me, I'm going to punch you in the mouth." Jail is safer than the mob.

Stokely checked out those with cars, assigning passengers. "Night begins at five," he said, which meant the period of utmost danger began then, when whites went home from work. (*Travel at night should be avoided unless absolutely necessary.*) The volunteers planned where to meet each other next morning and left. Some would be sleeping in the library as guards. Carol Kornfield, a tiny pretty girl with glasses on her nose and a pigtail to her waist, retired to "the little office"—a three-desk affair with our files, records, and phones—to type up the day's voter registration results and answer the crank calls, which came in by the dozen every hour. (Stu House, our temporary communications man, had just dealt with one, a man announcing: "There's another nigger dead tonight." "Oh, yes," Stu said neutrally. "Yeah, one committed suicide by jumpin' into the Yazoo River tonight." "Is that right?" said Stu; "well, it couldn't have been one of ours, or he'd have walked on the water." Slam.) Dick Frey, who had worked in Greenwood for a year, stalked around taking care of everything. An undernourished student from Pennsylvania, he seemed to subsist entirely on nervous dedication, as he seldom visibly ate or slept. Two or three others found typewriters on which to reassure their parents, sleeping bags unrolled on the floor, and the library was as empty as it would ever be.

I had only to cross the road to the Amoses'. The family had returned from church, where they went almost nightly, and had long been asleep, though it was just 11 o'clock. I stumbled in the dark to the bathroom, first through a room beside the kitchen where Mr. Amos and Earl Henry shared a double bed and Mrs. Amos slept on a mattress on the floor, then a smaller room where Cora Lou and Gloria Jean had one bed and Edgar the other. There were quantities of chests, trunks, and boxes spread around against the walls, and these, with the beds, left only narrow aisles through which to navigate. No one woke; the high-powered fans in both rooms made a steady mechanical hum. They were relatively prosperous to own such fans, and to have a bathtub and basin or a bathroom at all. In most of the homes washing could be accomplished—in this persistent, clammy heat—only by heating water on the stove to fill round tin tubs on the kitchen or living-room floor. Some houses had single cold-water taps, some only water outside. I felt guilty being so favored, but particularly in finding Mrs. Amos on the floor. The next morning she pointed out that it was cooler that way, and that she always slept there in the summer.

I crept past them again to the back room I shared with Lorna. Though very small, it somehow managed to contain, besides the huge bed, a wardrobe, dresser, small table, large trunk, a straight chair holding a fan—which ran off the light fixture hanging from the ceiling—and two armchairs, one missing an arm. The floor was of scrubbed bare boards, and all the furniture covered with bright stripes and flowers. Propped on the wardrobe were framed school photographs of the children; on one wall hung a calendar with a picture of a sexy white girl, and over the bed a pale portrait of Christ. The room, I noticed as I got into bed and looked through the blinds beside me, was not in the back of the house at all, but the very front, the window looking out on the porch and main street. (*If it can be avoided, try not to sleep near open windows. Try to sleep at the back of the house.*) Cars roared past all the hot night: sightseers come to view our office and, I imagined, case it for bombing. If any of them got trigger-happy, my middle was unavoidably included in the target range.

I slept anyway. "Orientation" is defined as "the act of being set right by adjusting to facts or principles; put into correct position or relation; acquainted with the existing situation." The facts were an abuse of power and a history of inhumanity; the principles, justice and nonviolence; the position—South?; the relation, race hatred; and the existing situation, one of extreme danger. The emphasis of the orientation in Ohio had been to teach us to live with fear as a condition, like heat or night or blue eyes. You had to learn to arrange your fear as a parallel element in the day and night, to exist beside it and try to function without its interference.

3. Occupied Mississippi

Q. What has four eyes and can't see?
A. Mississippi.

—Children's riddle

The early mornings were glassy and warm, with hardly a hint of the thick heat that would roll in later. The Amoses were always awake long before me, the children in the playground or giggling on the porch beyond the window by my bed, and Gloria Jean helping Mrs. Amos make biscuits or do the laundry in the kitchen. Glo-Jean did it alone three times a week when her mother had a part-time cooking job. The radio was tuned in loud to gravelly jazz or gospel singing, and friends dropped by for coffee and gossip. The noises stretched outward in diminishing volume through the neighborhood: it wasn't eight yet, but the men and many women had left for work and the children were yelling and leaping around the streets.

There were strong coffee, eggs, fried ham, and grits keeping warm on the stove, with children trotting through now and then for a plateful. They sat on the edges of chairs gulping down grits and smearing strawberry jam on hot fresh biscuits, and ran off again. The grits, which I'd imagined to be at least gritty, were like cream of wheat with salt and butter instead of milk and sugar. On the dining-room table was a sewing machine with some torn jeans still in the works, and through the screened window I could see a baby asleep on a rumpled bed a yard away in the next house. Pottering about, Mrs. Amos would worry aloud about Edgar on his paper route, all the trouble he could come to.

"Jus' one boy touch a white girl's hand," she said, "he be in the river in two hours. We raised them up never to even look at one— they passes on the street, don't even look, that's the way down here. But we has to work for them and many of our womens have a baby with their husbands. They don't seem to see that, though."

45

"But they must notice a lot of half-white Negro children. Where do they think they come from?"

"Oh, I guess they thinks the birds lays 'em."

She laughed, pausing before loading up the old washing machine again. The radio music paused too, for a commercial for a Greenwood insurance company. The voice had a clipped, Northern ring. "That's funny," I said, just to make conversation. "They don't have a Southern accent on the radio."

"They don't have nothin' here like other places," Mrs. Amos said. "They jus' as different here from other places as tar from biscuit dough."

I washed the dishes—as time went on, more to be able to stay with her than for my first reason: to try to allay the family's total impression of whites as the waited-on. She scolded and complained for some time when I did it, unable to believe I'd washed dishes all my life. These unearned elevations were hard to inhabit and the greatest job to tear down. It was some weeks before any of them would sit at the table and eat with me, and I never succeeded in getting Mr. Amos to stop saying "Miss Sally." And true to his mother's lesson, Edgar never, never looked at me. He seldom spoke to me at all, but when forced would call me "ma'am" and talk at the linoleum. He was sixteen.

He woke up now and wandered drowsily through the kitchen. He was used to spending his time at the pool, his mother explained, but on the day following the passage of the Civil Rights Act the city had drained both pools, the white and the Negro. "But they's gonna have to do something so's they can have theirs back. It get mighty hot."

I finished the dishes, and as I left for work she wrapped me up in a tremendous hug, trying to lift me off the ground. I was a head taller, but her strength was enormous and she nearly managed it.

There were at least a dozen children playing around our office building, running back and forth, sitting on a bench against the wall, pitching horseshoes in the dust. Beyond the few bare square feet was a row of oil drums overflowing with garbage and swarming with flies, an old shack SNCC used to store clothes sent down from the North, an abandoned frozen custard stand; then out past Avenue N a green space—the Negro park and playground, all the more expansive among the clutter of shanties. Our brick building was the handsomest short of the new high school three blocks down; SNCC had spent money and effort to make it a model community center for the Delta. At first it had consisted of little more than the chapel that gave on to the street—a stifling whitewashed little room with nothing to indicate its purpose but some rows of crude white benches. Behind it were the temporary SNCC national office quarters; above it, a room for the NAACP. The local project worked out of "the little office," an even littler mimeograph room, and the library—where order somehow had to be created.

People were gradually groaning awake. Dick Frey was asleep on his typewriter, having fallen where he sat at some point in the night. Other bodies still lay huddled up in sleeping bags, trying to drown out the day, but if someone on an urgent errand didn't jar them awake, curious neighborhood children kept stepping on them. I got going on the books. The remnants of a cataloguing system were falling out of various cigar boxes, but it looked as if it would have to be abandoned. The fiction shelves, where I began, were stocked with antiques, scores of Horatio Algers, nineteenth-century ladies' books, some valuable-looking first editions, numbered sets of Thackeray, Dickens, and Conan Doyle, eleven copies of *The Vicar of Wakefield*, a lot of esoteric modern fiction, and a very few novels which might conceivably generate some interest if they could be got at. Everything had been donated by Northerners whose good intentions were not so much in doubt as their grip on certain realities. Boxes kept arriving full of people's charitable throwouts, instead of anything new or imaginative, but now and then came a useful carton of new children's picture books; American, Southern, or Negro histories; how-to books—good things. I trundled between boxes and shelves in a sort of alphabetical rhythm, adding, discarding, arranging, and realizing only much later, when I paused to collapse for a moment, that the heat had risen to the strength of a furnace and the morning had gone. In the meantime, processions of volunteers had passed through, busy figuring out what to do or not do next, writing reports, sitting out the heat, picking at guitars, and meeting local movement people who came in to size up them and the summer's prospects.

Two reporters and a Justice Department lawyer chattered around, tending to merge with each other in the similarity of their questions and insistence on coats and ties. Stokely, in between bouts of hysterics over Lorna Smith's historical anecdotes ("Mrs. Smith, you're something *else!*"), shouted at people ("Stop sitting around the office, this has got to stop"), at which some left, others changed places. Then in the most crowded, hottest part of the afternoon, a white girl from the other side of town walked in.

For a moment no one realized who she was. A local Negro girl described her later as "all Snicked up": she wore sandals and a denim skirt, her hair in a long braid, and she was our age. No one's identity was firmly established yet, people from other projects stopped in frequently on their way through Greenwood, and she might have been another volunteer. But she asked a question in a lilting Southern voice, and in no time had attracted as much curiosity as if she had just descended from a saucer instead of a pastel sports car. "I jus' wanted to know," she said, "what y'all are up to over here."

There was too much competition in the answering and asking for the ensuing dialogue to be very intelligible. She was crowded into a corner and encircled by volunteers, who climbed on desks and shelves for a vantage point, shooting questions at her. She was a student who had just returned from four years in the North, she said, implying liberal credentials. But she nevertheless seemed to be confused by the Northern Negroes among us who spoke with "educated" accents. Hearing their voices, she focused on them perplexedly, soliciting more with gratuitous questions as if she suspected a ventriloquial act. Her name identified her to the local people as the daughter of one of Greenwood's rich men. Yes, she confirmed, her father owned a plantation just outside town.

"My mother works there," said Dorothy Higgins, the girl beside me. "You know what she earns?"

"Oh, I don't know anythin' about that," the white girl said.

"She earns three dollars a day."

The white girl looked around for an ashtray until someone took her cigarette and found a plate to put it out in. She immediately took another, which was lit for her. The volunteers themselves seldom used anything but the floor for butts and no one had ever been seen lighting anyone else's cigarette.

"You know what hours they work on your father's plantation?" Dorothy was persisting angrily.

"No, I really don't know anythin' about it."

"Six a.m. to six p.m. Twenty-five cents an hour. You *ought* to know." She tried to meet the white girl's eyes, but they were lowered. "And I've worked there too. They got a old foreman there who'd as soon fire you as let you rest five minutes."

A white volunteer tried to change the subject: the mood on the other side of town. "Why are they harassing us over there?"

"Oh, I don't think they're fixin' to bother y'all really," she said. "Most o' them don't mind, long's you limit it to schoolin' and votin' and don't go in for demonstratin' and trouble."

"That's not true," someone objected. "What about the crank calls we get all day, the bomb threats, the cars circling the office with paper bags on their license plates?"

Well, she said, she didn't know anything about that, there were always a few rabid people any place you looked, but most of them were just folks.

"Aren't you the girl whose mother killed herself?" a voice asked from behind the cluster of heads. Quickly Stokely broke in, wondering if she'd care to help us since, as she said, "schoolin' and votin'" were all right with her, "and that's just what we're doing." He turned the full force of his evil-eyed smile on her. "How about coming out to your plantation with us tomorrow morning to register some voters?"

She answered neutrally that she'd have to ask her father, and then she edged out, captured briefly on the way by one of the reporters. But our curiosity lingered—about her seeming fearlessness in driving over to see us so openly and in talking to the reporter. Naïveté or provocation: opinions split. In any case, we never saw her again. The newspaper story got no further than Greenville, fifty miles away, where it was stopped by a local man who understood its dangers to her. The next day the foreman of her father's plantation clubbed a woman worker on the head for asking for a three-dollar advance. She needed ten stitches. Stokely and a lawyer went to see her to try to get an affidavit. She refused, saying, "There ain't nothin' you can do about it to help me."

A mass meeting was scheduled for that night, as for up to half the subsequent nights—rallies for as many local people who would come, from a hundred to a thousand. Slips announcing time and place were mimeographed and given out to us to distribute in different areas. I was to go with Clara, a local girl, down Avenues K, L, and M. She had a round, dark, merry face, and wore a ragged black dress which, she said, was all she owned, and therefore she couldn't attend the mass meeting herself. It would be, as almost all were, in a church, and best clothes were worn. I offered to lend her something but everything was the wrong size; she remained as cheerful as she was resigned.

Long fat insects wandered brazenly across the street, with none of the modesty of their Northern cousins who at least wait for the dark. Dodging white-driven cars and pits and upheavals in the sidewalk, where there was any, Clara and I took opposite sides of the narrow street and handed out paper slips to people passing by or sitting on their porches. Hardly a house was empty—so many lived in each that someone was almost certain to be home. The tired frame shanties were propped on bricks, tilting and unkempt, with bits of cardboard stuck in broken windowpanes, weathered, peeling paint, and a view inside of jumbled, crowded, darkened sitting rooms stuffed with beds and makeshift funiture. Ghetto life had stagnated the sensibilities of some—their homes, most often owned by white men, were neglected by everyone involved. Others tried their best to fight the odds, the heat, the filth, the vermin and poverty that attacked them incessantly in different combinations but with equal deadly force. They filled their yards and porches with greenery and flowers, sewed frilly curtains and bedspreads, disguised the houses' scars with scraps of bright wallpaper, fabric, linoleum, and scrubbed it all shining.

People greeted us with smiles and waves, assuring their support. Some, anyway: others were polite but withdrawn, sitting on their porches as though bonded to them, rocking in apathy. They said of course, they would be there, but one knew they wouldn't be. Or they said more frankly, "I don't want to mess with that mess." Often the response matched the look of the house: it was simply a question of hope. Though all of life conspired to extinguish it, there it was anyway, all over the place, surviving, working, trying. It was our job, in a way, to find it and give it substance—the movement—for expression.

The children had their hope intact—those still free within slavery, anyway, those not yet old enough to know the other world beyond the tracks. "Hey, freedom!" they cried, and intercepted us for slips to hand out too, then galloped into side roads waving handfuls, bare feet skipping up dust. Clara and I walked together down a stretch of uninhabited street. Three boys of three shades of brown passed going the other way and smiled. "They looks at you," she said, "not at me." "Because they've never seen me before." "No. Because you are white, and I am black. You don't have to straighten your hair, do you?" she wondered, touching it.

I asked her how old she was and she said seventeen, eighteen next week. "My first baby gonna be four on my eighteenth birthday," she announced proudly. There were three children, the youngest a year old. They were born by Caesarean because she had been so young for the first. She never would have gone to a hospital otherwise, she said. "After the third I got my tubes cut. But sometime if a colored woman go to a hospital they does it without tellin' her. They just cuts her tubes, she don't know nothin' about it till she can't have no more babies. That's why they afraid to go to hospitals. But me, I aks them to do it. I don't want one o' them big families. I got eleven brothers. No sisters though. One woman I know have nineteen children, jus' two girls."

We separated again to hand out papers; one of the ubiquitous patrol cars swerved between us and around the corner, a white arm stuck out the window dragging a billy stick against the ground. "How're y'all this evenin'?" a very old man called out from his porch, where he was rocking and fanning. ("Evening" began at noon in Greenwood.) He took a slip and examined it, holding it upside down. I explained about the meeting and he said he never missed one. Hearing us, a younger woman carrying a baby emerged on the porch with a broad smile. "Hi," I said. "All right, how're you feelin'?" she answered. "I sure glad y'all's here. I don't understand it though, I ain't seen nothin' like it in all my days. What you want to come down here for? You got a nice home to live in up North. Why you want to help us?"

Feeling like some kind of saint, though knowing I was only a symbol, I said that my home wasn't so nice—just because there is a Mississippi. And that I liked it here, already I felt more at home here than where I really was at home. It was my fight too.

"Well, we gonna fight," the old man said, "and we gonna win. Don't nobody need to worry none about that."

The sky had clouded over, and when I found Clara again it had started to drizzle. The rain was warm, like falling soup. "Oh-oh," she muttered, "I got to get back quick, or my hair'll get all nappy." We had nearly finished anyway, and we ran back to the office, while I remembered how many white girls I had run somewhere with in the rain "or my hair will get all straight."

Just before we reached the office, a last car tried to run us down. Clara was so used to this that she seemed to have an instinct about the color of the driver before he was visible, stepping off the road without interrupting her sentence and not even bothering to dignify him with a glance. But I still looked. This car, a new model Plymouth, had a sticker in the rear window: YOU ARE IN OCCUPIED MISSIS-SIPPI: PROCEED WITH CAUTION.

At the mass meeting we were introduced to the Negro community. One by one the volunteers stood and gave their names, home towns, work. There was loud applause. I sat at the back of the stage, where we had been summoned from among the audience, and looked at the heads in the rows in front. Four shades of blond-haired boys in the first row, a couple of redheaded girls to the side, a complete array of browns, Lorna's blue, and scattered among them maybe half a dozen Negroes, most of them local movement workers. The voices were grave, timid, as strange to each other as to the people out front, and somehow terribly mortal. The fear of uncertainty still hovered over the summer, given shape by our suspended anxiety over the three missing boys, and aggravated by some leftover drama from Ohio: the question of survival couldn't help being prominent in everyone's mind. But considering the heads that way just made them the objects of some macabre lottery. Something in the substance of the idea blocked it. It wasn't a conscious decision, but after that moment I stopped considering death—mine, or anyone's—as if the thought itself were somehow lethal.

The meeting had begun, as they all did later, with freedom songs and Brother Williams, who led a prayer and delivered a short peptalk. An old man in shirtsleeves, he communicated with the soul of the crowd, arousing their enthusiasm, laughter, or indignation in a Southern patois so impenetrable that it took me half the summer to make out all the words. Biblical verse was stirred in liberally. " 'Of one blood He made all nations,' " Brother Williams would quote. "So if those people are so separate, who all these bright [light] Negroes?" The crowd would sway with reaction, in tune with him as they never were with a Northern speaker of either color. "Seem to me the white man done hisself some integratin' at *night*." "Yes!" voices answered him. At some point he would say, "No man can keep another man down without staying down there with him." "Amen!" He lambasted what he called "those ole Jeff Davis niggers who think the white man loves 'em"—the Uncle Toms who never came to meetings. But the term was really meant to include the reluctant among the audience, and they knew it. "If you don' wanna get hurt, don't let a dyin' mule kick you! You do what the young people say. You go on down to the courthouse and register! If all the Mississippi Negroes'd register, Senator Eastland'd be pickin' cotton nex' year. Won't nobody pray Eastland and Stennis out o' office, you got to *vote* 'em out. We been told too much about heaven and not enough about how to live *here*."

There were teen-agers and young working people at the mass meetings, but many were the same age as Brother Williams. Old women came as though to revival meetings; for them SNCC was a substitute heavenly host. Brother Williams *spoke* to them, if not quite so tellingly to the younger generation, who called him "the 'Look-out' man" and had the sort of fond disdain for him that others feel for a tiresome, embarrassing old grandfather who is still the wisest man around. "There's a law 'gainst shootin' deer," he would say, pausing. The audience knew what was coming. "There's a law 'gainst rabbit." "Yes, yes," some voices answered. "There's a law 'gainst possum." "That's right." ". . . but it's *always* open season on Negroes!" They would laugh wryly, as they always did, as though the joke were new. Brother Williams, winding up to a shouting finish, would finally threaten, "If you don' register to vote you goin' to *hell*, that's all they is to it!"

Then he would lead them in a hymn, a music always strange to me. Supplying the words of the line in quick time, he bade them follow, and they would repeat the same words in apparently rhythmless, tuneless song, each syllable stretched out indefinitely. But this was only to my ear; their voices were always in unison.

There was very little resemblance between the sounds of the freedom songs and the hymns. The voices changed in quality from determined to resigned, from fresh and young to generations old, from exuberant with hope to fatalistic with suffering. A fragile, ancient woman stood and sang an incantation far older than she herself, full of Africa and voodoo: "Now Lord," and the audience echoed, Now Lord, "Help us stand together Lord (Yes, yes), Now, now, now oh Lord (Yes, Lord), Oh Lord, sometime I can't jus' res' at night (Oh, yes), Now Lord (Yes), Now now now oh Lord (Oh yes), Now oh Jesus . . ." She continued, swaying and incoherent, a low moan, a deep black dirge. Then Sam Block stood, taking advantage of a pause; and she sat, as though she'd intended to.

Young, very black, intensely thin, Sam had come from his native Cleveland, Mississippi, to Greenwood three years earlier to start the movement there. Then, it had been weeks before anyone was brave enough to house him, still longer before he had a vehicle faster than a mule. The first place he found for a SNCC office was invaded by a mob armed with guns and chains, and Sam barely escaped out the window, across the rooftops, and down a television antenna into another house. The second office was set on fire, all its equipment and records destroyed. Shot at, jailed, and beaten to the point of losing the full use of his right thumb and left eye, Sam had used up many more than nine lives by now, but the one still left to him was painful with stress. His asthma left him only when he left Greenwood. He had the quality of a wire drawn so taut that a word might snap it, pulled narrow from his feet to his face, which had large sensitive features and enormous eyes magnified through thick lenses. He whipped out at the people irritably now as they joined with insufficient enthusiasm in the song he was leading. His voice rang out like a primitive instrument, overpowering the others however loud they sang. But they were oriented toward hymns, and he wanted them to sing the songs of freedom as fully and naturally as they sang of Jesus.

"It's that free-ee-dom train a-comin', comin', comin'," he began, and they responded, at first tentatively then louder and faster as the line was repeated and built up. "It's that free-ee-dom train a-comin', comin'," and finally all together, "Get on bo-o-oard, get on board." Verse after verse—"It'll be tra-avlin' through Mississippi, 'sippi, 'sippi," "It'll be ca-arryin' nothin' but freedom, freedom, freedom." And then they hummed it while Sam spoke, "You don't have to push to get on that train no more, you know, 'cause—" and then went into the song's last verse, "They'll be co-o-omin' by the thousan', thousan', thousan' . . ."

The moral came through the music and the people gave themselves the message of the meeting. Words could never rival its effectiveness, but there had to be words. Stokely spoke to them that night, grabbing the tension already built up and manipulating it to give them courage. "We've got a lot to do this summer," he told them. "While these people are here, national attention is here. The FBI isn't going to let anything happen to them. They let the murderers of Negroes off, but already men have been arrested in Itta Bena just for *threatening* white lives." He urged, cajoled, and ordered them down to Martha Lamb, the registrar of Leflore County and sole judge of the test she administered. Some had been there before, some of them more times, literally, than they could count. "What do we have to do?" Stokely asked. His audience knew. "REGISTER!" they shouted.

There were more songs, and finally we stood, everyone, crossed arms, clasped hands, and sang "We Shall Overcome." Ending every meeting of more than half a dozen with it, we sang out all fatigue and fear, each connected by this bond of hands to each other, communicating an infinite love and sadness. A few voices tried to harmonize, but in the end the one true tune welled up in them and overcame. It was not the song for harmony; it meant too much to change its shape for effect. All the verses were sung, and if there had been more to prolong it, it would have been prolonged, no matter how late, how tired they were. Finally the tune was hummed alone while someone spoke a prayer, and the verse struck up again, "We shall overcome," with all the voice, emotion, hope, and strength that each contained. Together they were an army.

Across the room I saw Clara; she had somewhere found a yellow dress to wear. There were tears on her cheeks. I looked for the Amoses, but they had gone to another church.

4. Christians, Cops, and Black-Eyed Peas

A Southern moderate is a cat who'll lynch you from a low tree.

—Dick Gregory

"The time is *now!*" Sam Block would harangue the crowd at mass meetings. "If we fail this summer, what's going to happen to us next winter? You tell your minister, the time is *now!* Some o' you go to a church that won't fight for freedom. Jesus is not *in* there!"

"*Look* out!" Brother Williams would shout from the audience.

"Where do we go from here?" the speaker, a local minister, would ask. "To the courthouse!" More gently: "I know how you feel, you who've never been down. The first time I went my throat was so dry I could hardly get the words out. The second time it was better, then the third, and by the fourth time I was talking as I am right now. . . ."

Supplementing the message of the meetings, the voter registration workers went from house to house explaining the importance of the trip to the courthouse, attempting to convince the people that the vote would make them free, that sacrifices *had to be made.* The people were frightened, centuries had frightened them, and explanations of historical necessities made little impact on those who knew their names would appear for a fortnight in the daily paper (ostensibly to provide the opportunity for public-minded complaints about an applicant's moral character), and that the advertisement would more than likely cost them their jobs and possibly their homes, if nothing more. Illiterates knew they had no chance, but even the educated had no hope of passing the test—which was really of skin color, not of knowledge. They would therefore have to take the test again, and again, a dozen times or more, the risks the same with each attempt. But every trip was essential if we were to build up a case

56

against the registrar, who might then be enjoined by the federal government from giving the test, a goal already achieved in two of the eighty-two counties. It was very hard to make it all seem worth the danger and the tedium to the registrants. But to a few it was: they had got in the courthouse habit since the movement came to Greenwood, and dogged Martha Lamb with maddening regularity, prepared to continue the confrontation all their lives. Others responded for the first time when our Project began its work.

July 1

Three old men appear at 708 Avenue N at dawn to be taken to the courthouse. None of the voter registration people is around, so Lorna and I go along. The car parks on Market near the white marble Confederate Memorial "erected as tribute to Gen B. G. Humphreys by Varina-Jefferson Davis Chapter of U.D.C." The old men are silent as we climb the Ionic-columned steps of the huge, anonymous-official county courthouse. A blast of cool air as we walk in: a forgotten sensation. The first door to the left, lettered CIRCUIT CLERK, opens on a counter, and facing us behind it, Martha Lamb, terror of Greenwood. An ordinary-looking woman, after all, a tailored housewife. "Form a line outside the door," she directs in a stainless-steel voice. "I can see only one at a time." She knows who we are, of course, and what our presence means, and can afford to be officious. Besides, taking the applicants one at a time intimidates them—just when they need it, they lose our support. Before I leave the room, she points at me. "You! What's your name?" I tell her and she writes it down, inquiring how to spell it. Then she asks me where I'm from, and notes it.

The first old man goes in, and I wait with the other two in the hall. Benches having recently been removed, there is nowhere to sit except a window ledge on which hangs a sign saying something like "do not sit on the window ledge." In the preceding months the public telephone has also been disconnected, and then the phone in the drugstore across the street. This means that if there is trouble, or we simply need to call the office for a car, someone has to walk four blocks.

Mr. Otis, one of the men standing with me, admits that he and his two friends are illiterate, but that he badly wants to learn to read and write. "We want to be free, have our rights!" He is nearly eighty, straight and tall, half toothless, with someone's castoff tie in a plain knot around his collarless neck, and an old coat. He goes in next when the first man, rejected, reappears not a minute after entering. I stand in the doorway then and watch. "Course you know," Martha Lamb snaps at once at Mr. Otis, "you can't read nor write a scratch, you can't pass the test." He says he knows. "Person ought to have sense enough to know that," Martha Lamb says, waving him out. Then: "You!" she says at me again, noticing me in the doorway. "Get on outside there now!"

The third man passes me with a tense smile and goes in; I move outside the door but lean around to see. "How many times you been here before?" Martha Lamb asks him. "Eight," he answers. "*You* can't read nor write. What you doing here?" "I'm a citizen o' the United States," the old man says, "and I want to make the attempt." She dismisses him. At the door, nodding and looking down, he says, "I want my freedom all right. I do mighty bad, I'll tell you that."

Lorna goes in now. She marches up to the desk, demanding, "What proportion of the Negroes in this county are registered?"

"I don't have that information," Martha Lamb replies without looking up.

"I should think a person in your position would have it," says Lorna, deadpan and implacable.

"I don't care what you think." Martha Lamb fixes her with a scornful look. "The people of Mississippi think enough of me to hire me for this job."

Turning to a sheriff's deputy who entered a moment before and now towers beside her, listening, Lorna perseveres. "Well? Where can I get this information?"

"708 Avenue N," he retorts.

Lorna smiles. No one else does.

When she emerges I decide to go in too, simply to see if I can. My legs are shaking and, when I speak, so are the words. "Could I see a form?" Silently Martha Lamb hands me one.

"May I keep it?"

"No," she says.

I began reading. The deputy, still idling nearby, says, "Look at her, she's memorizin' it."

"Really"—I point to the four pages of print—"could I memorize all this?"

"Well, you ask them niggers," he says, "they got a copy of it."

Not bothering to refute this, I finish reading and return the form to Martha Lamb with a tense smile. She says shrilly, "You *see* they can't read nor write, why y'all keep bringin' 'em down here when you know they can't pass the test?"

"They're illiterate because there were no schools; it's not their fault. They're still citizens and they have a Constitutional right to vote."

"Well, I just follow the law," she says. "That's the Mississippi law, nothin' to do with *rights*." Before I can answer, she goes on, "Why don't you stay home and clean up New York, anyhow? You got it worse up there. Our folks is happy down here." She produces a happy smile.

"Some are," I say, "and some aren't. I guess it depends on what color you are." The deputy sheriff is staring at me and I retreat, realizing that I'm still trembling.

A new carload of registrants has arrived with June Johnson, a tall, powerfully beautiful sixteen-year old who had been in Ohio; they are waiting in the hall. One of them goes in. I look for Lorna and find her standing by a candy-cigarette stall down the corridor, excoriating the white man behind the counter. "Where do all your taxes go?" she wants to know. "North Greenwood is as rich as Beverly Hills. And look at the condition of this courthouse! It's a disgrace!"

I look around at the "condition of the courthouse" and think it resembles most of its institutional equivalents around the country. The deputy sheriff has left the Circuit Clerk's office and is sauntering over to us. June, beside me, whispers, "That's Honey Styles."

"You people are being cheated," Lorna accuses, "that's all there is to it. If I were you I'd look into where your tax money is going."

Deputy Sheriff Styles breaks in. "Lot of it's goin' into fightin' outside agitators." He glowers.

Lorna turns on him, unamused. "Well, I'm from San José," she says, "and back home we know where our money is going."

"Why don't you gwan home to San José then?" the deputy says, bending over Lorna as though about to send her there with the force of his personality. She dismisses him and turns back to the candy vender. "How did you lose your sight?" she asks—and now I notice that his dark glasses are not just for protection from the sun.

"In the Second World War," he answers.

"Well, if you lost your sight fighting for freedom you'd think you'd continue to fight for freedom at home."

Hearing June's voice as she questions a returning registration applicant, the vender directs his answer at her. "You people are going about it the wrong way," he says. "You ought to get rid of these outsiders and organize yourselves, with your teachers."

"*You* got it wrong," June says. "Our teachers can't organize with us as long as they're employed by you. They'll lose their jobs."

Honey Styles, feeling left out, contributes a non sequitur. "These people got ten children and don't one o' them know who their father is. None of them's married. They come in here about to have a baby for a marriage license."

Lorna deigns to look at him again. "Well, from what I can see, there are a lot of mulatto children around here whose fathers didn't bother to marry their mothers." She lets that take over the silence for a moment, then adds, "Besides, if they're coming to get married, that's pretty good, isn't it?"

The deputy walks away, and the vender begins to rearrange his display of Life Savers.

Lorna has an errand to run: she has given away all the Sunday school leaflets she brought from California and wants more for the children she reads to in the park. We stand outside the courthouse dividing up, while cars pass and slow as they see the mixed group. I'm not accustomed yet to the faces, the way they make a split-second switch from indifference to hatred—it still seems a specific threat, not just a Southerner's duty.

Four of us, two local teen-agers and Lorna and I, go in Ed Bauer's car in search of the First Methodist Church. Neither of the Greenwood kids knows where it is. Dorothy Higgins says the worlds are so separate that the minister of the Negro Methodist Church had never met the white Methodist minister, though they live but five blocks apart, until a recent national Methodist convention in Chicago.

We pass a large, beautiful swimming pool with no one in it—the municipal pool for whites, closed in order not to integrate. "It's Olympic size," Dorothy says. "You could fit about ten of our pools in that one." The Negro pool, near the office, is about half the size of a basketball court. We're still looking for the church, when driving up and down a series of streets we pass a smooth lawn with a water sprinkler in the center shooting out a fine spray. "Hey, let's integrate that sprinkler!" Willie James Earl suggests. Such possibilities are only jokes.

We finally find the church, and Lorna and I go in. A motherly woman at a desk blocks access to the other offices. She listens to Lorna's story about giving out the papers and of the child who had taken one home and been told by his mother, "That woman's a missionary of the Lord." "Though in fact," Lorna appends, "I'm a sinner. I don't go to church."

"Why?" asks the woman.

"Well, I see so many people who pretend to be Christians, but they hate Jews, they hate Negroes."

The woman nods and smiles in unctuous agreement; but she has no authority, she says, nothing to do with leaflets for Negro children.

We circle the church and return by another entrance, hoping to get at the minister. This time Dorothy and Willie James come with us. Edging along various corridors, we come upon a door with the minister's name on it, enter when there is no answer to the knock, and feel distinctly that someone has just that instant fled. Proceeding to one door farther, we find ourselves again confronting the motherly woman. Never on the defensive for a second, Lorna immediately asks her, "Could these children come to your church?" She indicates Dorothy and Willie James.

"I am not in a position to say," the woman answers.

"You're not in a position to say? Do you mean there is some *doubt* as to whether or not these children of God could attend your church?" The woman fumbles with some papers. "Well, you're just not doing God's work. Now you see why I'm not a Christian. It says in the Bible to love the Lord thy God with all thy heart and with all thy soul and with all thy mind, and thy neighbor as thyself, but here these children of God, your neighbors, can't come to your church."

The woman, pretending to look for something, says nothing. Then Dorothy asks her, "If it was up to you, would you let us come?"

The woman says: "I can't answer that question. I'd have to pray on that."

We decide to try another church. The Catholics are down the street, the church open but unattended. We ring the bell of the next-door house. An old man in a clerical collar and a red velvet smoking jacket answers after two or three minutes. He looks with dismay at our array of colors and talks through the screen door. Tiny drafts of his air-conditioning drift through to us. He says immediately that he has absolutely no Sunday school material for Negro children. Noting Lorna's hand on the door, he pulls it more tightly toward him. He seems upset. Lorna points to Dorothy and asks him, "Can this girl come to your church?" He wants to know what church she goes to; Dorothy says Baptist, but she'd like to come to his church.

He thinks for a moment. "She belongs to another church, she goes to her church," he says.

"What about me?" pipes up Willie James. "I'm a Catholic." (He isn't, he admits later.)

"He's got his own parish," the priest says, refusing to address Willie James in the second person. "There is a line in the middle, he goes to the church in his parish. We provide for them."

Lorna glances at him askance. "I thought the Catholic Church wasn't segregated," she says.

"No, it isn't," he answers.

"But you won't let this boy come to your church."

"He has his church," snaps the priest, losing patience.

So is Lorna. "Well I'm certainly glad I'm not a Christian," she retorts.

The priest relaxes a little, pleased. "I see that," he says.

"I'm not a Christian," Lorna continues, "when I see how you people act. You don't give a damn about Christianity. I try to follow Christ's teachings, but I wouldn't call myself a Christian for anything."

"Ah well, it's easy to see, if you damn people, you are not a Christian." He gives her a holy smile. "Christ wouldn't damn anyone but hypocrites."

"And aren't you a hypocrite?" I break in. "You who say your church isn't segregated?"

"The church is not segregated," the priest says in benediction. "We have our parish, they have theirs." He draws back and shuts the door in our faces.

"Mrs. Smith has a strong heart," Willie James says, grinning on the way back to the car.

Lorna is not to be put off now. What other churches are there? The Presbyterian, Dorothy suggests. A man behind a desk in the first office we find there says the minister is out of town, that he is the "music minister," and can he help us? His manner is cordial enough, in spite of his integrated interlocutors. When Lorna explains about the literature, he responds immediately that he will see if they have any. He leaves us in his office to go to "the educational department."

About ten minutes pass while we wait for his return. We're sitting and gossiping, when all at once the door to the office swings open and five armed policemen stride in. "What y'all doin' here?" one of them asks. He has four gold stars on the shoulder of his shirt: Chief of Police Curtis Lary. We tell him the man has gone to get us some material; Dorothy takes two steps out of the room to indicate the direction in which he went, and a policeman springs after her, ordering her to "git back in there!" They stand around looking at us through half-closed eyes, rattling their weapons; Chief Lary asks questions long after the situation is obvious. He has a thin, weak, papery face, more pathetic than sinister, and keeps polishing his glasses. Finding the phone, he is about to dial a number when the "music minister" returns with an armful of pamphlets.

"Did you call the police?" Chief Lary asks him.

"No," the man answers too quickly, his expression of sudden fear rather startling.

Lorna, concerned with the business at hand, takes the pamphlets and expresses her gratitude. The policemen linger. "Are you segregated?" she asks the churchman.

"Yes," he answers.

"The Southern Presbyterians and the Northern Presbyterians are different, aren't they?" she says.

"Yes."

"Are you aware that a Negro is head of the Northern Presbyterians?"

"Yes," he says.

As we leave, Willie James mentions that a man had been watching us enter the church; it must have been he who called the cops. For a while we had been forced to suspect the "music minister," but everyone prefers to believe the best of him. He is praised all the way home, an honest man—when asked if his church was segregated, after all, he had simply said, "Yes."

Back at the office, Stokely was losing his daily temper. Even if what he said was not entirely rational, the volume of the voice got things done. Yesterday it had been: "Everyone in the office at nine! No one late, or I'll send you home! Across the board!" Now: "What's all this hanging around the office? No more of that! I don't want to see another person sitting around here tomorrow! Across the board!"

Volunteers got back to work; some went downstairs to help clear out the two rooms for the national SNCC office, about to move from Atlanta. Jesse Harrison, the SNCC man who was doing most of it, had stayed up for two nights now, wiring and putting up partitions. A crew of two came in and out the window from the roof, where they were attaching a thirty-foot aerial for our citizens' band radio transmitter, KUY 1106, part of the statewide communications network, growing as money and equipment—including two-way radio cars—trickled in from the North.

The traffic upstairs dwindled down to a dozen people, most of them with a purpose. A lawyer, one of those who spent a week or a fortnight away from their Northern jobs to help us, remarked that in picking up the phone just then he had heard a voice say, "Gimme a pencil." "That's okay," someone commented. "In some towns the cops can't even write. In Itta Bena the other day a SNCC man had to fill out his own ticket." Books, boxes, shelves. Some children who had taken out some picture books and returned to ask if they could help were toting armloads across the room. I was trying to get used to the idea that some books would have to be thrown out. The heat was wilting. Every now and then Carol Kornfield padded through on bare feet from her typing in the little office, doused her head with cold water in the bathroom, and reappeared scattering drops like a drenched puppy. She was busy all day answering obscene phone calls from the other side of town and trying to think of a good retort —the messages were repetitious—before the next. She had developed a superior degree of equanimity to deal with the voices asking, "How many nigger cocks y'all got to suck 'fore you can go to sleep at night?" But no one could answer: "Can I speak to Andy Goodman?"

There was a rush downstairs, where some women had brought us

food: basins of salad, pots of chicken and greens, a mound of cornbread, and a big glass jar of Kool-Aid. In five minutes not a scrap
was left; the children who played around outside had disposed of
the last crumb. The women packed up their dishes and left again.
They received nothing for the food or the time, and most of them
cooked for a white family as well as their own; but it was what they
had to give, and they wanted to give it to the movement.

Stokely, peaceable again, was calling people "Sweets" and laughing in a corner of the library with a group waiting for a car to return. Discussing local police procedures as though they were practi-
cal jokes, he described the burns produced by cattle prods—"I've
seen it! Man, they don't have to do anything but *show* it to me!"
And wrist-breakers, a gadget with a screw that tightens down the
center of the wrist, cutting into the vein. "They got that thing on
me and I couldn't move my hand for two weeks afterwards." He
demonstrated. Then a month ago he was hospitalized after
exposure to tear gas—"raking my insides, ripping me apart." Then
the time they beat him till he was more than happy to say "Yes,
suh." What it felt like to be on the wrong end of a gun: "I don't
worry about a gun pointing at me unless the guy is shaking. If he's
scared, I'm scared." It was all supposed to be funny; in any case the
group was nearly in tears with laughter. Stokely was in good spirits
—tomorrow was his birthday, the first he would spend out of jail
(he hoped) in three years.

The car returned and a group of voter registration workers piled
up the stairs. One of them announced that "Sister Martha" had just
transcended herself. To a man appearing for his test results, she had
said, "Well, you didn't pass, but would you bring me some good
green peas?"

"What we gonna do, we gonna take her the peas all right, but
they ain't gonna be green peas. We gonna take her a whole mess o'
black-eyed peas."

In the late afternoon I joined the Amoses in the living room. A
portrait of the Kennedys hung behind the television set, and Mrs.
Amos sat looking at it, waiting for the news. There was only one
electric outlet, which meant that none of the lamps in the room
could be used, only the bulb in the ceiling; and the light above the
Kennedy portrait had to be sacrificed when the television was on.

There was one like it in every home. One woman said to me, "The lady I worked for was happy when he died. There was a big black cloud that day, and right at the edge a blood-red cloud. You couldn't see the sun at all."

Walter Cronkite came on. The first item concerned the setting up of private schools in the South to combat desegregation. The second related that Schwerner, Chaney, and Goodman had still not been found, and showed pictures of sailors poking through Neshoba bayous. The third was a report of a speech by Roy Wilkins, Executive Director of the NAACP, demanding federal protection for civil rights workers in Mississippi. The fourth was datelined Hattiesburg, Mississippi: shots had been fired into two cars belonging to COFO. That strange feeling was maintained from Ohio: "world news" appeared to be happening entirely where we sat watching it.

The airwaves produced an equally curious, opposite sensation later on that night. Back at work in the library, I could hear behind me the music of the radio that sat on a shelf in the back. The sounds were suddenly familiar, and when I tuned myself in I realized it was Odetta singing "Oh Freedom" and "I'm on My Way." When the music stopped, a voice announced, "This program came to you from the United States of America."

It was the Voice of America, broadcasting to the most foreign of lands.

5. Free and Unfree

*No use you sayin' you ain't in the mess. 'Cause, baby,
if you born black, you born dead in the mess.*

—Sam Block

At some point in the summer all the local COFO workers started
wearing straw hats. They had colorful cotton bands and brims so
wide you couldn't always tell who was underneath—especially useful for assuming siesta positions in the library. Late in a July afternoon I noticed I was being looked at from under a new hat by a
new face. It was a boy, very young, hardly five feet tall, with a brilliant grin. The next day he sent me a letter.

Itta Bena

Dear Sally

How are you doing as a libarian. The first time I saw you, I
start thinking, she smiled at me it best for me to start smiling
back. Don't look at this letter and smack it up Please. I have something to tell you. I am 13 you are older than I am. I just tell you
my age and see how I'm standing. I am not back that far. Sally
come over to the office some time in Itta Bena. I'll visit you every
chance I can. I wish I could work in the libarie with you, do the
thing libarian should do. If I ever write a book I'll never forget
how to spell your name.

When I get 17 I'm going to San Diego California, and I'm going
to Manhattan New York. There I shall go my 10 years in College.
Five years for myself, five years for you.

Everyone mostly know me. I am not bad like the other boys
are. Hope I see you soon.

Your friend Lucius Murphy,
write me back.

There were more letters from Lucius, and he hitched a ride to
Greenwood with COFO volunteers when he could—not very often,

as he worked hard in the movement at home. I would look up from the books and there he'd be, keeping an eye on things. One day he sat down at a free desk and wrote me a report.

The Negroes has been taken it ruf. If the Negroes make a move and go violent, it would be more killing than anything in the world. That's why the Negroes has to go nonviolent. The southern white think that the Negroes is afraid of them. But that's not so. The white is really afraid of the Negroes. They can't fight fair, they have to use guns. They doesn't do it in the day, they wait until night come. From that statement that proves that they are afraid of the Negroes. The white man think if we get our equal rights, he thinks it mean the Negroes are trying to get over him. And he thinks we will be able to tell him what to do instead of him tell the black man what to do. But the reason we are trying to get freedom is because slavery is the next thing to hell. It is not fair to treat the Negroes like they are cat and dog and mules. Whip them when they don't do their work hard enough. We work very hard for little pay. We get cheated out of all our money the little we do get. Some still do that kind of work for little pay. Some like get cheating out of their money. Those kind the white man want.

You can see how much our own color is against us. Negroes always telling you that they are 100% with us. But when you bring those Freedom Registration Forms they get out of focus. That's the way you find them out. They won't sign the Freedom Registration Form. They think that they can fool you. But they really be fooling their self. As long as we have been in the movement people are saying you don't know what you are doing. I ask one man did the white man know what was *he* doing he said yes. Then I said Negroes don't *suppose* to know what he or she is doing. I told him you let your color get you scared. My brother ask him what about we go sit in the white cafe. He said that's for white people. I said go look at their cafe and then look at yours. Theirs look like a cafe but yours look beat up. They don't care what way our park look but we are showing them that if they don't care, we care and if they don't do anything about it we'll have to go to park they go to. I say we should have one school. One for colored and white both to go to. They think that they are more important than the Negroes. We are going to show them that we can get just as important as they can. They get mail at home, we got to go to the post office. If they can get

mail at home we can get mail at home also. I think that we have
slave to much we want our freedom now.

I've been working with the movement in Itta Bena for 3 year
and haven't ever been put in jail. I'm willing to go to jail if I
have to. If I have to died for freedom I don't mind. Because you
doesn't have to be in this to get kill. Because you have to go someday. It might not be now but someday. It doesn't matter what
color you are black or white. I'm glad I am a Negro. I'm proud
to be one. When I become older I'll join the Student Nonviolent
Coordinating Comittee. I'm working hard to get my freedom.

Expert Lucius Murphy I hope.

One day Samuel T. Mills came to the library. He said he was
eight, or nine, or seven, and he wrote his name on everything. He
didn't know his address or what the "T" stood for, though the
other children called him just that, and no one could explain his
origins, until Bambi Brown revealed he had followed her to the office
from Baptist Town, where his family lived. But once with us, he
seldom left. He was there at 5 a.m., often still crashing around
eighteen hours later, and he punctuated the day printing his name
on pieces of paper and presenting them to his latest friends like calling cards. Sometimes they would catch him sleeping in one of the
cars parked around the office and drag him off to an aunt's house
nearby, with attempted explanations about the police catching
him and arresting us all for contributing to the delinquency of a
minor. Failing to grasp this, he simply got better at recognizing
allies and enemies and eluding the latter. He could talk the
allies into making over much of their days to him, then their nights
—taking him along to mass meetings, or just finding him there,
however distant the church, waiting for them. He would fall asleep
in the pew about halfway through, worn out from his exhausting
schedule.

Samuel was smooth dark brown with skin the texture of a plum,
and a stomach the shape of one when he ate, which was almost constantly. He wore nothing but some crusty blue jeans riding precariously on his hips and dragging in the dust. Mrs. Amos gave him out-
grown shirts of Earl Henry's, I bought him two pairs of sandals at
Wing's, and he had an inexhaustible belt supply from someone worried about his pants falling off. But he would disappear for half a
day now and then, to resurface shoeless and topless from some

extraordinary adventure which was never articulable but always involved an awful fate to his clothes. In fact he just took them off wherever he happened to be when they got too hot or in the way.

He had a deep gravelly lisping voice which laughed with love for his friends. Eli asked him, "What are you going to be when you grow up, Sammy?" and he answered, "A Nick fiel thectay." "A SNCC field secretary? What do SNCC field secretaries do?" "Don' hit nobody." He was full of convincing, if improbable, stories to arouse sympathy, about the way his father mistreated him, his big sister pounced on him, his mother fed him nothing but cake, and (to others, never to me) that I was going to take him back to New York with me. Coaxing everyone "Gimme a nickel," he promoted himself to a dime, and when they got tired of that he had them pitching pennies, always winning and keeping the loot. Then, hitching up his pants, he trotted down the road to Wing's to buy an ice milk or a pop, depending on how rich he was. When he came back he had often cut his foot on something and would hobble around on one heel and one toe until someone noticed and put on a bandage, which he lost in the next trip, having cut himself somewhere else. In his back pocket was a tattered wallet with nothing in it but a smooth stone he saved to put between two toes of his right foot where an old cut rubbed open sometimes.

He moved with an athlete's speed and a dancer's grace, and his energy never faltered; when there was nothing else to do, he used it to empty ashtrays or sweep the dirt around the floor. No one ever asked him to do these things, and no one else (except Jim Forman) did them without being asked. The energy needed a lot of replenishing. An almost mystical instinct kept him informed about when I was awake in the morning, and within seconds he would scamper to the door, laughing and hungry. He would put away about half his weight in breakfast, hang around the library during the day, ramble off, return, pitch pennies with Eli, leave again, but turn up precisely as I sat down to dinner—which was never the same time—ready to go again. At this point he would be in the mood for half a fried chicken and a quart of buttermilk, a lot of which would end up smeared in a white foam all over his face. Mrs. Amos could refuse him nothing either. One night he stayed in my room after I had gone out to dinner, angry that I wouldn't take him with me. Afterwards I found my wallet open with a five-dollar bill and a toy-money thousand-dollar bill missing. Three singles were left scattered around the dresser. It was not the work of a master thief.

Outside there were already signs of Samuel's path of devastation. He had invited all the children around the office to come to Wing's with him; the word had spread, and by the time he got there a crowd was following. He bought them all candy and soda, but was then set upon by bigger boys and beaten up, and the rest of the money was snatched from him. Then he ran.

Pieces of this story got put together from various sources as I chased around the dark streets with Lucius, looking for him. Others had begun the search before I'd even known the money was missing, and a COFO radio car and various private posses were all out after him. Why they felt it a matter of such urgency was in doubt: some were worried about him, others seemed to need the thing to do from the momentum of their own tension, still others were just second-string vigilantes out to get some money themselves. Wing said he'd thought such a large bill peculiar, but Samuel had explained it as the gift of someone at the office. Across the street at the high school a floodlit baseball game was going on. Lucius and I ran into the emerald circle of light and around the bleachers in pursuit, but onlookers who were already in on the story said that Samuel had seen me coming and run. Where? No one knew, but there had been a couple of dozen kids following him, still hoping for a share of the cash. One of them had taken Samuel's shirt and belt, added a big boy who had apparently just stood there watching.

They looked for him until long past midnight without results. In the morning the neighborhood kids, each more self-righteous than the last, joined the search, and just before noon a large band of them dragged Samuel up the stairs and pushed him, trembling, in front of me. They envied his favored position with us and shouted gleefully, "Now you get a whuppin', Tee." I told them to leave, and they seemed to, but small heads bobbed up behind corners and pieces of furniture until I shouted louder.

Samuel was covered with grime and tears, and he stood with his head down, waiting. I didn't know what to do. Following the suggestion of a psychologist on the medical team, I told him we would make a chart of all the jobs around the library and that he could work off the money he owed me. We sat down and ruled up a large sheet of paper, giving prices to sweeping, mopping, emptying wastebaskets, dusting, cleaning the bathroom, and straightening the books. He had never heard of such a strange form of punishment. Snuffling, he found the mop and pail and scrubbed the floor from end to end, rubbing at it furiously, all afternoon. He did half-a-dollar's worth of work, and then his mother came.

She was as handsome as he, with a strong, well-boned face and huge slanting eyes, and spoke with the same voice. She talked as though she had stolen the money, and now, she said miserably, she wanted to pay it back. Her husband, she explained, had gone to Chicago several years ago when they had separated, and her job as waitress in a café lasted from midafternoon to midnight; she was afraid her children didn't get enough care, but without her job they would have nothing. I told her about the chart and that she didn't need to pay me back, and called Samuel to show her it was all right, but he had vanished. He didn't turn up again until three o'clock, the time his mother reported for work. Then I found him dusting in the mimeograph room. He hadn't eaten all day, but didn't complain, and wouldn't follow me to dinner until invited.

He suffered much, if stoically, for a week or two, more from the psychological lectures that everyone felt impelled to give him than from the work—because so attractive and adventurous did he make it seem that by the next day every child in the neighborhood less than three and a half feet high wanted to scrub and dust too, and the library was clogged with his helpers. Afterwards it was as though it hadn't happened, except that it never did again. And now whenever he was asked, "What do SNCC field secretaries do, Sammy?" he would answer, "Don' hit nobody, don' take nothin', don' tell 'tories."

On Saturday afternoons every fortnight or so there would be a very large cardboard box on the Amoses' dining table. Samuel's radar sent him messages about it, and for the next few days he would never wander far away. The box was full of candy, and it was Edgar Amos's recompense for an odd job he sometimes did: loading trucks at a local candy factory, the wages consisting of all the candy you could carry away. Other Amoses, Samuel, every child within blocks, and I made ourselves regularly ill on a diet of sourballs, peanut brittle, chocolate bars, jelly beans, cookie snacks, caramels, licorice treats, coconut marshmallows, and fudge. Edgar himself just doled it out to friends—he had eaten all he could while loading and

was too sick of it to want any more. It seemed a generous wage to
him because it would have cost so much in the store. That it was
waste from broken boxes, or broken itself, and cost the factory nothing, was not a consideration.

Three times a week, after Mrs. Amos came home from cooking for
the white folks, the diet changed too. They gave her all their leftover *boeuf Stroganoff* or *coq au vin*, which had something over *coq
au* deep-fat in the way of variety, but there was a constant humilia-
tion in living on the discards of others. The family dressed entirely
in the worn-out, shrunken, outmoded garments of their employers;
and now these were supplemented by the clothes that Northerners
donated to SNCC. Truckloads of clothing came in from everywhere.
Someone had gone to great trouble to package and mail them,
though often they seemed not altogether worth it, faded, misshapen,
and dirty. But the recipients resented it less than I did.

"They's white and we's colored"—Mrs. Amos rationalized it one
day. "They lives in the old plush, what we call the old plush, sendin'
us all them clothes. You wouldn't find nobody here with enough
clothes to send 'em away. . . . Things is better, though"—she
cheered up—"you don't see people in rags no more, and mos' people
got shoes in the winter now, or if not shoes at leas' tennis. But they
ain't used to them, they go out in the rain and bog 'em up, the children, jus' leave 'em there in the playground. My children do that, I
make 'em go back hunt all day for 'em."

Mrs. Amos had begun receiving such booty at thirteen, when she
got her first job with a newly married couple hardly older than she
was—the girl was seventeen at most, she said. She had cooked
bacon and eggs for them in the morning, and greens and meat and
bread at night, and stayed with the young wife all day, less to clean
—though she did that too—than to keep her company. "She were
'fraid to cook and 'fraid to be left alone. But she were very good to
me; I got a dollar-fifty a day and a lot o' clothes."

She had worked in white women's homes all her life, from 6 a.m.
to 7 at night, seven days a week, for a wage now risen to $2.50 a day.
"Takin' care of their children, and my own jus' havin' to stay home
all day. Couldn't let 'em run loose on the streets—I had to lock 'em
up. They was real good, but I sho' did wish I could see 'em some
more. Glo-Jean, she were so quiet, she jus' be settin' right where I
put her when I come home again. She still so quiet. . . ."

The only other variety of work she ever had was in the war, when for the first time there were different kinds of jobs available. She was hired "pickin' tops" for a soda-pop manufacturer. "They were a tin shortage, so they had to use old tops. We had a big old tub o' tops, and I had to pick out the good ones." She was paid five dollars a week; but it was a five-day week, and she got to see her children.

The Amoses were intensely religious. They didn't drink or curse and observed in their lives all the old Christian virtues—which uniquely included absolute tolerance of those who didn't. They couldn't go to mass meetings because these conflicted with church; their whole involvement with the movement was open, generous, but inactive except where its work was clearly God's. Since God was on the side of equality, and so were we, they filled out Freedom Democratic Party forms and gave food and comfort to the COFO workers. "I'll tell you somethin'," Mrs. Amos said, "God is so *just,* he jus' natchel-born so just, that they ain't *nothin'* you can't do for him." In a corner near a picture of Christ hung one of Bob Moses. She had cut it out of the *Saturday Evening Post,* put it in a frame, and often gazed at it with love. "When he first come here I'd *cry* over him. I thought sure they'd kill him. He'd jus' stand there and talk to them, then they'd go away, and he'd just be standin' there. Then they shot at him one day. I never thought they'd let him leave alive."

Mr. Amos, when he wasn't at work as an odd-jobber and gardener, or at church, or out fishing for our dinner, was usually in the street underneath his old car, tinkering with it. It almost never worked, though once in a while it briefly decided to, and the whole family would pile in for an excursion to "the rural," and it would lurch to a stop about a block away. He would get a friend to push it back and take it all apart again. Since I used the kitchen door, and the porch and the front of the house were off-limits—I could easily be seen there by whites driving past—I seldom saw Mr. Amos. He ate later than the rest of us because he needed the daylight for the car; I also thought he was avoiding me. But at last one day it rained and he came in early, washed, and filled a plate with food while I was still at the table writing something. I put it away to make room for him. "You ain't got to hide that from me, Miss Sally," he said, with his bright smile. "I can't read it nohow. That's white folks' writin'." He stood there eating. I denied, embarrassed, hiding anything from him. We smiled politely. I asked him please to sit down. He said he liked to eat standing up.

We were so scared of offending each other, with our roles so undefined, that each kept bowing to the other in an utterly foolish sort of dance. He had never sat at a table with a white woman, and since that situation is within the heart of the mess of the South, it was not something done easily. I had been trying to talk with him for weeks without success and now realized that in some extraordinary paradox he would never think of us as equal until I ordered him to. I begged him to sit down; he wouldn't; I *told* him to sit down. He did, in great confusion. Somehow or other, everything was all right after that. Later Mrs. Amos reported to me that he had been amazed to find we could be *friends.*

"You got to tell me all about them foreign countries," he said. "I never lef' right here. They speaks different over there, I know that. Like Wing. When he start talkin' to his wife they might be sayin' how they gonna shoot me—I don't stay around to find out. It's real *fun*ny-soundin'."

I asked him how far away he'd been, and he said Chicago once, very briefly; but also he had a brother in Tennessee whom he'd gone to visit three times. "Where he come from it's a hundred per cent better than down here. Up there the white people and the colored people go in and out of the same door, and lie in the same hospital, and eat in the same restaurant. Oh, it's *real* different up there. Now here, we got us a puzzle. This puzzle gonna take a heap o' subtractin' and multiplyin' and dividin' 'fore we get th'ough. Mm-mm!"

He went back to eating for a while, and thinking, then continued. "Got to do it with the young people, that's the only way. The young people is better than the old people. The old people get all slaveytown on you. Like in the old days, if the white folks told you to do somethin' you *did* it! Now'days you can jus' turn around if you don't want to. But the old people, they don't know times is changed."

"What did they do before if you didn't do what they wanted?"

"I don't know, I didn't want to know, I jus' did it. They made you get up when it were still night, and be out in the fields till dark again, and I *knowed* you could get jus' the same work done without all that, but that were how they wanted it, and I jus' did it. They paid us fifty cents a day. Two bits for the mornin', two bits for the evenin'. I never thought they was any other way to make a livin'."

"When did you start working in the fields?"

"Soon as I was old enough to know better, I reckon. 'Bout seven year old. My mother would give me the hoe halfway up the row, and by the time I were done she'd gone clear the way to the end and back." He had finished eating by now and just sat still, remembering.

"Didn't you go to school?"

"Well, it were a six-months' school, so's you could work most the year around, but I went. I'd have to get up early and work in the fields, then go to school, then go back to the fields after. See, they weren't money enough for books—books cost at least a dollar each, and tryin' to find a dollar then was bad as findin' five dollars now. You was supposed to go down to the drugstore and buy them, but I never could do that, 'count o' no money. I learned real quick when I was there, though. . . . But it were only six months o' the year, like I say, and after I learned to read and write some I had to quit. Didn't have no clothes to go in. We got one pair shoes for the winter, and if you wore them out you didn't get no more, so you had to treat 'em careful. But when I were thirteen they just wasn't no more clothes."

One of the puzzles of the movement was the way it seemed to attract more women than men. At the mass meetings the audience was preponderantly female, and among the women were the most articulate, active workers, the most responsive group for literacy classes. Since just about as many women as men were breadwinners, they had as many jobs to lose; and after a ten-hour day of cleaning, cooking, and child-watching for white families and then their own, they were no less tired. At the Freedom Democratic Party county convention, thirteen of seventeen delegates whom the people chose from among themselves were women. When the FDP ran three candidates for Congress, the most obviously qualified were Mrs. Hamer, Victoria Gray, and Annie Devine.

Later, when the Summer Project ended and its recruits left Greenwood, the question arose of who among the local people could replace Bob Zellner as Project Director. One name was obvious to everyone but its owner: Mary Lane. A thin dark girl of twenty-four with a kind and gentle face, she seldom smiled and never spoke except to *say* something. Now she just sat quietly, then said finally, "I can't make those decisions." Eli complained, "Mary, be honest, you've done it before—who did it all spring?" "I can't do it," she said, shrugging unhappily.

It was hard to get her to talk about herself: "You know how it is. These are memories I try to forget." But after a summer with her it was possible to worm some of it out. She had joined the movement in February 1963, when SNCC had just got its office on McLaurin Street—the office which was subsequently burned. She had had a job at a cabstand opposite, and would go to work early to hang around the SNCC office—"because they were nice people, and I was wondering what was going on." Bob Moses was there, and Jim Forman. Many of her friends warned her, "Don't connect with that mess." "But SNCC was making people realize they had problems, and they offered a way out." So she started doing little jobs for them, helping to distribute the food that was coming in from the North (this was the winter when Leflore County had rejected the federal surplus foods). After waging a small campaign against her self-abasement, they got her to agree to work with them full time. I asked her what the pay was then. "When I first began we weren't getting anything but satisfaction," she said. "That was enough. Then sometime later we started getting five dollars a week."

She organized a food and clothing distribution committee, and worked in voter registration, "carrying people to the courthouse." At some point she began to try to register herself but, though an exceptionally bright girl and a high school graduate, she was turned down again and again by Martha Lamb. Martha Lamb was making a mistake. For one thing, Mary wouldn't stop taking the test. For another, she ran for Martha's job in the first mock election in 1963, and again in 1964.

In June 1963 she and George Greene, another local worker, brought a group of people to the courthouse, where they were told to wait, as Martha Lamb was "busy." Martha Lamb was reading a newspaper and gossiping with her assistant. Some of the others left; Mary stayed. "Mary, what do you want?" said Martha. "I came to check if I passed the test," said Mary. "I told you I was busy," said Martha. "You're not too busy," Mary said.

After being asked to leave four times, they were threatened with arrest unless they complied. Twenty-three were arrested. They were tried four hours later, without permission to make a phone call, charged with breach of the peace and disorderly conduct, found guilty, and sentenced to six months and a $750 fine. The first four days were spent in the county jail, then a week on the county farm. The men were worked on road gangs. Carloads of whites followed them daily, threatening them with guns. Afraid for their lives, they went on strike, and were then all moved to Parchman State Penitentiary. There, Mary's shoes were taken and she was put in solitary. The nights were very cold: the air conditioning was turned off in the day and on at night, and there was no covering on the steel bed, "which had forty-four holes in it." This was standard treatment. One night she woke with cramps in her legs, told the authorities, but was refused a blanket or medical attention.

Her legs still ached more than a year later, though she never talked about it. Doctors offered various diagnostic theories involving the circulation, and gave her heat and other treatments, but Mary remained in almost constant pain, and no one knew it unless they observed her limp. No one noticed her much at all, until they needed something done.

During July, Mary failed the registration test for the tenth time. For the eleventh, she took U.S. Representative William Fitts Ryan of New York with her. Ryan and three other congressmen had been touring the state after the disappearance, and he was interested in registration procedure. Shown Mary's last flunked test, he observed that he couldn't see anything wrong with it and that apparently Registrar Lamb hadn't either, as she had marked no mistakes on the paper. Martha Lamb administered the test again, while Ryan waited. Mary Lane stood at a mass meeting three weeks later to announce: "Tomorrow I'm going down to the courthouse for the eleventh time to find out if I passed. But if I didn't pass, I'm not going back there again; I'm going to file a suit against Martha Lamb."

She passed.

Lucius, Samuel, the Amoses, and Mary Lane were free already in the important sense—"freed even from the need to hate," as Vincent Harding had put it in Ohio. They disarmed the enemy with their gift of sight beyond surfaces. But "the enemy" was not a category; their love was color-blind and reserved for what was important. Mrs. Hamer was free. She represented a challenge that few could understand: how it was possible to arrive at a place past suffering, to a concern for her torturers as deep as that for her friends. Such people were rare. All of them began by refusing to hate or despise themselves.

"It has never been proven that Negroes are not inferior to whites," said a Negro doctor. "There isn't a colored man in Mississippi I'd vote for over Governor Johnson."

"Wasn't it a Negro," Lorna Smith asked him, "who developed blood plasma in the Second World War?"

"He just developed it," the doctor said. "White men started it." The doctor refused to sign a freedom registration form.

Another man who was well educated in Mississippi terms—a graduate of a local Negro college—signed the form, though later admitted he believed it hopeless. "After all," he said, "didn't Noah curse Ham—'a servant of servants shall he be unto his brethren' —and wasn't Ham the father of the Negro race?"

A third man who had lived half his life away from the atmosphere that produced these attitudes had learned theoretically that black and white were only colors, and had returned to his native Delta to try to make equality work, for himself as much as for others. His intelligence was warped and frustrated from lack of training, lack of self-respect; a semi-literate Bohemian, he was constantly forced, through confrontations with white volunteers, to see the inadequacy of his weapons to fight or tools to build as well as they. It drove him to blind spells of arbitrariness, silence, aggression; one moment he took off on a flight of meaningless pomposity, the next he was unable to function at all.

Similar reactions were displayed by others in the movement who resented the hundreds of smart, sharp, articulate white students coming down and taking over. Not only were they taking over, they were doing pretty well—they led at meetings, knew something about organization, set up schools and political programs, and in discussion were often *right*. Some of the local SNCC workers faded into the background, away from this onslaught of insensitive Northern energy, becoming sullen from guilt to the extent they felt unjustified in their sullenness. Before the summer they had been a small tight group, bonded together in trust and friendship and in deep understanding of their cause, since they *were* their cause. Now the nation's press was hailing the bravery of the young white army gone to save the Negroes of Mississippi, failing at every point to credit the grass roots. This was aggravated by some volunteers convinced that they personally were working out a set of historic principles, of which they felt they had a special view. "The people who come here and think you can do it like in the thirties"—someone described them—"they're hallucinated. You could write O'Neill plays about their efforts."

The movement, despite any white illusions and black resentments, was and is an indigenous one, before, during, and after the summer. Black and white had to fight together in the movement, but the fight was as much against its own internal racism as the outer world's. The only difference was that the movement was in the middle of the mess, acting on it immediately, while the rest of America preferred to ignore it.

In describing the then Chairman of SNCC, with whom he was sharing a Mississippi jail cell, Bob Moses wrote in 1961 that "[Charles] McDew . . . has taken on the deep hates and deep loves which America, and the world, reserve for those who dare to stand in a strong sun and cast a sharp shadow." This could as well describe many SNCC Negroes, whose deep hates and loves were often translated into simple whites and blacks. They were automatically suspicious of us, the white volunteers; throughout the summer they put us to the test, and few, if any, could pass. Implicit in all the songs, tears, speeches, work, laughter, was the knowledge secure in both them and us that ultimately we could return to a white refuge. The struggle was their life sentence, implanted in their pigment, and ours for only so long as we cared to identify with them. They resented us, and this was as difficult for some volunteers to assimilate as it was understandable: the volunteers wanted gratitude, and couldn't understand why there was instead a tendency to use them simply as the most accessible objects for Negro anger.

This was manifested most often in exercises of status, subtle condescensions which acted to diminish any self-important, bloated white prides. It humbled, if not humiliated, one to realize that *finally, they will never accept me.* And this raised the question: Why, then, am I here? If they're not grateful for my help, if we are supposed to be struggling for brotherhood and can't even find it among ourselves, why am I here?

This was each one's private battle, rarely discussed. To do so would have meant admissions, giving words to certain uncomfortable doubts. Over and over in Ohio they had told us that we were all the victims of the very prejudice we fought. How could this be so? We were forced to examine ourselves meticulously for symptoms of the disease. Yet those who exonerated themselves could see no contradiction in their innocence and their parallel desire for gratitude. Why gratitude? The battle was as much ours as theirs, and to expect thanks was somewhere to feel superior to that battle. But we didn't *have* to come, did we? We could have stayed at home and gone to the beach, or earned the money we so badly needed for next semester at old Northern White. And here we are: We Came. Among all the millions who could have realized their responsibility to this revolution, we alone came. Few Northern Negroes even came. We came. Don't we earn some recognition, if not praise? *I want to be your friend, you black idiot,* was the contradiction evident everywhere.

SNCC is not populated with Toms who would wish to be white. They are not the ones who fill closets with bleaches and straighteners, who lead compromise existences between reality and illusion. They accept their color and are engaged in working out its destiny. To bend to us was to corrupt the purity of their goal. To understand us meant to become like us, and the situation was too tenuous for the risk—though the temptations to be a white's intimate, whatever the principle involved, must sometimes be strong.

Once I heard a white man say to James Baldwin, "I am Mister Charlie. I feel victimized by some of the things you write in your books. I feel personal guilt for your condition. But it's not my fault. What can I do?" Baldwin answered, "That you are guilty and I am bitter is the state of things. It may not be your fault. But it's not *my* fault. It's not enough to feel guilty. Change things."

How does one bear this responsibility? Was it guilt, after all, which lay behind the thousand motivations a thousand volunteers produced for the television cameras? Was that the answer the reporters sought? It was not the one they were ever given. Is that why they kept asking?

Try it. Yes, I feel guilty. I am guilty of the sins of the world, the sins of the past, the sins of the foreign; the most outlandish and alien of sins are all mine. I am the underdog in the guise of the top dog. I take the next, most logical move. I go where they are changing things. Not to Harlem, a subway ride away, where on my own I might do penance for my city's sins. I go where the view is a different one, my responsibility somewhat less oppressive, my guilt less evident. In the backside of America there is little danger of discerning a face at all, much less my own. It is a pilgrimage to a foreign country; traveling there, I can leave my guilt behind and atone for someone else's. There are others with me in the movement to endow our fight with solidarity, morale. Who are they? Most of them are like me, but some are black. They understand what it's all about; and through them, a new guilt flourishes. They feed it. Why shouldn't they? *It's not their fault.* I try to join them, to acquire their ease in hating the color white, and thereby hate myself. Since I do not, cannot hate myself, I can never be one of them.

At least the Southerners are not dishonestly color-blind, any more than SNCC Negroes are. And at least the white volunteers did not succumb to the liberal alternative to hate, a pretense of sameness. There he is, the token Negro at the cocktail party, unable for a second to avoid the solicitations of the others, forced to represent "his people" in eternal talk of civil rights bills, conditions in Harlem, last Sunday's demonstration. They cannot face him as a man and speak to him as to each other; but neither can they admit the truth of his difference. He stands, say, in a group over there, and here with me a man refers to him in conversation. "Which one do you mean?" I ask, and he says uneasily, "You know, that man over there, the one in the red socks." Hate is better than that.

Do I hate? Whom? Do I hate them as they insist I do, or is this insistence their necessity, to excuse their hatred of me? I can't really believe in my own innocence when they confront me—we are opposites, and we balance one another. Try that. I am the oppressor: I look the way he looks, the way America has decided one *should* look. Perhaps it is possible to reduce the question to one of appearances. I examine all the hatreds I have ever known. During the war I remember asking an adult to explain why Jews were being killed. The concept of the Herrenvolk was explained to me; I heard the word Aryan. "What are Aryans?" I asked, and the answer was: "People who look like you." The Negro maid who brought me up, an old woman whose mother had been a slave, hated Jews. The Jewish mothers of my schoolmates hated me. My English relatives hated the lower classes. The lower classes hated Negroes. I have always felt as if I inhabited a place in the center of this circle, ringed round by it, untouched. But am I in too, linking them all together?

Or is it all an oversensitive invention? Is there a possibility that something simple is being lost in complications? Maybe these clothes, this guilt and hate, don't fit me at all. Maybe it is just a cool question of feeling, impersonally, that some things are right and others wrong, and that I must do what I can for the right. But how many people say this to themselves? And saying it, in no way solve or resolve the problem: the hate is there. If it's not mine, then whose? To act at all, perhaps one has to assume the sins which led to the need to act, whether or not they fit, make them one's own. To take on the deep hates with the deep loves, exist inside them, and somehow find a way out.

6. The Nitty Gritty

I think the Negro is well off and that he knows he's well off. He has confidence in the white and Negro leadership of his state. He's like the Filipino. He just wants to be left alone.

—Governor Paul Johnson

Voter Registration

The Mississippi registration application is four pages long and consists of twenty questions and an oath. The applicant must copy a section of the Constitution of Mississippi chosen by the county registrar; write "a reasonable interpretation (the meaning)" of the section copied; and define "the duties and obligations of citizenship." These parts must be completed to the satisfaction of the registrar, whose decisions cannot be appealed.

The movement in Greenwood had been conducting citizenship classes for more than a year before the Summer Project began, to help train registrants to overcome these "booby traps," so called by Professor Russell Barrett of Ole Miss. The first and the third could be learned; but there are 285 sections in the Mississippi Constitution, many of which could trap boobies of any color. Other sections, simple on their face, must confuse those denied the rights they guarantee. Section 14, for example, reads: "No person shall be deprived of life, liberty, or property, except by due process of law"; and Section 23: "The people shall be secure in their persons, houses, and possessions. . . ."

Mississippi has had to be artful for the sake of a clause under which it was readmitted to the Union in 1870: "The Constitution of Mississippi shall never be so amended or changed as to deprive any citizen or class of citizen of the United States of the right to vote who are entitled to vote by the constitution herein recognized." That (1869) constitution guaranteed the vote to all sane male residents

over twenty-one. However, while 190,000 Negroes were registered
in 1890 (70,000 higher than white registration), the number had
been reduced by 1961 to 20,000. According to the *Congressional
Quarterly* of July 5, 1963, there were 268 Negroes registered in Leflore County out of a potential 13,567, or 1.9 per cent. The percent-
age is typical, though in eight counties no Negroes are registered at
all.

Shut out of all participation in the political process, eighty-three
thousand Negroes demonstrated their desire to vote by joining in a
mock gubernatorial race in November 1963. The following April, the
Mississippi Freedom Democratic Party was set up, pledging its loyalty to the National Democratic Party and attempting to establish
itself as the legitimate party of the state. In Atlantic City, at the National Democratic Convention, the FDP was to challenge the seating of the "regulars." During the summer the voter registration staff,
and everyone else who wasn't busy, had the job of registering local
people on freedom registration forms, which asked nine legitimate
questions similar to those on applications in most Northern states.
The drive had another purpose: it was the best means of physically
organizing the Negroes of Mississippi, of finding indigenous leadership, and building a political structure.

"Dick Frey's so *nice*," Mrs. Amos said. "I *never* saw a white boy
nice as Dick."

Pathetically thin in his baggy overalls, his body bent toward the
audience with nervous concentration, Dick tried to explain the mysteries of the Freedom Democratic Party to a mass meeting. Searching for the simplest word (hearing himself say "individual" he
would switch to "one man"), he outlined the schedule. It was essential that everyone freedom-register; volunteers would be canvassing
from house to house with forms, and through a system of block captains the people themselves could register their friends. He explained about the precinct meetings, the county and district meetings, and finally on August 24 the "national meeting" in Atlantic
City. We would send sixty-eight of our own delegates, bolstered by
tens of thousands of forms filled out by everyone in Mississippi who
wanted to vote, and it would all be the work of the people themselves.

Some time would pass before anyone was clear on what it all meant, but Dick made a brave beginning. He worked hard at it, pausing often, punctuating points with awkward, jagged jerks of elbows, fingers pushing back the floppy black hair from his face, as he struggled for a simplicity unnatural to him. But his passionate conviction and sincerity worked for him in a way he didn't seem to know.

"I think he's like Jimmy Stewart," one girl said to another later that night.

"I think he's like young Abe Lincoln," the other answered.

"He's not like Abe Lincoln. He's more sensitive."

"Who said Abe Lincoln wasn't sensitive?"

"Oh I don't know, it's just that—the way he talks, he doesn't come on strong or anything, but he really gets it over. Some quality. I don't know what you call it."

At the mass meeting, he was succeeded by Bob Zellner. When the SNCC national office moved to Greenwood, it brought the Zellners, Bob and Dotty, with it. Dotty worked downstairs on communications: the WATS line, the press, and the FBI; Bob had joined the local Project in voter registration, later becoming Project director. He was from Alabama, a Methodist minister's son, SNCC's first white field secretary, a graduate of the best Southern prisons and a master of the language, a solid, brown-haired, gentle man. His confident grin and gestures supplemented his words; and he had the cadence, he spoke just as they did.

"Sure was hot today," he began easily, "till that cloud come along. . . ."

"That's right!" they responded immediately.

". . . and we were sittin' on the front porch talkin' 'bout freedom. I think we gonna get us some freedom. Do you?"

The crowd registered an excess of enthusiasm for him, a white Southerner with them, of them. "The people in Greenwood are gettin' shook up," he said.

"Amen!"

"Now I'm from Alabama. I been in Alabama all my life. And I know you know white people, and I know I know white people. And I know when they're gettin' shook up."

He attacked the question of the block captains—their jobs would be to "find out who-all is registered, and who-all is not registered. Now, some o' you might have agreed to be a block captain," he suggested, "and forgotten about it. . . ." He encouraged more to volunteer, removed some of their doubts, and tried to clarify the distinction between registering at the courthouse and freedom-registering. "It's still important to go right on down and stand outside Lady Lamb's door," he said. "And nobody got to worry none 'bout the lil ole deputy with the big ole gun. You tell Miz Jones that they don't have no horns—they never did have, only now we *know* it. . . . If Miz Jones tells you she gonna lose her job if she goes down to the courthouse, you just tell her that you don't get freedom for nothin'. We been sufferin' so long, and we don't have anythin' to begin with, so you might as well give up those three pennies. If *ever*body goes down, you know, they cain't fire *ever*body in town. If they have trouble with their job, they should come to us and make out an affidavit, and we'll do our best. After that it's up to the Lord."

"You tell 'em, brother!" When Bob spoke, it was always a dialogue. He was the only white man who could do that. But to them, very soon, he almost stopped being white. "What does your father think of you?" I asked him once. He smiled his slow, lit-up smile. "He thinks a lot o' me," he answered. "He's an ole rabblerouser too." "And *his* father?" "Oh, before that they was just a lawng line o' rednecks."

Early in the morning and late at night both Bob and Dick would be wandering around trying to sort out the latest crises. They were both effective, if only because of the respect they earned for their endless energy and the love the local people felt for them. But the contrast between them was deeper than their speaking techniques.

Dick had come to Greenwood the year before from Phoenixville, Pennsylvania, via San José, California, where he had been an architectural student. For much of the year he had been the only white civil rights worker in town, and as such had come in for white Greenwood's entire allocation of abuse and threats for "white niggers," and done time in the county jail. He was rarely unengaged in helping someone, and it was hard to find a space to talk to him. Sometimes he came to dinner at Mrs. Amos's, but even then people constantly tumbled in to consult him; he often abandoned his half-nibbled meal to congeal while he answered the office phone or attended to the newspaperman, the Justice Department man, the sheriff, or anyone in trouble. Once I asked him how things had changed since his arrival a year before.

"It used to be much . . . calmer," he said, still automatically simplifying his language. "It's more desperate now. No, more militant. People have begun to see what they can achieve, and they're impatient to get it."

"How long are you staying?"

"No longer than the challenge."

For a moment I took his words literally, repeating them to myself. Then I remembered: "the challenge" referred to the convention in Atlantic City.

"And then back to California?"

"Yes," he said.

"To study architecture?"

"Yes."

"I guess it will seem pretty unreal after a year here." He didn't answer, sat and thought. It was fully five minutes before he moved; the chicken was cold beneath his fork; and then, in a burst: "I get so *frustrated* about so many things! I haven't painted a picture or done anything creative in so long. I want to make a mobile."

He was silent again. "Why don't you go to the community center and make one?" He didn't answer. "Have you painted a lot?" I asked.

"I don't draw very well," was all he said. After a minute or more, he continued. "I wonder if *every*one carries around pictures in their heads? I mean, whole paintings?"

"Do you have many pictures in your head?"

"Oh, not so many. I don't know. Maybe twelve."

"All complete in your head?"

"Yes." He studied the middle distance.

"What kind?" I asked.

He gestured with his hands. "Symbolic," he said. "Realistic."

"Like what?"

"Are you familiar with the *Aeneid*?"

"Not very."

"Well, I have a picture of Aeneas, when he's on the path to hell, and he meets Dido, and she turns from him. It's very clear in my mind, the rocks, the path, the ferns. Their positions. If only I could draw it. It's like a dream." He gestured again. "Like some dreams. Something you can hardly explain."

"To yourself or to others?"

"Even to yourself. Although you could write a poem about it." Someone called him from the screen door. He left.

Freedom School

The children sat in small groups under trees on the lawn or on the steps of the church. More than a dozen were learning to speak French with a drawl; nearby, half as many were studying Spanish; and a group of three, German. Foreign languages, not taught in their schools, were the most eagerly chosen elective subjects—they suggested other worlds and possibilities. A few yards away another half dozen were conducting a creative writing class. Bret Breneman, their teacher, was asking them to describe the difference between two stones, a rough light one and a smooth dark one. By the end of the summer they had their own mimeographed newspaper, the *Freedom Carrier,* and had written and performed a play.

At first there were difficulties in finding a place for the school; pressure was put on ministers, who offered their churches. For a fortnight they were on the move, with no one certain where tomorrow's school would be. Eventually they settled in the Friendship Baptist Church, and separated among the pews for their various classes or joined again for general sessions on the subjects in which all participated: English, citizenship, Negro history. On a typical day, the French class was singing old Edith Piaf songs around the piano, Bret's group was upstairs in the sacristy where they were learning lines, and an English class was discussing *Moby Dick* and variations of whiteness—white doesn't *have* to be bad (if it's a whale). They finished and everyone listened to "Freedom Now," a Pacifica broadcast on the Birmingham crisis. Judy Walborn asked the children to keep some questions in mind as they listened: What was the object of the Birmingham demonstrations? What was the reaction of the white community?

There were interviews with or commentaries on the major figures in the crisis—Bull Connor, Martin Luther King, representatives of U.S. Steel, the mayor, Burke Marshall, President Kennedy, and a white businessman on the bi-racial committee that solved the problem by employing "one Nigra in one store." Judy got them role-playing afterwards. The children volunteered for the parts of all the cast of characters and got inside the drama. They knew the Southern types backwards, but even the boy playing President Kennedy spoke on the phone to Martin Luther King in a powerful Boston accent, "The federal government is not empowahed to act." In the end they connected Birmingham to Greenwood: "If there were a thousand people demonstrating in the streets of Greenwood, what would be done?"

Mississippi is the only state with no compulsory education law. Negro children in many communities have to go to school in mid-summer in order to work in the cotton fields in the spring and fall. Throughout the state more than two thousand students, twice the expected number—most of them high school sophomores and juniors but spreading out to include the aged and the toddlers—enrolled in forty-one two-month Freedom Schools. (Thirty-four of these were to continue into the winter.) The teachers were ordinary college students with no special training; the curriculum and its presentation were as unorthodox as the classrooms, which were often little better than the few feet of grass, in the hundred-degree weather, on which they began in Greenwood. There were few textbooks and blackboards, and no examinations; the student body shifted, as did the lessons—which often sprang spontaneously from the events of the day, the newspapers, the questions of the children, the lives of the teachers. Discussion could go off on any sort of tangent, depending only on everyone's curiosity, responsiveness, and energy. In the words of the curriculum, the goals were "to provide remedial instruction in basic educational skills, but more importantly, to implant habits of free thinking and ideas of how a free society works, and to lay a groundwork for a statewide youth movement."

The effort to stimulate the students to think out their problems and possible methods of dealing with them depended more on questions than on answers. The citizenship curriculum, for example, examined such realities as the Negro in the North, the poor Negro and the poor white, the movement, the power structure; but implicit in the facts were recurrent questions: Why are we (teachers and students) in Freedom Schools? What is the freedom movement and what alternative does it offer us? What does the majority culture

have that we want? That we don't want? And what do we have that
we want to keep?

Popular beliefs were examined—that Negroes are inferior, lazy,
happy and satisfied, incapable or unwilling to participate in government; and the reasons for the beliefs—that there are those who
profit from their perpetuation.

The problem of overcoming them was defined in the curriculum:

1. The "power structure" is one force that helps to maintain the
   world; in the South, that helps to maintain the terrible world
   of segregation.
2. That "power structure" derives its power, in the final analysis,
   from the fears of both whites and Negroes.
3. Poor whites and Negroes are oppressed by the "power structure." We have much in common.
4. If poor whites and Negroes could get together and move out
   from under the "power structure," it would fall.
5. We do not move because we are afraid.
6. Generally, the Negro's fear is based upon very real danger.
7. Generally, the white's fear is based upon guilt.
8. Fear—whatever the cause—produces lies.
9. Living lies bends and breaks us.
10. That is to say—keeps us from being whole.
    That is to say—keeps us from being free.

And finally, "If lies enslave us, then truth will free us. What is the
truth? Or, the same question, What is freedom?"

There were discussions of Negro history, of Reconstruction—from
a point of view denied the students in their regular schools—and of
African culture; of the movement, its tactics and goals, of Mississippi politics and the FDP, and the Civil Rights Act.

The schools really accomplished something by the time the summer was out. Most students had begun with no higher ambition than
to leave Mississippi the moment they were independent enough:
just get *out* of there, seek the good life they felt sure existed in Chicago, San Francisco, anywhere North. They learned they would not
find it there; more important, what they might accomplish at home
through organization, understanding, work. No one really taught
them these things: they pooled what they knew, and they were for
the first time taken seriously. Probably more than half of them

changed their minds about migrating, and then they set about changing what they had. In one community they decided to boycott the public school until their demands were met. In August Freedom School students met in a state convention in Meridian, and compiled their grievances into an immense platform, covering everything from education (better teachers and facilities, integration, academic freedom, nine *consecutive* months of school), through health (school health programs, mental health facilities, Medicare, "all patients should be addressed properly"), voting, housing, civil liberties, law enforcement (protection from mobs, abolition of punitive sterilization laws, Negro policemen able to arrest anyone, federal trials of cases against law enforcement agencies, police must possess warrants), to foreign affairs ("The United States should stop supporting dictatorships in other countries and should support that government which the majority of the people want").

They did much more: they taught their teachers.

Literacy

"This is a bird with a long neck and a round body. This *looks* like a bird with a long neck and a round body. 'Bird' begins with the sound 'buh.' Say 'buh.'"

"Buh."

"That's right! Every letter has a sound and a name, and the name of this letter is 'B.' Say 'B.'"

"B."

"Good. And this is a capital B. Say 'capital B.'"

"Capital B."

"Right. If your name were Bob or Barbara you would write it with a capital B."

"Capital B."

"Very good! . . . Now, buh, buh, buh . . . b,b,b."

"Buh, buh, buh . . . b,b,b."

"Fine! Now, this is a cup spilling coffee. This *looks* like a cup spilling coffee. . . ."

The Laubach system of teaching literacy to adults is based on learning by association rather than by rote. There were booklets with simple pictures, followed by stories using the letters learned, and other books in which to copy the letters over. If the pupil had never written before, it was necessary to start large on a blackboard or with a stick in the dirt, because it took some time to develop the muscles which could maneuver a pencil. That was all there was to it, that and one principle: praise. Confidence was as absent or atrophied as pencil muscles. Therefore "Good," "Right," and "Yes," were the only judgments the teacher expressed. If the pupil mistook an "n" for an "m," for example, the response was "Yes, *this* is an 'm'. Say 'm'. And *this* is . . . ?"

Three of us taught literacy in Greenwood, Ray and Rita Rohrbaugh and I. Ray had a small class of women who could read a little. I started with a fragile old woman who was blind in one eye and nearly blind in the other, but who struggled eagerly to learn. She could hardly make out the letters, and it was hard to get past the first page, which had to be repeated every day she came. In contrast there was Amanda, a woman of thirty. We first met over a chocolate cake she baked for the volunteers, and again at the courthouse when I accompanied a group to register; it was her fifth failure, and she wanted to remedy the cause.

"I went to school for two years," she told me when we started, "but they didn't have no books and we wasn't learnin' nothin', so my father took us out and made us chop cotton."

She remembered a few of the letters and, in daily sessions of an hour each, mastered many more. She was quick and bright, but it was a discouraging process for her more than for me: she expected results as magical and immediate as the movement itself.

At the start of the summer she had been looking for work; she was so poor that she couldn't afford a cigarette, and would take one of mine with the gratitude of one just handed a fortune. One evening she turned up exhausted, reporting that she had found a job. She was always cheerful, with an enormous, gold-toothed smile, but this time she had great difficulty mustering any energy behind the laughter—she had spent ten hours scrubbing floors and dirty clothes —so we just sat and talked. Two days later she appeared without even the smile. She had been fired. Why? The woman who had hired her was a Texan, and to Amanda Texas was as distant a place as New York or Calcutta—people must be different there. She had asked the woman if she ever went to mass meetings. "I said I didn't mean no harm, but that y'all done told me that people all over the world is on our side, so I just wanted to know if they was like that in

Texas." I tried to explain about Texas; Amanda nearly wept in despair. "I didn't know, I never saw nothin' like this movement before."

By the end of the summer she knew a great deal, though not much of it was reading. She would rush to finish the day's allotted letters, then ask me questions about the movement, the FDP, the world; the questions had stimulated others by the next lesson, but she had forgotten the letters we had done and they had to be repeated. We never got as far as "w," but Amanda became a block captain.

Community Center/Federal Programs

The community center couldn't really get off the ground in Greenwood—among other reasons, because a permanent building wasn't found. Three tiny shabby rooms were rented, and Bambi brightened them up with soap and water, maps and posters, and held art classes for young children in the mornings. Typing was taught to Freedom School girls in the afternoons. The library was theoretically a part of the community center apparatus, and the hope was to take over more space in our building after the summer if another house couldn't be found.

The federal programs workers were concerned with various forms of aid from Washington which local white authorities obstructed, either simply for Negroes, or altogether because such programs were desegregated and anti-discriminatory. Linda Wetmore took on anybody who wanted to fight about getting free lunches in the public schools—the money came from Washington, but it went to the white schools. The other goal she set herself was a day-care center for the children of working mothers. COFO was the liaison with such agencies as the Farmers' Home Administration and the Office of Manpower, Automation and Training, and investigated abuses of the Area Redevelopment Act and the Manpower Development and Training Act. But on a daily level, much of the work involved helping people straighten out their Social Security and welfare problems.

Harry Simpson, a man of over seventy, had had his welfare checks cut off. He came to the office for advice and assistance, and Ed Bauer and I went with him to the local agency to find out what had happened. There was a motto on the desk: THIS OFFICE BELONGS TO

THE PEOPLE. WE ARE HERE TO SERVE. Two stringy career women, one of them with a trembling tic, gathered Mr. Simpson's enormous dossier and sat us down opposite their desk.

"What have you come for, Harry?" the trembly woman asked.

"See about my pension, ma'am," he answered, crushing his hat in his hands, then sitting on it. He was large and muscular, but his hair was gray and he walked slowly, with a cane, which he now and then waved in the air to make a point—the gesture might have seemed threatening until one saw the man behind it.

"We don't have pensions here, Harry, we have old-age assistance." The women scarcely looked at Ed and me, but were clearly set to make an example of "Harry" for us. Mr. Simpson just nodded yes, that was what he wanted to see them about.

"You have to be in need, Harry," the first woman said. She was half his age. "What did we tell you, Harry? Didn't we tell you you had to keep a record of your earnin's? You told me you hadn't worked all last year, then we checked and found out you'd been workin' for the Lashleys and for Mr. Coot. Why'd you say that, Harry? Why've you been tellin' us stories?"

"I didn't tell you no stories, ma'am," said Mr. Simpson, clutching his cane.

"But we called Mr. Lashley and he told us you did a paintin' job for him. Now you got to tell the *truth*. You can go to Mr. Lashley and get a paper sayin' you didn't do any work for him. Would you like to do that, Harry?"

"I don't know Mr. Lashley, ma'am."

"When did you go to Detroit, Harry?" the other woman broke in, with a patient air.

"For Christmas, ma'am."

"Did you work up there, Harry?"

"No'm, I went for a visit with my son."

"You sure you didn't work up there?"

"No'm."

"Harry, we been helpin' you since nineteen hundred and sixty. And we can't get the truth out o' you. Would you like to be reported for fraud?"

"No'm."

"Well you got to tell us when you work. Harry, we *want* you to work. It makes people well and happy to work."

He explained that he couldn't work, as he had suffered a stroke and was disabled. "I ain't worked since the end of May nineteen hundred and sixty-three," he said.

The trembly woman resumed the questioning then. "Where y'all livin' now, Harry?"

"At home with my wife."

"Harry," the first woman broke in scoldingly, "what you mean with your wife? Here you been tellin' me you and your wife was separated."

He shrugged.

"How'd y'all make up with your wife, Harry?"

He didn't answer. Then they asked him who paid the rent (his children), how he had afforded the trip to Detroit (again, his children), and how many children his daughter Lulabelle had now, Harry?

"She ain't got but two, ma'am."

"Only two? She married?"

"Yes'm."

"They got a *license?*"

"Yes'm."

The two women assumed independent but identical expressions of patronizing amusement. Then the next question: "How'd you and your wife separate, Harry?" They accused him of drunkenness ("Everbody in *Green*wood know how much you drink") and of lying again, then brought up the subject of his wife yet again, and "You know what I mean by *fraud,* Harry?"

The money in question amounted to forty dollars a month, most of which was paid by the federal government.

By now I was thinking of Mr. Simpson as "Harry" myself; when we left, I inadvertently called him that. We had got nowhere. The women refused all assistance unless he produced various notes proving he hadn't lied. I considered Mr. Simpson entirely in the right. We took him home to his wife and discussed the possibilities of getting a doctor's note from Detroit and statements from the men he said he hadn't worked for—whom he had not, he repeated, ever even seen. Then, however, he admitted that two boys had done the painting job for him, and that he had got the check and paid them out of it. Various other minor discrepancies emerged. Who knew, any more, what the facts were? As far as Mr. Simpson was concerned, we were white too and not to be trusted with them. He never appeared at mass meetings, but would wander by most mornings through the summer and sit on a bench outside the office, waiting for nothing he could identify.

The Medical Team

The Medical Committee for Human Rights, set up in support of COFO and now permanent, sent more than a hundred volunteer doctors and nurses to different parts of the state for short periods throughout the summer. Health conditions were horrible. It was difficult for civil rights workers to get medical attention: many doctors simply refused. The worst abuse was in a doctor's office where an Iowa minister had gone with a volunteer whose feet needed treatment. The doctor told them that what they really needed was "forgiveness for what you are doing," then summoned half a dozen men who, still in the office, knocked the minister unconscious and kicked and trampled the volunteer. A deputy sheriff appeared, handcuffed the injured men, and arrested them for disturbing the peace; they were later released on hundred-dollar bonds and taken to the county hospital.

The attitude of the local doctors was illustrated by two letters published one day in the *Greenwood Commonwealth:*

DEAR DOCTORS:

For the past two weeks we have been caring for several hundred American college students preparing themselves in Ohio for a summer's work in Mississippi. . . .

We fully understand that the activities of these students working for civil rights in Mississippi may be strongly resisted by many people of the state. As physicians we are concerned that they continue to receive adequate medical care.

We are hopeful that the doctors of this nation, wherever they live, whatever their social or political views, will respond fully and without reservation to the words of the Hippocratic oath: "The regimen I adopt shall be for the benefit of my patients according to my ability and judgment, and not for their hurt or for any wrong. . . ."

We are sending this short letter to our fellow physicians of Mississippi and to the county medical societies, in the sincere hope that a clear separation between social upheaval and medical need will be maintained.

> Sincerely,
> Joseph H. Brenner, M.D.
> Massachusetts Institute of Technology
>
> Robert Coles, M.D.
> Harvard University

"Dr. W. L. Waldron's Tart Reply," the *Commonwealth* headed the answer:

O GREAT PHYSICIANS, LEARNED SIRS:

Deep devotion to the humanitarian principals [*sic*] which constitute a great and motivating part of the art of medicine leads me to hasten to stanch the flow from your bleeding hearts. Possibly your anxiety will be somewhat allayed if you can be reassured that we, too, went to medical schools which somehow had heard, perhaps by grapevine from enlightened areas, of the obligations assumed by physicians, and had not neglected to attempt to indoctrinate us in our responsibilities. . . . Speaking for a number of my colleagues, we question the sincerity of your desire to maintain a "clear separation between social upheaval and medical need." We are agreed, however, that you, by writing as you have, have clearly demonstrated an appalling ignorance regarding the area and the issues in which you are meddling. It is you who have forsaken Medicine to dabble in sociology to diagnose social illnesses and prescribe treatments without taking the history or examining the patient. The tenor of your letter suggests that you may adopt the same method in your medical practices, since you have been instrumental in sending several hundred obviously physically unfit American college students, whose health causes great concern, into the swamps of Mississippi, where they may be beset by malaria, snake bite, starvation, exposure, and pollens.

Now that the hundreds of American college students are on safari in the hinterlands, and since your practices do not keep you busy, may I suggest that you devote some time to an unbiased study of the racial tragedy which appears once again to have divided our nation. Perhaps you can, if freed from prejudice, assist in finding a solution by other means than radical, mutilating surgery. Had your medical education included psychology and psychiatry, you would be reluctant to encourage mass release of primitive emotional reactions. . . .

> Most sincerely yours,
> W. L. Waldron, M.D.
> 950 N. State Street, Jackson

The first few doctors who came to help us hesitated to venture out after 4 p.m. for fear the sun might set before they could get back again. They were unlicensed to practice in the state and could think of little else to do. Medical people lurked around the library using up some of their endless good will by sprinkling the books with Borax, which was supposed to be lethal to cockroaches but only made the bindings soapy; assigning a variety of vitamin, iron, and salt pills to staff stomachs; directing "Now we will wash our hands" to those seen petting the resident kittens, Freedom and Now; and asking me to make posters reading PLEASE FLUSH THE TOILET. I tried to explain that those who didn't flush the toilet couldn't read either, being for the most part under seven, but didn't make any headway.

Cars for project work were always scarce, and the doctors always had a car, so they were exploited as chauffeurs. But in midsummer an effective new team, headed by Martin Gittelman, a psychologist, and June Finer, a physician, arrived to show what could be done. They spoke to old SNCC hands suffering from battle fatigue, providing on-the-spot therapy for people who were being ripped apart by the danger of their lives. They supplied information about birth control to local women who had never known an alternative to "having their tubes cut," and arranged for them to get Enovid at cost from the Public Health Service. They inoculated everyone they could catch against typhoid and tetanus, in the process integrating the Public Health waiting room. Dressed in business suits, they went to see the local Red Cross, Salvation Army, Catholic charities, Elks, and Lions to find out what services were offered and under-utilized by the community, such as visiting nurses and free eyeglasses or dental care. They visited jailed civil rights workers to improve their morale, and the Freedom School to lecture on the subject the students voted for: sex. And when they had nothing else to do they took off their ties and jackets and organized the kids who hung around the office to build an outdoor shower and some flower boxes.

The Clergy

The National Council of Churches sponsored 250 ministers who came down to the state. One of those who stayed in Greenwood for a fortnight, David Hall from Connecticut, worked with the people and the volunteers as though Christianity still meant something. He was quiet and courageous; he shared in the work, the fear, the joy, and the punishment; he couldn't condescend; he treated the local people with respect because he saw how much they had to teach him; and he was the only adult adviser, religious, legal, or medical, who didn't immediately, compulsively instruct COFO workers in what they were doing wrong, or get in their way as though they were irrelevant. After he left, we heard he had lost his rich Connecticut parish.

The Library

My own daily work settled down mainly to signing books in and out for children. It was soon clear that few adults would be customers: many couldn't read well enough, but even for those who could, reading was not an item in life. In an overcrowded shack after a day's work there was no appeal in much but the television; space alone determined it, if all the other factors—heat, noise, exhaustion, and crowds—were not so overpowering too. The children loved the picture books to pieces inside three readings, if the books did not simply disappear before then anyway. There were no fines for unreturned books, as no one could have paid them, and the idea was to encourage them to read, not for the library to collect shelf-fuls of useless, unused printed matter. Even the older children liked the picture books—the level of reading in their higher grades seemed barely beyond Dick and Jane. They struggled over James Baldwin, however, or Richard Wright—the white, sophisticated novels were simply too removed from their existence; and teen-agers asked for books on the law, teaching, the ministry, or mechanics, the only professions they knew that were open to them.

There were boxes arriving with new donations every day, letters of acknowledgment to write, and vain efforts at quietmaking. (Lorna Smith, forceful and authoritative in the office as out of it, had returned to California.) I went out canvassing whenever I could, helped the lawyers, and most of the time engaged in a battle with trivia.

It was impossible to be alone. All the other deprivations, the total lack of recreation, relaxation, or release, might have been supportable if only there had ever been a chance to be alone. Outside the office it was unsafe. Inside there were never less than two or three dozen local people and children and staff, with constant interruptions and distractions, accumulations of tensions and numbers. It would take half a day to write a letter, if you could muster the will, the space, and the typewriter to do it to begin with, and it ended up a mass of lost trains of thought, the half day gone you had no idea where. This person needs housing—stop and search the file of names and addresses, then call up or go hunting; that one wants a colored marker to make a poster—try to find one but they've all disappeared, the children took them; simultaneous discovery that most of the rest of the office supplies have disappeared as well; nag the man who promised weeks ago to build me a shelf with a lock; a field secretary arrives from Tallahatchie and sits on my desk—talk about what it was like; four children have a battle about who got hold of the book each one wants first—mediate and dry the tears, find a coloring book for the injured party; someone feeling bossy shouts about the children cluttering up the office with their coloring—discuss it, calm it down; a volunteer must go out this minute and hasn't time to see to the mimeographing of some leaflets for canvassing—find Matthew Hughes and give him the stencils; Samuel T. Mills, in an excess of helpfulness, has refilled the air cooler with water so full that it overflows—protect the books and papers being sprayed, mop up the puddle, stop people stepping in it, give Samuel something to do; a woman wants to go to the courthouse to register—find a car and someone to drive it; an affidavit has to be witnessed—sign it; some children knock over a vast stack of *National Geographics*—pick them up and shelve them; a voter registration worker has just found a place for the next mass meeting—add it to the big schedule at the top of the stairs; a truck pulls in from Holly Springs with seventeen

cartons of identical arithmetic textbooks missing their teachers'
guides—clear a space on the floor and find help to carry them up,
never mind what to do with them after that; someone arrives from
the field and has to have his shirt laundered because he's due for an
interview with the FBI—wash it or find someone to; three women
come with a pot of meat and greens—borrow some forks from Mrs.
Amos; June and Willie bring their stew upstairs—explain to them
about cockroaches and no eating in the library; Willie thinks I am a
white supremacist and for revenge picks up Freedom, the kitten,
and swings him around by the tail—get Willie under control before
anything worse happens, and see if Freedom is still alive; someone
says all the typewriters are broken except the one I'm using and he
has a historically important report to get out—give him the typewriter and continue the letter by hand; a volunteer cries that he
can't find his spare pair of pants, which were right here last night, he
used them as a pillow—see if they have been mixed up with the
clothes for local distribution; Zellner appears and tries to do something about all the local people parked around and cooling off:
"Anybody with some long settin' around to do better do it downstairs"—assorted grumbles, no one leaves; Monroe strides in and de-
nounces me because the library is in such a mess and I never do any
work—explain about crowds and arithmetic textbooks, and find out
if possible what's really bothering him.

"Dear whoever-you-are," I have written (and forgotten by then
who it was anyway, probably my mother, who at this rate received
one letter all summer): "It all goes so quickly and remarkably
peacefully—no problems in Greenwood yet. . . ."

After Work

There was only one place to go for a brief respite: Blood's. Its correct name was Bullin's Café, but Blood was the manager; and
though there were other cafés and a dingy, wooden-seated theater,
nothing else in Negro Greenwood except a market or two was air-
conditioned. In Blood's was a moment's peace, despite the raucous
music of the jukebox and the bells of the pinball machines, the
laughter and wide-open talk. It was cool, lit dimly by some neon ads
on the walls, and there was beer and the only chance to sit for any

length of time with nothing to do: necessary, because the cook was so slow. Behind the counter in the back was a crude sign:

NOTICE!
Jobs in California
Free transport by
Greyhound bus—Round Trip
Free Housing
ages 18 years up
Guarantee $15.00 per day

Once they got there, the wages were about thirty cents a day and the trip was no longer round.

The first break of any length was a wedding. One night after the mass meeting Paul Klein and Wendy Weiner were married. June and Willie James had collected donations for punch, and spent the whole afternoon covering themselves with glue and sparkles for the decorations. Wendy put on jeans and sandals and a blue denim workshirt with the tails out, and wore her long black hair loose down her back. The chapel under the office was laden with flowers and pine twigs, and *Mississippi Freedom Summer* pamphlets twined with leaves around a string that crisscrossed the low ceiling. Behind the altar on the whitewashed wall were a cross and a star of David made of red glitter (for Paul, Christian, and Wendy, Jewish) and a SNCC poster, surrounded with more leaves and flowers, of two children sitting on a stoop with the motto: GIVE THEM A FUTURE IN MISSISSIPPI.

The Reverend Aaron Johnson, the first minister to open his church to the movement, conducted the ceremony, which was short, solemn, and to the point. The three knelt in prayer, then, "You may salute the bride, sir," said the Reverend Mr. Johnson as they stood again. Paul and Wendy kissed and Jim Forman called out, "One man, one woman—two votes!" The air was filled with rice and freedom songs; the punch, vaguely spiked with wine, was served with cookies and potato chips; the songs got faster, and outside some volunteers taught the *hora* to local teen-agers. Everybody stopped worrying for almost two hours.

7. White Greenwood

THE KLAN LEDGER

An Official Publication of the WHITE KNIGHTS
of THE KU KLUX KLAN of Mississippi

DEDICATED TO THE PRESERVATION OF CHRISTIAN CIVILIZATION

JULY 4, 1964

We are now in the midst of the "long, hot summer" of agitation which was promised to the Innocent People of Mississippi by the savage blacks and their communist masters. On this Famous Date, the Anniversary of the founding of the American Republic, under the auspices and blessings of Almighty God, we ask that each Mississippian, each American, get down upon his knees and offer up thanks to our Creator, Savior and Inspiration for his manifold grace and blessings.

THIS THEN IS OUR PRAYER

OUR FATHER, GOD OF LIFE AND LIBERTY, WE HUMBLY THANK THEE FOR THE STRENGTH, COURAGE AND INTELLIGENCE WHICH THOU HAST GIVEN TO OUR PERSECUTED PEOPLE. WE THANK THEE THAT OUR SATANIC ENEMIES, THE DOMESTIC COMMUNISTS WHO OCCUPY THE SEATS OF POWER IN OUR GOVERNMENT HAVE FAILED TO PROVOKE THE VIOLENCE IN OUR GREAT STATE WHICH WOULD BRING DOWN MARTIAL LAW AND COMPLETE DICTATORSHIP. THANK YOU O LORD, FOR OPENING THE EYES OF ALL THE GOOD PEOPLE OF OUR GREAT NATION TO THE EVIL WHICH HAS BEEN FORCED UPON US. HELP US TO OVERCOME OUR ENEMIES, KEEP OUR FEET ALWAYS UPON THE PATH OF RIGHTEOUSNESS, AND PURGE OUR HEARTS FROM MALICE AND VENGEANCE, GIVE OUR ARMS THE STRENGTH, OUR HEARTS THE COURAGE, AND OUR MINDS THE WILL TO DESTROY THESE AGENTS OF SATAN. . . . AMEN.

The recent events in Neshoba County and Statewide call for a message to the general public and the citizens of the great State of Mississippi. [Regarding] the so-called "disappearance" . . . we were NOT involved, and there was NO DISAPPEARANCE. Any-

*one who is so simple that he cannot recognize a communist hoax
which is as plain as the one they pulled on Kennedy in Dallas,
had better do a little reading in J. Edgar Hoover's primer on communism: "MASTERS OF DECEIT.". . .*

*We are going to serve notice that we are not going to recognize
the authority of any bi-racial group,* NOR THE AUTHORITY OF ANY
PUBLIC OFFICIAL WHO ENTERS INTO ANY AGREEMENT WITH ANY
SUCH SOVIET ORGANIZATION. *We Knights are working day and
night to perserve Law and Order here in Mississippi, in the only
way that it can be perserved: by strict segretation of the races,
and the control of the social structure in the hands of the Christian, Anglo-Saxon White men, the only race on earth that can
build and maintain just and stable governments. We are deadly
serious about this business. We have taken no action as yet
against the enemies of our State, our Nation and our Civilization,
but we are not going to sit back and permit our rights and the
rights of our posterity to be negotiated away by a group composed of athestic priests, brainwashed black savages, and mongrelized money-worshippers, meeting with some stupid or cow-
ardly politician. Take heed, atheists and mongrels, we will not
travel your path to a Leninist Hell, but we will buy* YOU *a ticket
to the Eternal if you insist. Take your choice,* SEGRETATION, TRAN-
QUILITY AND JUSTICE, *or,* BI-RACISM, CHAOS AND DEATH. . . .

The White Knights of the Ku Klux Klan had been formed in February 1964. Since few had ever dangerously disagreed in Mississippi before, there had been no need for a well-organized Klan to
deal with the "too dumb to learn, filthy, diseased, evil-minded
nigger." The impending passage of the Civil Rights Bill and news of
the Summer Project brought the competing United Klans of America, Inc., into the state in May; on a single night they burned crosses
in sixty-four of the eighty-two counties to signal that recruiting was
open. The recruits, however, were attracted instead to the White
Knights, whose money didn't leave the state and who had a no-
nonsense preference for burning churches to crosses.

A similar organization, the Americans for the Preservation of the White Race, was formed in the southwest by those disgruntled at the Citizens' Councils' excessive dues and lack of interest in "doing a grass-roots job." Membership estimates gave the White Knights one hundred thousand and the APWR thirty thousand; accurate figures were impossible because, as the Klan put it to lure recruits, "it is a very secret organization and no one will know you are a member."

The Klan's Greenwood strength and influence were also impossible to calculate. I was told by a Northern journalist who was on speaking terms with the people in charge that "the vigilante group" was tied in with Greenwood's law enforcers, who had passed on a warning to "cool it for the summer"—because protecting them would be so difficult with all the feds around. Whether this proscription extended to the rest of the state was in doubt. More than thirty churches were burned in July and August by somebody.

It was easy to forget that not only the Negroes were undereducated, undernourished, underemployed. Mississippi is the nation's neediest state, ranking fiftieth in most economic and educational categories. Per capita income in 1960 was $1,285, 47.2 per cent below the national average. For every $218 paid per Mississippian to the federal government, $327 went the other way: the state has become a national charity case. Half the white adults had received less than nine years of education. In two decades emigration has accounted for the loss of two congressmen (leaving five). Much of the exodus has been Negro; among the rest have gone some of the best of white Mississippi. What of those remaining?

COFO organized a pilot project in white relations for the summer in Biloxi, on the Gulf Coast. It was the safest place to start, because it attracts Northern tourists (though only half as many after the murders in Neshoba, a statistic of great concern to the local chambers of commerce), is only fifteen per cent Negro, and is "open" to alcohol, gambling, and all the vices the rest of the state disdains (in public). To Jackson came Northern women for "Wednesdays in Mississippi"—flying down for the day to meet their opposite numbers. In a third town, on the pretext of writing an academic paper on "the Southern city," a white student was assigned the job of infiltrating the white community to do research on its political and economic structure—information easily accessible to any ordinary person in any ordinary community, but unavailable to SNCC. He made friends with the police chief, bank president, and mayor, passed reports to COFO through an out-of-state address, and never, of course, made any contact with the local project. The result of this experiment, according to a story which no one cared to verify, was a series of impressively detailed reports, followed by the student's resignation on the grounds that he had begun to find some plausibility in the arguments of the whites, and was "confused."

In our town no organized effort was made. The summer was two months short. There was hostility toward the idea besides—most of it realistic—from those who knew how poor were the odds for success. It was first expressed in a staff discussion on the holding of precinct meetings for the Freedom Democratic Party: to be legal, in contradistinction to the white party, the FDP had to provide opportunity for everyone to join, and therefore had to communicate with the other Greenwood. Bulk mail? Too expensive. Leafleting? Too dangerous. An ad in the paper, similar to those the white party ran, was finally decided upon, but the paper refused to publish it.

The ministers and doctors went scouting over the tracks, coming up with a friend. Arriving at different stages of the summer, they each managed to find the same man independently, to return in wild optimism announcing the introduction of the thin edge of the wedge, and to discover that they were not the first and it did no good in any case. The "friend," who obviously can't be identified, was afraid to reveal his aberrant beliefs to anyone in town for fear of reprisals. But it was comforting to some that he existed at all.

The dangers facing him were well illustrated by the fate of another, lesser deviant whom no imagination could transform into a friend. Thatcher Walt, editor of the evening *Commonwealth*, the only Greenwood newspaper, and as such a respected member of the town's power group, had come at the start of the summer to request an interview with three volunteers. Three were produced, but since one was Negro, Walt changed his mind. Then one Friday night he took his wife and two children to the movies. *The Chalk Garden* was playing at the Leflore Theater. A picket line was also featured: local vigilantes had been marching daily past its doors, advising customers that a nigger had been in there. That was enough to keep most of them away. But Editor Walt told the picketers not to be silly, bought tickets, and saw the show. That night his house was shot at and he received a series of threatening phone calls. Thinking it would all blow over, he took his family out of town for the weekend. On Monday he was told he had been fired. The *Commonwealth's* owner refused even to print the story; Walt's name was simply missing from the masthead. The paper never mentioned the picket line, but a buried inch a few days later noted that "police are investigating several broken windows at the Leflore Theater." No other Mississippi paper printed the Walt story either. He left the state.

A more outspoken liberal was Hazel Brannon Smith, Pulitzer Prize-winning editor of the *Lexington Advertiser,* thirty-six miles from Greenwood. Mrs. Smith ran constant courageous front-page editorials excoriating vigilantism, church-bombings, and related acts of violence; then the paper's plant itself was bombed in the fall.

Hodding Carter III, liberal editor of the *Delta Democrat-Times,* was in a slightly more favorable position. His father had run the newspaper before him and had also won a Pulitzer Prize. The paper had a tradition, and was published in the relatively relaxed and civilized city of Greenville: the Carter paper has helped to make it so. Though (or because) they were the best sources of news in the state, the *Democrat-Times* and the *Advertiser* were not imported by their nearest town, Greenwood, which instead sent for the Jackson papers or, out of state, for the Memphis *Commercial Appeal.* Carter was no more welcome in Greenwood than his paper. After a brief meeting with him in Greenville, and imagining he possessed some sort of native immunity, I asked him if he was coming to visit us, as he had earlier in the summer. He mentioned having to go there anyway that week to a party, and "the idea of having to drive back in the dark—uh-oh," he said, was enough without turning up at the COFO office.

I asked him if there was anyone in white Greenwood whom he could recommend I see. He thought for a moment, then shook his head. "Greenwood isn't run by the city government, but by a bunch of thugs. If you went to see them they'd just bring out all their obscenities for you. If nothing worse."

He had little optimism for Mississippi's future. "Automation is hitting us at a time we can least afford it. The manpower released from the cotton fields is by and large untrainable for anything else. Industries are leaving. Even if everyone gets the vote, it won't solve the economic problem." He shook his head again with discouragement. "I don't know what we're going to do."

"But you're sticking it out."

"This is an *exciting* place to live," he said.

How is the solid surface ever to be cracked? In a police state, the means of information are controlled. In Mississippi, the newspapers reserve their largest type faces for such matters as the annual obsession over the Miss Mississippi Contest. (Two recent winners had gone on to become Miss America, so she, whoever she was, was one of the state's few successful commodities; in the *Mississippi Official and Statistical Register* for 1960–1964 a whole page was given over to the production of such ornaments, under the heading, its *double-entendre* too subtle for the statisticians, MISSISSIPPI MISSES AMERICA.) There were subsidiary headlines in the papers for "Miss Hospitality," "Little Mr. and Miss Greenwood" (five and four years old respectively); and then the normal run of Billy Graham and "Helen Help Us" advice columns; news of the Lions Club, sports, fashions, nuptials; and editorials about topless bathing suits. For a touch of Southern individuality, there were announcements of revival meetings; and in the *Commercial Appeal* a particularly repulsive front-page feature called "Hambone's Meditations," in which Hambone, a patient old-style darky figure, expressed such fitting sentiments as "Kun'l Bob talk 'bout de 'fiel' uv thought,' but all de wu'k in *dat* fiel', I gwine leave to *him!*" Local news was fairly well covered, but when it involved us, only events that rated AP or UPI attention: then the *Commonwealth* would run the agency story of news originating half a mile away. Stories about Negroes called them by their first names ("Chief Lary said, Saturday afternoon Claudia got into an argument with another Negro woman. . . ."). There was news of civil rights, particularly when it was threatening and came from Washington, little else from Washington, and hardly ever a mention of the rest of the world.

Other information sources: When James Baldwin was to appear on the *Today* program, the show was interrupted for an old film about football. A network broadcast on social matters was introduced with: "The following program is Northern-managed news." On the radio, there is H. L. Hunt's *Lifeline,* and a daily inflammation called *Know Your Enemy,* motivated by "concern with the communist infiltration and influence in this country and in all of the Free World." A typical *Know Your Enemy* program attacked the three major networks—"leftwing microphone charlatans" leading the nation "toward a socialistic, one-world slaughterhouse" by, for example, insinuating that Governor Wallace was responsible for the murder of the children in Birmingham instead of the "civil rights agitators who are arrogantly and braggadociously carrying their demands to the extreme." That "countless [Southern] policemen, who made every effort to be fair and considerate, often received severe wounds and even threats to their lives" is a fact of which the nation is unaware because of the cover-up of "leftwing propagandists, better than any the Communists could produce." And so on, with the final remedial suggestion that "five hundred thousand patriotic protestors march on Washington, armed only with brooms," and, should they fail to sweep out the mess, "start 'negotiating' directly with the sponsors."

The local stationery store, the only place where books were sold, offered among its adult reading three books on the Civil War, three on World War II, one on fighter planes and another on battleships, one book by and another about Barry Goldwater, one current fiction best-seller, and several shelves each for cooking and religion. Anyone interested in reading James Silver's *Mississippi: The Closed Society* (then a best-seller in the North) had to seek it out underground. (This was in fact done, I was told later by a native Mississippi woman who left the state years ago and had recently returned for a visit. Although she had never engaged in political or civil rights activity, her mail was opened for the first two weeks of her visit. A friend of hers confessed to receiving a subscription to the *Saturday Review* by way of New Orleans, where it was readdressed and forwarded in plain wrapper. A friend of another sort told her that she made it a custom to change her Mississippi license plates when she left the state, "because otherwise I might be shot at by one of those Northern communist radicals.")

There was, of course, Dr. Silver at the University of Mississippi; and as long as there was a Dr. Silver the world seemed brighter. He came to see us at the office one day with Wofford Smith, the Episcopal chaplain of the university. Silver's deep-lined face has been well lived in, with honesty. People were eager to meet him and immediately expressed their admiration. "You've been doing so much," one said. "I have terrific respect for you." He laughed. "That has been a mythology that you are helping to perpetuate," he said, pointing to Wofford Smith: "This is the really decent man. He's done ten times what I've done." To the volunteers, smiling: "I haven't done anything. You're the troublemakers around here."

There were only about five people in Oxford who deliberately avoided speaking to him, he said, and harassment had lessened lately. "You people have saved me from that," because of the national spotlight on the state. He admitted to being "pretty unpopular," however. "What I did in my book was tell them that everything they have been taught for three generations is not only false but immoral. There's nothing worse you could say to them."

"But aren't you in danger?" a Negro lawyer asked him.

"No, not really," he said—though he was taking a year's leave of absence to teach at Notre Dame.

"What about things like driving at night?"

"I don't drive at night," Silver said.

The sight of white people in "Niggertown" was not unusual. Servants were often picked up and brought home. The route to Highway 82 could just be imagined as Avenue N, for those who felt an itch to check up on us or to try to run down a volunteer. And for generations they had been coming over to indulge in what the Negro community called "nighttime integration." Whatever the rhetoric about "race-mixing" and "the mongrelization of the white race," the principle is one-sided, depending on the color of the man involved. As one Mississippi Negro woman wrote to the *New York Times*, "It's too late for the white man to start worrying about integration, because you have already mongrelized the white race and the black one, too. The only thing you haven't done is claim your children."

Light-skinned products of the "illegal, immoral, and sinful doctrine of racial amalgamation" were everywhere; and those of us who got up early met the not infrequent sight of white men driving out of the Negro neighborhood at dawn. One SNCC field secretary (stationed in another part of the state) was the cousin of a Greenwood policeman who, on his one summer appearance in town, arrested him "for investigation." The policeman's father was the Negro's grandfather's brother, he elaborately explained, or in other words "my father's father was white." His grandmother raised Chief

Lary—"she whupped his ass many a time." This young man was darker than many; the others were simply less precisely aware of their lineage.

Whites who actually came to see us were of a different kind. Two young men called Leon and Herman came to the office or to Blood's quite regularly. Leon did all the talking, explaining that as a result of his superior education he was able to see our point of view. In return for bits of gossip—about, for example, his friend at the local radio station who had been assigned by the authorities to monitor our citizens' band station—he attempted to elicit information about our activities. There was very little information that was not public anyway. A few volunteers trusted him, though not enough to accept an invitation to a nighttime picnic he thought of once; others were violently distrustful. One day George Johnson was in the police station, waiting to bail somebody out, when Leon walked in and whispered something to the desk sergeant. The policeman nodded significantly toward George. Leon reddened and left instantly. He never came to see us again.

A sports car drove up one night with a white boy, a student, asking to see Phil Moore. He said he had spoken to him on the phone and now he thought they should meet. The volunteer who came forward to deal with him was edgy and questioning. "You don't have to be so hostile," the white boy said. "I'm not hostile, I'm suspicious," answered the volunteer. "I just wondered how you got our phone number."

"Oh everyone has *that*," the boy said.

Phil Moore had gone home already, his address of course could not be supplied, and the white boy drove off in disgust. He might have been a sympathetic contact, and our paranoia our biggest mistake. Perhaps, I thought then, there was an excess of the cloak-and-dagger obscuring our sight of the objective, which was finally to achieve a change in the Southern white man. But there was no way of knowing, and too many lives were at stake.

We had a desperate need to understand these people, and so few realistic chances to try. There was hearsay—once, the tapes of a Northern radio interviewer who had gone to a café in a nearby town and spoken to the customers: something I could never do. They were unfriendly but her credentials won their partial cooperation. She asked how they felt about the present state of affairs.

"I feel like I felt a hundred years," one farmer answered. "Same way I always felt. It's hard to tell just what you're feelin'. Kind for to grow on you, I reckon."

"Do you like Mississippi?"

"Yeah."

"Everything about it?"

"Like it all."

"What aspects of it do you like most?" she asked.

"Don't know nothin' 'bout any other state. Not interested in learnin'."

On his farm, he said then, the workers were all Negro. Did they like him? Sure they liked him. They've always liked him. Why shouldn't they like him?

"What jobs do they do?"

"All of it."

"How much do you pay them? Do you think you pay them well?"

"They live on my land. They're happy. I never hear anythin' out of 'em. They're drivin' cars and sleepin' in my homes, what else could they want?"

Another farmer joined in then. "We like the niggah," he said. "If we didn't, we wouldn't treat them the way we do. We furnish his house, we pay his doctor bills and his light bills, and I *know* they don't do that in the North. His house is furnished and his water is furnished and his field supply is furnished and at the end of the year they just about all get a bonus. They got better school facilities, better public places . . ."

A third voice then, a deputy sheriff's: "A niggah's like a mule," he said. "You feed him day in, day out, and then you git him in the stall and he'll kick your brains out."

There was also hearsay from the "mule." One night, waiting for a block captains' meeting to begin, I sat near Anna Mae, a robust, good-looking girl who told me about the woman she worked for—"a big *round* woman," Anna Mae described her. "They gonna have to make somethin' *special* to bury her in." The job, besides cleaning and cooking, involved listening to Miz McCaster's chatter, and to keep it Anna Mae was forced to play "the happy nigger, don't know nothin'."

"You hear about those three civil rights workers that disappeared?" Miz McCaster had asked her.

"Silver rights workers?" Anna Mae had replied. "You mean they stole silver?"

"No, no, *civil* rights workers," Miz McCaster had said. "You know, those three, that were taken out and they're dead."

"Sho' nuff!" Anna Mae had said.

"See, you a good person, you don't hear about these things." Miz McCaster had been very pleased. "I saw a big ole fat Nigra," she continued, "down on Johnson Street shouting 'Freedom! Freedom!' Like to fall off his stool. You know anythin' about freedom?"

"No *ma'am*," Anna Mae had said.

"Well, God's goin' to come strike lightnin', strike a sign right in the middle of their foreheads! They're so dirty, those freedom riders, what do they know about freedom?"

Anna Mae had answered cautiously: "I think I ought to know what they look like. How do I recognize one?"

"Well, they're just so *dirty*," Miz McCaster had said. "And they'll come to your door and ask you for somethin' to eat, and if you don't give it to them, they'll get you. But don't you talk to one, or the police'll get you. You'll know one when you see one, all right. They smell so bad! Course they haven't had as much education as we've had."

Anna Mae, wearing an old yellow dress cast off by some woman she had worked for, one of the best block captains and most militant civil rights workers in Greenwood, sat there and laughed her head off. Before the summer was out she had been fired for having once been driven to talk too much; between looking for jobs she worked nearly full time canvassing for the Freedom Democratic Party.

One of the few direct forms of communication, and about the worst, was the crank call. The phone rang often in the day and constantly at night, with the same voices repeating the same curses and threats at the other end, or one particular charmer who kept blowing a trumpet into the phone, maybe on the theory that he could deafen COFO piecemeal. Others who called regularly and liked to talk began to give us their names (assumed, they admitted, but it gave the calls a personal note), learn ours, and play favorites. We were polite to them. "John Cage" was on almost every night delivering himself of some foul abuse, softened over the summer after repeated conversations with Carol and Eli. Someone told him that "niggers" was offensive, and since he was unable to say "Negroes," couldn't he at least compromise with "black people." Afterwards he usually cooperated, to that extent anyway. Anything else would be "givin' in," and "the American people didn't give in when we fought Japan, did we? Why, if we give in we'll git complete lawlessness." "Like what, John?" "Like rape any woman you want. That's what happens in all them Northern states."

I listened on an extension one night to Eli trying to talk to him about school integration, and meeting with the full strength of John's resistance. "I don't want my children to 'sociate with black people," he said. "Mine's not goin' to school with 'em. Mine'll stay home. I'd rather they stay dumb the rest of their life."

"How many children you have, John?" Eli asked.

"I got three daughters. And they'll dig my grave 'fore any o' mine goes to school with 'em. Have to dig four more, too. 'Cause I'd kill my wife and the children along with me."

"You'd kill your own children?"

"Well what would they have to live for?" said John.

One day I picked up the phone in the library. It was "Casey," another of the regulars.

"Say, you the blondie?" he began.

"I don't know. I'm blond."

"Well I wanted to ask you somethin'. You peroxide your hair?"

"No."

"You don't?"

"It wouldn't be very easy around here, anyway."

"Oh, I thought one o' them nigger places might do it for you." (Pause.) "You don't value your life much, do you?"

"Sure I do. As much as you value yours."

"You're a troublemaker."

"I haven't made any trouble lately that I know of. Not enough, maybe."

"Well I want to ask you somethin'."

"What?"

"I know you'll lie."

"I'm not lying to you. What do you want to know?"

"Are you a communist?"

"No."

"Have you ever had any affiliations with communistic organizations?"

"I don't belong to any organizations."

"Oh well, I knew you'd lie." (Pause.) "Listen, tell me, you an American?"

"Yes."

"But what race are you? I mean, what country your folks come from?"

"England."

"*Eng*land. Oh well, that explains it."

"Explains what?"

"What you're doing."

"What I'm doing?"

"Sure. England's run by the reds. Socialistic place. They even admit it."

"I was born in California."

"Cali*for*nia? Oh well, that explains it."

"Explains what?"

"Those commies in California. Listen, tell me, if you're white, why you givin' away your freedom?"

"I'm not giving away anything I haven't got. I'm not free and you're not either until everybody is."

"Oh don't gimme that. Anyway I bet you're not *all* white. I bet you got a black *heart*."

"I don't know what color it is. Probably heart-colored."

"Well I bet if you took a X-ray of it, it'd come out black. The niggers that works for me, you know what they call you? White trash."

"They have a right to say anything. They have a right to believe anything else."

"You know, the South has more respect for its niggers than for you. There's a nigger works where I work makes more than I do. He gets two weeks' vacation just like I do."

"Fine. Should be more like that."

"And you know, in the evenin' he's dressed up in better clothes than I got at home in my closet. And you know who gets the food down here? The niggers."

"You mean you don't have anything to eat?"

"Sure I do. I *work* for it."

"Negroes work for it too."

"Aaa, they jus' get it from the state."

"The ones I see work pretty hard. Most of them working for you."

"You're messin' in business has nothin' to do with you. You see me comin' up North messin' in your business?"

"Well, you're welcome any time you like. It's one country."

"Hell, I don't want to go up there. This is the best place. 'Cept for you agitators."

"It's a little too hot down here for me."

"It's a lot hotter'n it used to be. The temperature's gone up since you arrived."

"Is that it?"

"Yeah, you know, all this hot air. Say, I want to ask you somethin'."

"What?"

"You ever been raped by a nigger?"

"No."

"You ain't, eh? Well would you *marry* a nigger?"

"Which one?"

"What's that supposed to mean?"

"I'd marry anyone I loved."

"I bet you go out with niggers, don't you?"

"If it's any comfort no one goes out with anyone. We have to watch out for people like you."

"Oh, don't be like that. Listen, I want to ask you a favor."

"What's that?"

"When you ridin' around town, will you sit by a white man?"

"Oh, so that's what's bothering you. I sit by whoever's there."

"I thought you'd say that. You're from up North. You don't have a prejudice about it. You were brought up that way. Right?"

"Right."

"All you Northerners are like that."

"As a matter of fact, all Northerners aren't like that."

"Well, I got to go now."

"Okay. So long."

"Bye."

He called the library fairly often after that, beginning conversations with: "Hey, peroxy?" One day it was: "You got any big white boys around there? I want me a big white boy."

"What for?"

"I want to come over there and have me a fight. If you can't find a big one I'll send my little brother. I'd jus' like to *whup* one of 'em. You find out if there's one over there wants his tail whupped."

There weren't any customers.

8. The Law

*Of course I don't approve of murder, but those kids
were asking for trouble.*

—Ross Barnett
June 1964

Behind the work of voter registration, the Freedom School, community center, and research in federal projects, there was a curtain
lowering. The center of the stage was still reserved for the plain,
constructive, humdrum job, but the backdrop didn't match the
drama. Harassment, intimidation, violence: each action provoked its
counteraction. Greenwood may have been more conscious of the
summer opposition, because the job of the SNCC national office on
the ground floor of our building was that of trouble center—receiving, sifting, filing reports of incidents throughout the state, and, on
the basis of this evidence, attempting to push against the immovable
object of the nation's apathy toward Mississippi.

Our enemies lacked originality of style, and after the first church-
burnings, beatings, and bombings their imaginative resources failed.
They found no further means to express their indignation than more
church-burnings, beatings, and bombings. The press was soon jaded.
Fewer reporters arrived, then none. They were not, of course, immune to the charge of "invader" any more than we were, and it was
not a favorite assignment. "You live in this county?" a dozen reporters were asked, two days after the disappearance, by a local mob in
Philadelphia. "Well we live here and we don't want you in here. You
better leave, and quick."

In July the FBI released the crime statistics of the year: comfort-
ingly, Mississippi had the lowest crime rate in the nation. Missing
from both the report and its news coverage was the qualification
that Mississippi does not list a great proportion of the crimes committed against Negroes, either by whites or by other Negroes. No

white man has ever been convicted in Mississippi for first degree murder when the victim was a Negro.

In Greenwood, they began with simple obscenity on the telephone, obscenity in the street, obscenity from passing cars. No one had to learn a new vocabulary: it had been polished in two years of use against SNCC. Someone was nearly run over almost daily. Our own cars were run off the road into ditches. One morning there were tacks strewn under our cars; they weighed two pounds when collected. The police helped, arresting civil rights workers on minor traffic violations, usually trumped up, throwing them in jail instead of issuing tickets, charging exorbitant fines, and impounding their cars. Typically, one staff member was arrested for driving without a license—the license was in the glove compartment but he was not permitted to look for it, and it was taken, together with the rest of the contents of the compartment, while he was detained at the station. After his release he found that sugar had been poured in the gas tank, a Southern *specialité* which wrecks car engines.

In early July, the Pleasant Plain Baptist Church burned down. It was in Browning, a small group of houses, not quite a village, three miles out, on a bit of land near that of the McGhees, a family to become famous. Browning was being slowly bought out from under its original Negro inhabitants by whites, who for some sudden reason found it desirable. The church, which had no record of involvement with the movement, occupied land that white men coveted. They had failed to induce the Negro congregation to sell, so other action was required. The white fraternal lodge down the road held extra meetings all that week. The night of the fire, they hadn't dispersed until after midnight and then were seen circling the area for two hours in cars without lights.

According to a COFO lawyer, insurance companies have never paid claims on destroyed Negro churches in Mississippi; it has been a still more efficient practice to cancel insurance the day before a fire. In Browning the fire truck had parked two blocks away for the burning, while firemen posted in front waved on anyone who tried to stop. A policeman explained that there was no water near the church, and the water on the truck had to be conserved to protect the other (white) buildings in the area. The church was demolished. Passing it the next day—quickly, as the ruin was covered with white men—we saw a yard-high remnant of wall, oddly smashed and sagging, one side apparently blown out, blackened timbers, nothing left. The Bible belt, "the last great bulwark of Christianity," where every other man is a preacher and the adjective "God-fearing" is reserved for the virtuous, where services for both colors are full not just Sundays but throughout the week, where the Scriptures salt the talk of men, here they burn the churches.

Local people had been suffering direct reprisals as long as the movement had been in the state. Greenwood was put on the map in 1963 when Byron de La Beckwith, a descendant of one of its oldest families, was accused of the sniper murder of NAACP field secretary Medgar Evers. Fifteen thousand dollars was raised for Beckwith's defense by the local White Citizens' Defense Fund (which still, for its more current needs, broadcast frequent commercials on the Greenwood radio), and one of the town's most prominent citizens, Hardy Lott—head of the local Democratic Party—defended him. While the jury was deliberating, "Delay," as he is known to his friends, received courtroom visits from former Governor Ross Barnett and General Edwin Walker. After eleven hours, the jury was deadlocked. A second trial resulted in a second hung jury. Beckwith is still under indictment, but the discomfort such a condition might be expected to inflict on him has been alleviated by Greenwood's rallying round the native son. They greeted him with welcome signs when he returned home from jail. A year later he had resumed his job as tobacco salesman and his hobby of gun collecting, but was to be found much of the time in the bar at the Travel Inn. Among what Beckwith had to celebrate was the federal government's purchase of a tract of his land for twenty-five thousand dollars, to build a post office; and his elevation to auxiliary policeman, enabling him to ride around in a patrol car with his own gun and club.

If you were black, you could expect other rewards. Reprisals hit all levels. It was one thing to react against the civil rights workers directly by arresting their leaders and burning down their office; it was another for Leflore County to withdraw from the Federal Surplus Food Program, as it did in 1962–1963. In "the winter of starvation" the Leflore County Board of Supervisors cut off twenty-two thousand people, almost all Negro, from what in many cases represented survival. No one doubted the Board's motives; they announced they could no longer afford to store and distribute the free food—but they had always found the means before the movement began its voter registration campaign. The deprived turned to SNCC, which organized a food drive and distributed supplies collected in the North. The first truckload of commodities was confiscated, and the two SNCC drivers jailed for "possession of narcotics" —aspirin and vitamin pills. But others got through, and the response in the Negro community was beyond SNCC's expectations: they connected with the movement and began regularly to besiege the courthouse to try to register to vote, and to participate in Freedom Days—mass registration attempts at the courthouse. White Greenwood followed up with group arrests, using cattle prods and a dog (the first: Birmingham was later), and by wrecking SNCC cars, destroying the office, and shooting Jimmy Travis. On a quieter level, those who moved with the movement were harassed, threatened, fired, evicted, struck from the relief rolls, had their taxes raised or their cotton acreage allotments reduced or their credit discontinued or their bank loans called in, or (since sheriffs in Mississippi are paid on the piecework system—a fixed sum for each arrest—and they have to live too) arrested for resisting arrest, or for drunken driving while walking down the street. Economic reprisal against those attempting to vote is a federal crime under the 1960 Civil Rights Act, but the Justice Department has not prosecuted the offenders in these cases.

June Johnson was at sixteen a veteran of the movement, and knew its risks precisely: they had been imprinted on her skin. She was one of twelve children, all of them tall, powerful, and angry. Mrs. Johnson and her children were still as outraged at the smallest injustice as if they had spent their lives wrapped in fleece linings protected from the sight of it.

In 1963 June was arrested at Winona, twenty-seven miles east of Greenwood, with five others, including Mrs. Hamer and Annelle Ponder. They were traveling by bus from South Carolina to Greenwood, and all but Mrs. Hamer had gone into the "white" waiting room during a brief stop. When they got to the jail, the state trooper who had made the arrest said, "I been hearing about you black sons of bitches over in Greenwood, raising all that hell—you come over here to Winona, you'll get the hell whipped out of you."

In her deposition, June said:

He opened the door to the cell block and told everybody to get inside. I started to go in with the rest of them and he said, "Not you, you black-assed nigger." He asked me, "Are you a member of the NAACP?" I said "yes." Then he hit me on the cheek and chin. I raised my arm to protect my face and he hit me in the stomach. He asked, "Who runs that thing?" I answered, "The people." He asked, "Who pays you?" I said, "Nobody." He said, "Nigger, you're lying. You done enough already to get your neck broken." Then the four of them—the sheriff, the chief of police, the state trooper, and the white man that had brought Mrs. Hamer in—threw me on the floor and beat me. After they finished stomping me, they said, "Get up, nigger." I raised my head and the white man hit me on the back of the head with a club wrapped in black leather. Then they made me get up.

She was locked up with her head cut open and her dress torn and bloody; then the others were beaten, one by one. They heard Mrs. Hamer being moved to another part of the building.

A little while later we heard Mrs. Hamer hollering, "Don't beat me no more—don't beat me no more." Later they brought her back to her cell crying. She cried at intervals during the night, saying that the leg afflicted with polio was hurting her terribly.

They were denied a doctor and a lawyer for three days, at which point they were booked and charged with disorderly conduct and resisting arrest.

AFFIDAVIT

STATE OF MISSISSIPPI
COUNTY OF LEFLORE
    NAME: Silas McGhee   AGE: 21
    ADDRESS: Browning
BEING DULY SWORN DEPOSES AND SAYS, TO WIT:

I am a Negro citizen of the United States. On the evening of July 5th, 1964, I went to the Leflore Theater in Greenwood, Mississippi, and asked to buy a ticket. The Leflore Theater had previously been [until three days before, when the Civil Rights Act was born] for "whites only." The ticket taker sold me a ticket and

I went in and sat down. I had only been sitting for a few minutes when whites in back of me started throwing papers and trash at me. I didn't say anything. Then a white man came up behind me and hit me on the head with his elbow. I still didn't say anything, but I got up and went to see the manager. The manager didn't offer me any protection. He only told me to go back and sit down if I wanted to. While walking back to my seat, I heard one of the whites say "He's going back!" Another said, "If he goes back, he won't be able to get up." When I took my seat, about 15 whites jumped me. I doubled up on the floor. They pounded me and kicked me. When I was able to get up, I ran out to the lobby and went into the manager's office. I asked if I could use the phone to call the police. He refused. I asked again. He refused. Finally, he agreed to come to the police station with me.

We walked to the city police station. I went in and told them what had happened. They took my name and address and asked me "Who put you up to this?" I told them that I only wanted to see a movie.

(SIGNED) Silas McGhee

Silas went to the movies seven times in the month of July but he didn't get to see any of them all the way through. White men, among them Byron de La Beckwith, began to picket the theater (evidently immune to the state anti-picketing law)—in the line that Editor Walt crossed. On the sixteenth, three men in a pickup truck stopped him on the road to Browning, took him at pistol point to a plumbing shop and beat him with a pipe and a plank. The local authorities took no action at any point, but the FBI arrested the three men on charges of conspiring to violate the Civil Rights Act—the first arrests made under the law in the country (and the last, despite innumerable similar incidents, for the summer). Silas went back to the Leflore, alternating with his older brother Jake; they always informed the FBI when they were going, were refused protection, never escaped without a beating, but they wouldn't stop.

"I want to take advantage of the Civil Rights Law," Silas said. "I want to assure the white folks I'm not scared and they can't push me around. They beat you anyway. Once I set my mind to something I don't stop."

"They're kind of brave," his widowed mother said. "I always

taught my sons not to break the law but to obey the law, and when they're trying to uphold the law I think that's right."

None of the McGhees said much unless asked; they had all just set their minds to something. The same men who burned down Pleasant Plain had long been after the McGhee fifty-eight-acre farm as well. In the course of their campaign they had arranged to have Mrs. McGhee committed to an insane asylum for a year, got the bank to initiate foreclosure proceedings, and shot into the house at night. When Mrs. McGhee invited the movement to hold a freedom rally on her place, the police surrounded it with signs reading NO PARKING ANY TIME. In May 1963 her eldest son, Clarence Robinson, returned on leave from the Army and went to register at the courthouse, was refused the right to take the test on the grounds that "his military duties take him away from home for long periods," and immediately set out for Memphis with his mother to file a suit. The next afternoon while Mrs. McGhee was cooking dinner she glanced out the window and saw two white men digging a huge ditch in her field with a steam shovel. Clarence ordered them off the land. He was arrested for disturbing the peace, fined five hundred dollars, and sentenced to six months in jail. The case was still on appeal.

The family owned an 1873 Winchester, but no one in town would sell them bullets. It didn't seem to matter: no one, yet, had found the way to stop a McGhee.

Phil Moore, a volunteer from Harvard, was beaten by an insurance salesman while he made his voter registration rounds. The judge, at whose house Phil and others applied for a warrant for the assailant's arrest, refused to comply on the grounds that the salesman's identity—from his name, occupation, and license plate number—was "not definite enough." Then they went to the police station, where they finally persuaded Chief Lary, after a three-hour argument, to call the insurance company and summon the salesman, Pruitt. He was charged with assault and battery and released on his own recognizance, to appear for trial the next day. The office tried for twenty-four hours to interest the local FBI in arresting Pruitt, as they were entitled to do; but "We have to be told by the Justice Department," they said on the phone. The Justice Department said they'd look into it. Nothing happened.

AFFIDAVIT

STATE OF MISSISSIPPI
COUNTY OF LEFLORE
NAME: Paul Klein   AGE: 22
ADDRESS: 708 Avenue N, Greenwood, Mississippi
BEING DULY SWORN DEPOSES AND SAYS, TO WIT:

On July 9, 1964 Mary Lane, George Johnson and I accompanied Phillip Moore to the Greenwood Police Station. His purpose was to swear out a warrant against one of the local whites who had beaten him on the street. While Moore was thus occupied in another room, Miss Lane (Negro), Johnson (white) and I waited in the station room. There were three officers present—Desk Sergeant Simpson, Officer Logan and another unidentified officer. Logan was not in uniform—evidently off duty.

Logan took a long knife out of his pocket and started to sharpen it, [directing] a running stream of threats at the three of us. He asked Johnson how he liked "screwing that nigger" (indicating Miss Lane). Then he said, while sharpening the knife: "sounds like rubbing up against nigger pussy." He poked the knife up against my ribs a few times; then he held it out toward me, told me to put my hand on it and asked: "Think it's sharp enough to cut your cock off?" Then he looked at Officer Simpson and said "You'd better get me out of here before I do what I'd like to do." At no time did Simpson or the other officer make any move to restrain him or protect us.

Shortly thereafter, he walked over behind the desk and took out a pistol from his trousers pocket. He brandished it in our direction and spun the chamber, then tucked it in his shirt front. He walked over to the door. Miss Lane was standing about eight feet from the door in front of him with her back turned to him. He took out his gun again, pointed it at Miss Lane for a few seconds and put it in his pants pocket. Then he opened the door with his left hand and simultaneously reached out and gave Miss Lane a shove with his right fist, knocking her several feet across the room. He swore at her; then Officer Simpson joined in and told Miss Lane: "Nigger, you get your ass away from that door." Miss Lane refused to move, explaining that she wasn't in the doorway, especially since Logan had knocked her practically across the room. Both the officers shouted threats at her, threatening to throw her in jail if she didn't move.

We went out about 15 minutes later and found that the tires of my car had been slashed. We went back in and reported the vandalism to the police but to no avail.

(SIGNED) Paul Klein

Beside the entrance to the courtroom in the city hall was a water cooler with the sign WHITE ONLY. Bill Hodes, a white voter registration worker, noticed the sign as he bent to drink, straightened again and walked away, as a matter of principle. A moment later Albert Garner, a local Negro movement man who knew the sign was there already, bent and drank, as a matter of principle.

In the courtroom two cases concerning us were to be staged. Three carloads of friends accompanied Phil Moore, plaintiff, and Fred Mangrum, defendant, to their trials. I walked in with Sue Taylor, the young girl in charge of SCLC business at the office, and sat with her in the second of two rows of spectators' seats. She seemed amazed, looking at the rest of the audience, that we had been permitted in together. "It's the first time I seen this courtroom integrated," she said. "Usually a man at the door stops the Negroes comin' in."

The room was tiny and jammed with incongruous furniture: a dozen metal lockers painted pink, khaki, and pale green, a refrigerator and two air conditioners the size of upright double beds. Up front were the judge's stand and a table pushed together, with an American flag behind them on the wall. In the remaining space, and seated in the row in front of me or along a bench to the side, were on- and off-duty policemen and some spectating whites. Among them stood a handsome young man in a policeman's summer suit: white shirt, blue trousers, a lot of brass, and his dark hair slicked back into a pompadour. Officer Logan. More policemen bunched in the doorway near the desk, talking among themselves and glowering at us. An auburn-haired policewoman with a bone-white face stared at the integrated group in measured thrusts as though to pierce us through. The cops—guns and whistles, straps, belts, badges, buckles, insignia—I tried to remember each one for the next encounter, which might not be as restrained. But it frightened me that we could belong to the same race, not only white, but human—their bland, vapid faces alight with hatred, gum chewers hiding behind their guns. The rednecks in the row just in front of me had such red necks. I turned to Sue to get my mind off them and asked, "Why do you have an 'A' on your blouse?" She said, "It's my sister's." "What's her name?" "Frances."

Judge Orman Kimbrough and Chief Lary entered the room; the former seated himself beneath the American flag as the latter called out, "The Police Court of Greenwood is in session." Two Lawyers' Guild attorneys with us were allowed to participate. Our first case involved Freddy Mangrum, who had been arrested the night before for "profanity in a public place." He pleaded not guilty. (He was, in fact: the cops had arrested the wrong man. Monroe Sharpe had called out "damn" about something. The police, driving Freddy to the station, had twice called him "son of a bitch.")

The arresting officer turned out to be Logan. At 1:30 a.m., he testified, he had been patrolling near Bullin's Café and saw "several people, about a dozen, in the street, several people runnin' back and forth across the street." "Fred," he said—employing the first name pointedly, because Freddy was a Negro, though from New York and unknown to Logan—"was on the west side of the street," and "Fred" said, " 'What the goddam hell did you do that for?' " Then "Fred" crossed the street and used those very words again. "Could it have been anyone else?" Logan was asked in cross-examination. No, it couldn't. "He was standin' right beside the car and I was lookin' him right in the face. He was standin' all by hisself."

The policeman with him when the incident occurred, an older, paunchy man, was called in from the next room. The words "Fred" used, he said, were, " 'I'll be goddamned, why did you do it?' " There was no mistaking who it was, though he had been quite a distance away at the time—about as far as that man in the back of the room (twenty feet away). "How many people were there?" the prosecuting attorney questioned—and prompted when the policeman hesitated: "Five, six, eight, ten . . . *twelve* people?" "Oh no, I imagine there were twenty-five, thirty or more."

After all the testimony, the lawyers asked the judge for the legal definition of profanity, maintaining that the words in question didn't constitute it. The judge snapped, "He is guilty of profanity; it doesn't matter what words he used." Fined fifteen dollars.

In the intermission between cases, a hale middle-aged fellow joined the cops on the side bench and chatted with them convivially. "That's Hardy Lott," Sue whispered, "Beckwith's lawyer." Glancing beyond him, I noticed Logan directing a furious, glittering stare at me. I looked away. A moment later, turned toward him again without thinking, I saw he hadn't moved. I looked at him back for a while to see if he'd blink.

Phil Moore was called. He had arrived in Greenwood on the twenty-first of June, he said. He spoke in low key, quite differently from his normal frantic good spirits. Canvassing the day before, he related, he had been approached on the street by a man who had hit him and told him to get out of town. (Pruitt, the defendant, sat near Phil at the table, looking straight ahead.) Phil had backed off and walked away, turning the corner to seek a friend who was canvassing nearby. A block later a car caught up with him, stopped and discharged Pruitt, who hit him again. Phil fell into a ditch. "And you didn't hit him *back?*" an astonished voice asked now. Phil tried to explain that he was nonviolent. The cops and others in the courtroom exchanged glances, sniggering. Pruitt, who had pleaded innocent, was fined twenty-five dollars. It was the first time in anyone's memory that a Mississippi court had decided in favor of a civil rights worker.

Scattered harassments and acts of violence occurred every day throughout the state, each—when you got the habit—insignificant on its own. Every statistic and minor outrage had been catalogued by newsmen in June, but the "Negro page" that Mississippi had brought to the front at the beginning fell back to page 14, page 36, then was left out altogether. Betty Garman, Judy Richardson, Dotty Zellner, Ed Rudd, and others in the SNCC national office nagged and bullied the outside to care. In day and night shifts and in varying numbers and combinations, SNCC staff members manned the WATS lines, compiled daily reports, dealt with long-distance crises as well as one can on a tapped telephone, and tried to urge Washington into action. A sign on the wall read:

> There's a street in Itta Bena called FREEDOM
> There's a town in Mississippi called LIBERTY
> There's a department in Washington called JUSTICE

Only people traveling through, for whom the SNCC office was a sort of Southern tourist attraction, found the sign amusing. For those at the phones, the Justice Department often held the key to survival, but the "J.D." was part of an administration with an election coming up.

In the 1964 FBI *Annual Report,* which devoted four pages to "the insidious nature of the communist threat" and slightly more than two inches to civil rights, the agency reported having handled 3,340 civil rights cases in the year ended June 30, 1964. "Each of these cases received thorough, impartial attention by experienced Agents specially trained in this field." The results were five convictions.

Then two white boys disappeared. The nation was aroused; the Navy came to search, Allen Dulles to fact-find, and J. Edgar Hoover to open Jackson's first FBI bureau. Five Negroes had been murdered in the first five months of the year without interest to the local or national authorities, or so much as an inch on page 36; in the course of the search for Schwerner, Chaney, and Goodman the mutilated bodies of two others were found in the Mississippi River, but no one besides their own mothers had previously noted their disappearance. Since 1900, 1,797 lynchings of Southern Negroes have been *documented*—but documented by the (Negro) Tuskegee Institute; these murders are not an item in the white conscious or conscience. More frequent, so less conspicuous, were the incidents of federal officials standing by while Negroes were beaten and jailed for attempting to register to vote in federal elections, standing by and taking notes; they are "not a police force." That a significant proportion of the only alternative "police force," Mississippi's, were active members of the Klan or the Americans for the Preservation of the White Race, did not interfere with such statements issuing from Washington as "the [Justice] Department and the Bureau uphold the value of cooperation with local authorities. They see this as the essence of the nation's Federal system." To encourage such "cooperation" the local federal agents were often local people, Southerners. Even if they were not, they were on good terms with local law enforcement officials through having collaborated with them on bank robbery or car theft cases. But even the liaison natural to law-enforcers failed to explain such phenomena as the remarkable job-shifting capacity of a former Meridian FBI agent who subsequently volunteered to defend the accused murderers of Schwerner, Chaney, and Goodman; or of another agent who in August 1963 left his post as Greenwood's FBI agent to run for Leflore County District Attorney, with the campaign slogan: "The South has no friends in the legal staff of the Justice Department." Such remarks only helped the J.D. to ward off attacks from the other side, and to feel like the lady with the scales, in a state of equilibrium. On Burke Marshall's wall, according to one newspaper interview, hung the sign BLESSED ARE THE PEACEMAKERS, FOR THEY CATCH HELL FROM BOTH SIDES.

The U.S. Commission on Civil Rights had concluded unanimously that "only further steps by the Federal government can arrest the subversion of the Constitution in Mississippi." Twenty-nine law professors pointed out that statutory authority existed for these "further steps," that the President would be "within his rights to send in troops or deputize U.S. marshals to prevent violence." Deputy Attorney General Nicholas deB. Katzenbach, however, replied that the professors had failed to prove that "there has been such a complete breakdown of law and order that civilian law enforcement measures are overwhelmed."

Dick Gregory summed it up: "No politician is about to send troops into *any* state this close to an election. A statesman would, but not a politician." In his book, *Nigger,* he said, "You never know what fear is until you walk through the streets of a quiet town at night and it suddenly dawns on you that if anyone attacked you, you couldn't even call the police." The "quiet town" was Greenwood, but it could have been any in Mississippi. We had no protection: responsibility for our lives extended no further than ourselves individually. And the important point, which no one had thought to mention until there were whites, too, involved: the Negroes of Mississippi, historically denied rights guaranteed by legislation enacted long before the Civil Rights Act but unenforced, were the helpless victims of a continuing injustice.

There were only four Negro members of the bar in Mississippi; white lawyers, when court appointed, have been willing to handle civil rights cases, largely in order to keep outside lawyers out, but they have refused to raise Constitutional questions such as jury composition. To fill our need, members of the National Lawyers' Guild came to Greenwood at their own expense, often sacrificing their summer vacations, just as members of the NAACP Legal Defense and Educational Fund and the Lawyers' Constitutional Defense

Committee did to other parts of the state; and scattered among the COFO projects were twenty law students, all attempting to influence the situation.

George Johnson, Greenwood's law student, spent his time compiling heaps of affidavits which might or might not be acted on, besides supplementing next year's FBI statistics and drawing up petitions of removal. After each arrest the local federal judge was requested to remove the case to federal jurisdiction on the grounds that a Southern jury trial was automatically prejudicial to the defendant. While Claude Clayton, the federal judge for the northern half of the state, moved from town to town, the lawyers chased him with their documents and attempted to persuade him to grant the petitions and lower excessive bail. More creative legal work was seldom possible, although New York attorneys William Kunstler and Michael Standard filed a suit attempting to reactivate an 1866 statute authorizing the appointment of federal commissioners to sit in every county of the state to insure the safety of Negro citizens and civil rights workers. The plaintiffs included COFO, Rita Schwerner, Mrs. Fannie Lee Chaney, Mrs. Fannie Lou Hamer. The defendants: Sheriff Rainey and Deputy Price of Neshoba, the KKK, APWR, the Citizens' Councils. And the Lawyers' Guild initiated a case to enjoin the state from enforcing a collection of unconstitutional laws which were specifically enacted against the movement —e.g., prohibiting obscenity on the telephone (a fancy way of legalizing wiretapping) and picketing, both laws violations of the First Amendment; and the "criminal syndicalism" law, making it a felony to "suggest . . . any political or social change."

The law students had another valuable function—just talking to the local people, who had never had any idea of their rights. "Is it lawful to say 'yassah' and 'nossuh'?" I heard an old man ask. "Do you have to? I heard it was the law."

Every week there were more arrests on sillier charges requiring trips to the police department to bail somebody out. For a while it seemed usually to be George Albertz, a white volunteer whom the police arrested nearly every day for reckless driving, until his car was smashed with bricks one night; then he was arrested for walking, on the charge of "parading without a permit." We got used to the policemen's faces, the desk sergeant's stare, the big ledger where the names and charges were inscribed; and used to waiting, for the judge or Chief Lary or the man with the keys. There was always time to see, among the WANTED posters behind the desk, a much larger one reading: MISSING: CALL FBI. THE FBI IS SEEKING INFORMATION CONCERNING THE DISAPPEARANCE AT PHILADELPHIA, MISSISSIPPI, OF THESE THREE INDIVIDUALS ON JUNE 21, 1964. . . . Their pictures, their descriptions, and SHOULD YOU HAVE OR IN THE FUTURE RECEIVE ANY INFORMATION CONCERNING THE WHEREABOUTS OF THESE INDIVIDUALS, YOU ARE REQUESTED TO NOTIFY ME. . . . Signed, J. EDGAR HOOVER. One day there was a change in the poster: someone had drawn a mustache on the picture of Andrew Goodman.

A poem was framed and hung above the entrance to the courtroom.

> When the hours seem long and the going, rough
> When the pay seems small and the criminals, tough
> Just square your shoulders and call their bluff
> Let them be the ones to cry, "Enough"
> You're a policeman.

It continued for several verses, ending:

> When you leave at last this worldly din
> And seek, like mortals, Paradise to win,
> St. Peter, I trust, will o'erlook ev'ry sin
> And say, "Well done, my boy, come right in.
> You're a policeman."

This one was signed, "W. H. Drane Lester, Inspector, FBI."

On a third wall hung a copper plaque etched in cursive script: "In appreciation for outstanding service to our community for a job 'Well Done' during near riot conditions erupting March 27th, 1963." Underneath was a list of heroes, starting with Mayor C. E. Sampson, Comm. B. A. Hammond, Comm. W. G. Mize, Police Chief Curtis Lary, with Officer Logan included in the middle, and finishing with "Police Dog 'Tiger.'" March 27, 1963, was the day Jim Forman, Bob Moses, and eight others were arrested leading a march to the courthouse to ask for police protection after the burning of the SNCC office and the subsequent shooting into the home of Dewey Greene, whose son had applied for admission to Ole Miss. Tiger had been honored for biting SNCC worker Matthew Hughes.

One afternoon I was standing by the plaque and looking at it again when a policeman coming from the courtroom noticed me and snarled, "You better quit readin' that."

"Why is it hanging here if I'm not allowed to read it?" I asked, watching him try to take the plaque down, though it was obviously nailed to the wall.

"It ain't for the public," he said, wrenching at it.

"Maybe you should hang it somewhere else then, in the men's room or someplace."

His hand left the plaque and moved in the direction of his holster. I went to the other side of the room.

Stokely got to spend his birthday out of jail, but was arrested within the week, for the fourth time in a month, on a false traffic charge. He burst into the office freshly sprung with nothing more urgent on his mind than had anything arrived from FASC? FASC was the Friends and Admirers of Stokely Carmichael, a nationwide organization whose membership included an entire order of Carmelite nuns somewhere in the Midwest. There was, as usual, an enormous package from FASC, filled with insect repellent, shaving cream, shoe polish, shampoo, Camels, baby powder, prickly heat powder, foot powder, and other more or less essential items which Stokely proceeded to brandish and distribute about the office, to the irritation of local representatives of rival groups like FAJR (Friends and Admirers of Judy Richardson). Then he got down to telling the story.

AFFIDAVIT

STATE OF MISSISSIPPI
COUNTY OF COAHOMA
    NAME: Stokely Carmichael   AGE: 23
    OCCUPATION: SNCC Field Secretary

I was driving away from the Clarksdale COFO office down Yazoo St. when I was pulled to the side by police chief Ben Collins. He said, "Gimme your license, boy." I replied, "What did you say?" He said, "I said, gimme your license." I said, "That's what I thought you said." He replied, "You're a smart nigger, ain't you?" He looked at my license and then said, "You didn't signal." I said I didn't have to, because I hadn't made a turn. He jumped

out of the car and told me I was under arrest, and started searching me. I put my hands over my head. He told me to get in his
car. I asked if I could move my car. He said, "Get in the car
and shut up." I acquiesced. We got to the station where I was
booked for failing to signal. Collins told me to take everything
out of my pockets . . .

". . . and then," Stokely said that night at the mass meeting,
where he repeated the story, "he found some dice I had on me and
asked me what I used them for. I told him that my grandmother gave
them to me and that I always carry them for luck. He says, 'I didn't
know a nigger could use those for anything but gambling. Niggers
don't do nothin' but gamble and drink wine.' I said, 'That's right,
niggers don't do nothin' but gamble and drink wine. But who taught
us how? We know who makes wine. Negroes don't make wine.'
'Why're you smilin'?' he says to me. 'Niggers always smile,' I said."
He made a smiling bow to the audience, which was heaving with
laughter.

"Ben Collins said I'm the orneriest nigger he ever saw. Then he
said this was the worst generation of niggers yet." Applause. "When
the lawyer came and asked for Mr. Carmichael, Ben Collins said,
'We don't have a Mr. Carmichael, we got a nigger Carmichael.'"

They laughed again, and Stokely slid right into his next subject. "I
was talking to a woman yesterday, trying to get her to go to register,
and she said (he mimicked), 'Our people are dirty, they don't go to
school, they're lazy, they smell,' and that we weren't ready for the
vote. We had to be more like white folks to be ready for the vote.
'That's right!' I said to her. 'We got to bomb their churches, shoot
them at night, wear hoods, lynch them, beat on their heads, be just
like they are, *then* we'll be ready for the vote!'"

Tomorrow, Thursday, was Freedom Day. Meetings had been held
throughout the week to encourage everyone to go to the courthouse
in a mass attempt to move Martha Lamb, and to sign up as many as
possible on freedom registration forms. At the same time, some of
the volunteers and as many local people as wanted to would picket
the courthouse to protest discrimination in voting and to test the
anti-picketing law. Four store windows in the Negro neighborhood
had been broken that week for displaying Freedom Day signs; but
the more the resistance, the greater the enthusiasm. Pickup points
had been established for people who needed a ride to the court-

house. Now Stokely exhorted them all to go. *"Everyone!"* he shouted, and everyone shouted back. "The only thing keeps white folks together is keeping black folks apart!"

None of the high feeling weakened after the meeting. They sang and held together in the streets long afterwards while white-driven cars circled. Aware of an impending crisis in tomorrow's Freedom Day, the whites had crossed the tracks to have a look. Many of the same cars returned again and again; George Johnson and Bob Zellner stood outside noting down license numbers. Now, the meeting over, the crowd surged along the street shouting at the cars as they began to recognize them, and it was late before Bob and George talked them into dispersing. COFO workers walked back to the office for a late staff meeting.

Stokely was addressing the volunteers in a fierce voice, alluding to a couple who had scoffed at danger. "Now look! *I'm nervous.* There've been eight cars circling the place, one of them with a piece of paper over the license plate. There's been a car with Georgia plates circling the office all day." Some stragglers wandered in, sensed his tension, didn't move. "Now I don't want any funny business here! Anybody wants to get killed, they can just go out in the middle of the street, but leave the office. Now that goes. Across the board."

They sat down, sobered. Assignments were given out for Freedom Day. Names had been chosen at random to fill the picket line, because the marchers would be arrested—a fate almost universally considered desirable. As Eli had put it the week before, "I want to go to jail. I'm honest. I've never been." Others did too. "Ellis *v.* the State of Mississippi," Evelyn said. "Doesn't that sound *great?*" "Well *I* ain't goin' to no jail," Stokely had broken in. That's what he thought.

The list was read. Two of everything: white men and women, anyway, had to be arrested together, "because you won't find very many friends in there." My name was called. It was a relief just to know. Others were given stations at the Elks' Hall, or Baptist Town, or the office. No one contested the decisions.

9. Jail

It is to be confessed, too, that the naïve, off-hand information that he was to be thrown into jail by no means produced an agreeable impression on a poor fellow who had always prided himself on a strictly honest and upright course of life. Yes, Tom, we must confess it, was rather proud of his honesty, poor fellow, —not having very much else to be proud of;—if he had belonged to some of the higher walks of society, he, perhaps, would never have been reduced to such straits.

—Harriet Beecher Stowe, UNCLE TOM'S CABIN

At seven on Freedom Day I dressed in cut-off jeans, filled the pockets with a toothbrush and paste, cigarettes, comb, pencil and paper, two dollars, and a handkerchief of Mrs. Amos's, put a skirt on top, smoothed out the lumps, and sat down to a big breakfast of eggs and sausages. "When y'all gets in jail," Mrs. Amos said, "I'm gonna have to cook you up some food and bring it to you."

"Don't they feed you in jail?"

"Oh, they feeds you, but you ain't gonna want it." She piled more sausages on my plate. "Some of the children gets in jail, they never saw bugs in the bed before. You know, lice and crabs. Oh-oh, like to scares 'em to death!"

The morning was misty and bland. Bambi arrived bearing dozens of signs she had painted for the picket line, and the first group left. After a tearful hug from Mrs. Amos, I joined a carload of local people who were going to stand on line to try to register. We drove over the tracks to white Greenwood, which looked quite normal, as if the Freedom in Freedom Day reminded it of nothing. The woman beside me said she'd heard they had taken out the "Colored" drinking fountain in the courthouse and locked up the restrooms. From the back seat, a very old man said, "Don't you worry. When the

137

great day come, we gonna lock up heaven so they can't get in there."

The car dropped us in front of the courthouse. All the police were there, with their voluntary auxiliary force, and the sheriff, deputies, highway patrol, and white men arranged like the audience of a parade behind wooden horses on the other side of the street. There were reporters and photographers, some of them SNCC workers in disguise, in more intricate viewing positions—on ledges and upper floors or parked innocently in cars. The old man and others with us joined the end of the line of registrants, which stretched down the steps and walk from the courthouse and around the pavement in front; Martha Lamb refused to permit them to take the test more than three at a time. Then the picketers arrived, held their signs high—ONE MAN ONE VOTE, WE WANT TO REGISTER, END VOTING DISCRIMINATION—and began a slow procession down the walk, turning at the end and marching back. Chief Lary was upon us in an instant, bellowing through a megaphone, "There'll be no picketin'. We will not interfere with you goin' to register to vote, but there'll be no picketin'." The paddy wagon, a bus, pulled up in the center of the street like a big black animal hungry for a meal of picketers. "You are free to register, but no picketin'." The police, helmeted, their billy sticks swinging, arranged themselves strategically along the line. "There'll be no picketin'." As they reached the point nearest the bus, marchers were picked off arbitrarily, told "You are under arrest," their signs torn across, and pushed inside. In decreasing numbers the others continued around, like a children's party game in which the last one left is It. I passed a parked car and greeted the *Time* reporter, whom I knew, sitting in it; he looked through me in an attempt to prove that one or other of us was invisible. It wasn't me. Coming around to the front again, I felt a hand seize my arm and shove me toward the bus through thickets of guns and clubs. Up the steps and in, where a dozen or more were already pounding, shouting, thumping on the windows, "FREEDOM! FREEDOM! FREEDOM! FREEDOM!" while others in cadence sang: "Ain't gonna let Chief Lary turn me round, turn me round, turn me round. . . . Keep on a-walkin', Keep on a-talkin', Marchin' on to freedom land. . . ." A frail old woman beat an umbrella on the floor in time, a slight, wiry girl stamped rhythmically in the aisle, and more of us were flung in, more and more, roughly and triumphantly. The bus was packed; it began to move. "FREEDOM! FREEDOM! FREE-DOM! FREE-DOM!" The shout ripped the air apart as we drove off, building a wild elation and sense of power. If only the movement's success could be measured like a noise contest, I thought irrelevantly, remembering the applause meters on TV quiz shows, and shouted.

There wasn't far to go. The bus turned left, left, left, and into the parking lot behind the courthouse. The door swung open and we were summoned out by cops, down and hurriedly over to the door of the jail. "What happened to you, pretty?" a policeman sneered, shoving me into a dank hallway full of mops and pails, where I followed those ahead up a flight of stairs and waited. A man was taking down names and home towns on a yellow legal pad in a slow, childish hand, spelling, erasing, respelling with infinite stubborn clumsiness. A sign behind him ordered prisoners to bathe twice a week, not to put mattresses on the floor, and No KANGAROO COURTS PERMITTED. My name was on the pad and I went up more stairs to be put away. The jailer, his face sunlessly white, appeared and unlocked a door in the middle of three. Hovering behind him was Honey Styles, deputy sheriff, male version of the warty, snaggle-toothed old witch in primitive picture-book illustrations. Linda Wetmore was inside already. "It's segregated here?" she asked. Honey said, "I wouldn't put you in with them dirty niggers, Red." The door slammed shut, heavy and metal. A moment later it opened once again for Margaret Aley. "Another one of them nigger-huggers," Honey said.

We sank onto bunks. From down the hall came the clank of keys, slam of doors, and the Negro girls singing: "Ain't scared o' your jails because I want my freedom, I want my freedom, I want my freedom . . ." We joined them and the building rattled with our voices. Between choruses another voice rang out: "Hey! Y'all want some tear gas bombs in there? Shut up!" A moment later the jailer came in a side door and down a narrow aisle outside the bars, closing the windows.

The songs gradually lost their momentum and we our frenzied voices. We began to examine our new home. Margaret got up and paced the cell. "This is for my diary," she said. "Fifteen . . . by ten." There were three lower bunks and two uppers, metal shelves hanging down on chains and covered with ancient fetid mattresses. Another lower and two uppers were broken, propped up against the bars. Bars made up two walls, beyond them the closed windows, two on the short end, three on the long. In the third wall was the door to the rest of the world; in the fourth, a curtainless, concrete showerstall, a basin, a seatless hole that was a toilet. On the ledge above the shower sat one tin cup, half a bar of Ivory soap, a roll of toilet paper, and a green block of worn-out air purifier.

It was still an adventure, and we were in a hurry—surely we'd be out by night? Possibly any minute. So we busied ourselves observing it all, speleologists stumbling on a new cave, and reading aloud the bits of information, advice, and other graffiti that covered the walls like primitive art. JESUS SAVE, read a motto beneath a penciled picture of a crowned, benevolent face on the bottom of a propped-up bunk: KING OF GLORY. Beside it someone had daubed in lipstick: "Where is he at? Name_____, St._____, Zone_____." Scratched into the tarnished silver paint on another bunk: "My phone no. is GL 3-5950. Call me if I can help. I had so much while I was here." A third: "Greenwood: This is the place for all weaklings. I have been one for 22 years. Does one's luck ever change?"

And: "I love Clyde Kidd so much it is hurting to stay in this jail without him. But I will get out of here and I will see him real soon and it won't be long. Zona Bollard, Charleston, Arkansas."

And:

> Sun Feb 26 1961
> Mon Feb 27 1961
> Tues Feb 28 1961
> Wed Mar 1 1961

> Hurrah! I'm leaving this hole! It's all yours, baby. Why don't you put in wall-to-walls and drapes and a poker table—with the traffic going through here, someone could make a killing.

Inscribed in a heart:

I
Clovis
know
God is
love

Then Linda discovered in tiny crude print near the door: "Man is the only animal that can be skinned more than once. He is a creature that is always looking for home atmosphere in a hotel and hotel service at home. A self-made man is one who started from scratch and now itches all over."

There were names and dates and invitations to mysterious obscene acts, and after we'd learned them all by heart we lay down again and laughed, chattered, sang, and only very slowly ran out of adrenalin and retired into ourselves. Doors still slammed somewhere and keys jangled, a far-off phone rang, and other strange metallic sounds made a distant, hollow din. There were undercurrents of fear, but I could examine them in the same scientific spirit as the cave, because more powerfully I found I still retained a child's faith in the law, born in the era of *Gangbusters, The FBI in Peace and War,* and *Mr. Keen, Tracer of Lost Persons.* I *know* what can happen here, I kept thinking, but I can't believe it *will.* Some of the strange metallic sounds were finally identified: the door opened, and the pale-faced jailer, with two Negro trusties, set three tin plates on the floor. They had a trolley outside and, one assumed, some sort of dumbwaiter. "We want a lawyer!" I shouted; they didn't look at us. "We want to make a phone call!" No answer. They left.

Rice with red sauce, lima beans, cornbread. We picked up the plates and held them tentatively on our laps. Next door the girls were being given theirs. "We want to get out!" a shrill voice shouted. Sounds of Honey Styles again: "Act like human beings and you wouldn't be here in the first place."

"We are human beings! We want freedom!"

"Well, you ain't gonna git it." Slam.

Margaret and I discussed the possibility of a hunger strike. Why not? "You talk about it," Linda said, "while I eat." She spooned up a mouthful of rice, instantly spat it out and rushed for the tin cup and water faucet. "Pepper," she choked. We agreed to fast.

The plates were piled up by the door, and I thought of Bayard Rustin's saying during the orientation in Ohio, "We always have mixed motives. Once I was halfway through a ten-day fast for peace, when I noticed among the group an *enormous* woman. I realized that one of the reasons for the fast was that I wanted to lose weight."

Songs reverberated down the stone and metal corridors. Now and then we joined in, but our voices so drowned out theirs to us that we found ourselves ending the lines too late or too soon—it was impossible to come out together with the others so far away. We lapsed into daydreams with their music beyond us. I felt as if I were falling away and yet into myself, losing contact with something important that I couldn't identify. The smell seemed to battle the air and gradually subdue it. Heat had risen with the windows shut, and the sweat—our own, each other's, and all the years of it gone stale on every mattress—throbbed almost tangibly, as though it had a color or a shape and was pushing at the tiny space to suffocate our bodies. There was already, after a couple of hours, a *physical* sense of oppression at not being able to move, go anywhere, get out, find an enemy to fight, breathe the air beyond the bars. The sudden vanishing of a predictable future, a minute or a month away, and the enclosedness of the walls so vivid they seemed to be a live force.

The door swung open abruptly, interrupting my musing, and Bambi, Carol, and two other girls were flung in—weaving and bubbling with all the sense of discovery we three had lost. They introduced Erin Simms, from the Atlanta SNCC office, and Iris Greenberg from the Jackson Project. For different reasons, they had found themselves in Greenwood on Freedom Day and had accompanied the others when the policy changed: to the courthouse, *pack the jails.*

Seven now, too many to lie down, we squatted, crouched, and tangled limbs on the sticky mattresses while they told us what had happened. It seemed many years and miles away. They had left their stations at pickup points in the Negro neighborhood, where their job had been to encourage as many as possible to attempt registration, and gone to join the picket line. Chief Lary resumed his megaphone chant, the black bus drew up again, and the police began to swing their clubs and kick the demonstrators into it. This time a cattle prod was used; in the scuffle Monroe Sharpe had been clubbed and a pregnant woman dragged down the street to the paddy wagon. The four girls had been taken to the city jail, then out again and back to the county jail. Still others—all Negro—had been taken to the county farm. Unlike us, the second wave had been searched and their possessions taken, though some carefully concealed toothbrushes and a few bent cigarettes remained. There was relief that, although denied a phone call or even the formality of being charged, we had not been stripped and searched vaginally "for narcotics," as has been a practice with arrested civil rights workers.

The toothbrushes were exhumed and propped into the center of the toilet roll. There was nothing else to housekeep. The wall messages were reread and songs resumed. New girls sang out from the other cell nearby, and with the music came the heat, as though our voices were a function of the temperature, or the other way around. A motor started chugging somewhere, and we wondered if they'd turned the heat on or if it was just the air conditioner for the rest of the courthouse. Raucous cries to shut up interrupted choruses, but the windows were already closed.

Hours rushed away as minutes dragged and darkness came. Everyone wanted to hunger-strike, but no more meals were served. Whenever footsteps or key noises indicated anyone outside we shouted for a lawyer, for a phone call, or was there going to be any dinner. No one ever answered. It was as though the sounds were uninvolved with life, but simply made themselves. We tried calling to the other girls but we only managed to bellow out about the hunger strike, heard muffled replies, and hoped they understood. Someone thought we ought to play some games, and pitching pennies was the first suggestion. Taking turns sitting on the same spot of bunk, we tried to get them nearest to the wall. It soon got boring. Night came like a destination; we lit our single bulb. Iris thought of hopscotch and, leaping up, Erin unwrapped the bar of Ivory soap and drew squares on the floor. All we had for a potsy was a fifty-cent piece, which rolled around and wouldn't cooperate; then some discontents set in, displays of local patriotism involving variations of the rules of hopscotch in New York and Los Angeles. It all stopped somehow. We were beginning to feel very hungry, and annoyed that there had been no word from our lawyers. The cigarettes were running low; we lit one for all, less and less often. Carol split our few matches down the middle, a trick she remembered from Dick Tracy's *Crimestoppers' Textbook*. The comb got passed around and braids and buns constructed. We sat.

Suddenly, a tapping on the Judas-hole. It opened and a face showed through its bars. Negro: a friend. It was one of the trusties. Someone had the presence of mind to turn off the light to prevent his silhouette showing in the hall, and we mobbed at the window for the precious sight of someone else. He pushed a couple of candy bars into the nearest hands, then a note, and shut the window, promising to return.

"We are not going to eat. Send us cigs. We don't have light." It was from the girls. Someone was splitting the candy bars into minuscule allotments. There were sticky peanuts in them that lodged in the teeth for a second helping. Everyone gloated with the miracle and comfort of a respite from isolation. A return note to the girls was composed, then one to each set of boys, whereabouts unknown. There wasn't much to say: "How are you? We're fine. Are you going to eat tomorrow? We're not."

The creak of the little window again; light out; to the door. Like captive animals in the ape cage we swung on bars, over bunks to the face at the peephole. "Oh God, thanks for the *candy*." "How did you *do* it?" "Can you get cigarettes?" "Let's give him some money." "Did the other girls get some?" "What's your name?" Patterson, he said, and he had given the other girls a couple of bars too. He glanced in the direction of their cell—which was the other way from where their voices sounded. There was more metal between us than around corners, we could see now, so to yell to them meant to yell away from them. "We don't have light" was accounted for: though we had a cord for ours, theirs was controlled from the hall, and no one had seen fit to turn the switch. Patterson described his case, eighteen-month sentence, innocence; he explained that as a trusty he lived in an ordinary room, not a cell, and was permitted to go outside at certain hours of the day and home some weekends. The alternative was parole to a farmer, who would "own me like a slave"; he preferred jail.

He had seen many prisoners come and go: the eighteen months were almost up. Our cell was not necessarily reserved for whites; they didn't mind our sharing a shower and mattresses with Negroes as long as we didn't share them at the same time. He described the pattern of prison life as he had seen it: the first day or two are fine, you tell each other stories, and if you're in for different things you talk about them, and it's entertaining for a while. After the third or fourth day, you run out of things to say. "You looks at each other, and suddenly you begins to fade out. . . ." Of course, we all smiled confidently to ourselves, we would avoid this experience. We would be out the next day.

A thousand questions, some of them answered. Nearly forty of us were in the jail, fifteen Negro girls in a cell the size of ours (capacity eight, assuming no bunks were broken), a similar number of Negro boys across the hall—Patterson pointed to the right where we could just make out some bars. The white boys, half a dozen of them, were downstairs in an open cell block. We gave him the notes and a dollar for cigarettes. The little door popped open once more for the briefest second and another scrap of paper thrust through, then clanked finally shut for the night.

"We won't eat tomorrow. We will sing loud about daybreak. Freedom." It was from the Negro boys.

The two most disgusting mattresses and most of the heat were on the top bunks: you had your choice of them or sharing a bottom. Nobody else apparently found any appeal in the upstairs, so I had it to myself, folded my skirt for a pillow and tried to forget the hot stench. Pieces of filthy mattress-stuffing stuck out in lumps, crusted with years of vomit, urine, sweat. It was easier to sleep than to stay awake.

Early in the morning the jailer opened the windows. I woke to his sound and the smell of frying fish competing with the mattress. It was 5 a.m. From the high perch I could see four floors down to the Yazoo, flowing to the Mississippi, past New Orleans to the sea; an odd color, cocoa made with water instead of milk. The sun was rising and the boys began their song.

> Woke up this morning with my mind
> Stayed on freedom . . .

Other voices and another song joined them then: the white boys downstairs.

> I'm so glad
> That we shall brothers be . . .

They were unable to hear each other, and made a strangely lovely counterpoint of song.

> Halleloo-oo, halleloo-oo, halleloo-oo-oo . . .
> Singin' glo-ory hallelujah, glo-ory hallelujah, glo-ory hallelujah,
> I'm so glad.

Below me the girls dozed, tried to turn over, couldn't, dozed again. Carol's long black braid and Linda's red curls were spread among bars in the center of the last bed, where their heads met, Carol's feet on the next bunk and Linda's in the air propped on the bars. Between them and the windows the floor was littered with butts and debris. Early morning at the zoo. I slept and woke to freedom songs.

At seven, the jailer brought the tin plates again. Patterson was with him, but he looked at no one—a study in three centuries of Negro rebelliousness masked in servility. "When can we make a phone call?" Weakly now. "We want a lawyer." No reaction. Hungry bodies stirred, remembered, remained where they were. Fishcakes, grits, and cornbread. I swung down and sat on the hole, brushed my teeth, and had a cup of water, passing it to the nearest groping hand. It became orange juice, milk, and coffee according to request. Then a cigarette, sucked in so deeply it made no more than a couple of rounds. What else was there to do? Take a shower.

Others joined me in an attempt to wash some of the smell away. Naked bodies lounged around waiting to dry (no towel) while others tried to aim the spray at themselves, but the fixture was broken and water sloshed around the room, forming slimy puddles on the floor. When the jailer came again to take the breakfast away, we asked for a mop as well as a lawyer. "And a Bible!" someone shouted after him. "And more mattresses!" Slam.

The mop and the mattresses arrived—two of them, *new*—and a broom, and a copy each of some religious tracts stamped FIRST METHODIST CHURCH, GREENWOOD. No Bible around, the jailer mumbled; he had obviously sent for the tracts or gone for them himself, ignorant of the precise nature of our religious interest. One of the tracts, *Emergency Rations,* was read aloud in squealing voices of discovery from various parts of the cell.

" 'You can always do something about youself. No matter how bad your environment may be, you can always do something to improve it. You can never get to the place where you are completely helpless. No man is ever completely the victim of circumstances. Fight the good fight with all thy might.' "

" 'If the people around you are unfriendly, try changing yourself. Try putting on a smile in the presence of those who are storming. You will be surprised how quickly the world about you changes when you change your approach to it.' "

The length of the pamphlets equaled their inspiration; we turned to mopping up the puddles. Time was galloping along; someone looked at a watch: it was 8 a.m. The new mattresses were a coup, anyway. Spread together on the floor, they provided a stinkless refuge for four. We dozed.

A small breeze was blowing from the window. I woke up cramped and stiffened, my mind as numb as my stomach. A telephone was ringing. From the bunk I could see cars drive past and turn into the parking lot below. Martha Lamb descended from one and trotted past the others, checking her reflection in their windows. A lovely day. Even the traffic looked pretty—the colors of the cars, reds and blues and oranges, and behind them a row of houses, a Negro man mowing a lawn. Back and forth, back and forth, hypnotic, musical clip of the mower.

When I woke again the parking lot was full and the colors only hot. A voice was shouting. The girls on the floor joined me on the bunk to see: two Negro women outside were calling up to our friends in the next cell, *"There's seventy-six on the county farm."* Unintelligible answer. *"You'll be out tomorrow."* A motorcycle policeman wheeled into an aisle between the cars, and, spotting him, the women walked away as though they had never stopped. A moment later two deputy sheriffs appeared and closed our windows. "We want to see a lawyer!" No answer. They left. The lovely day was shut behind the mottled glass.

"You'll be out tomorrow"? Where were the lawyers? Grumbles and moans. Someone thought of the broom and mop as window openers, and poking through the bars in teams we had one window flung up in no time. The others stuck, all the ones with a view. A metal door at one end of the aisle outside the bars was successfully wedged ajar too, and through it we could communicate with the other girls more clearly. There wasn't much to say, but it felt less lonely.

What do people do in jail? In solitary, you have to try to learn the tapping code. (A nightmare of mine. How do you ever figure it out? Panic.) Alone, even with others, you think. But it seemed so hard to dredge up even the thought of a thought. Once I had a friend who said he learned poetry by heart because "I always think I'm going to be imprisoned with nothing to do." It had seemed an odd idea to me. "But you won't be imprisoned, because you're so absorbed in things they don't imprison you for. Like learning poetry by heart." All right. I tried to remember a poem of Yeats'. Lines kept getting lost in tiredness, couldn't keep track of them. Took out my tract and wrote them down on it. For some reason the key word of every line and key verse of the whole thing disappeared from my mind altogether. It was like a helpless fever, the whole sensation of being in a hospital: sick and immobilized, responsibility gone, at the mercy of someone's tender sadistic care; and all those terrible institutional clanking noises, unidentifiable motors, anonymous bells, footsteps rushing around toting one's destiny back and forth to the operating room/death row. Drowse, sleep it away, get well soon.

11:30. What *do* people do in jail? "We could play checkers," Iris suggests, and begins to draw a board on the floor with soap. Counters? Carol makes thick, packed wads of toilet paper, dousing them in the cup of water to stick, and arrays them on the crossbars to dry. Linda takes off with mad trapped energy and tries to scale the walls, her laughter half a scream. The comb is passed around, and Carol finds a piece of mattress thread to tie her pigtails. The songs, inevitable signal for window-shutting and invitations to a fire hose, begin again and gain enthusiasm until our limited energy or repertoire fail. Some self-consciously sober conversations start up, reach momentary elevations, fall away in doze.

12:30. Dinner served. ("We want to see our lawyer . . .") Beans, mashed potatoes, cornbread. Discussion about eating it. There are four backaches, three headaches, two concerns with failing health, and a general nebulous suspicion that the news is going no further than the jailer anyway. The score is three to four, with one of each group insisting she won't obey the majority rule whatever happens. "I have to go right back to Atlanta and work fifteen hours a day." "We were arrested illegally and we must not cooperate." "It's never happened in Greenwood before; they won't even think of it in the other jails. What good is it if it isn't everyone?" "A strike isn't effective until it's for more than two weeks, and we'll be out tomorrow." "Says who? Where are the lawyers?" "Two *weeks?*" Finally Bambi's suggestion is accepted: that we wait until tonight and see if we can get a message out.

12:35. Dinner removed. The argument had taken that long anyway.

12:45. The distant sound of male voices, "Everybody sing Free-eedom, Free-eedom, Free-eedom, Free*dom!* Free*dom!*" Everybody sings, two sets of girls, two sets of boys, no one together, in key or rhythm, lovely chaos.

1:30. The Judas-hole opens and we converge on it. A deputy, several men in civilian clothes, one of them an FBI-looking man. The deputy says cheerfully, "They look all right!" and bangs the window shut again. It all happens so quickly that no one can muster the alertness to bring up the lawyer-phone call question. After they're gone, I crouch on the side bunk and shout around the corner, "Mr. Sheriff, are we going to be able to see a lawyer?" "Hell no!" he booms back. Finding the tin cup, I bang on the door with it—if that *was* an FBI man, he ought to know what's happening. Simultaneously everyone joins in, picking up the broom and mop, swinging a loose chain against a metal bunk, or just using fists and feet until the noise is a hideous offense. Pausing, exhausted, we shout to the girls down the hall, *"Make noise!"* and their clatter soon beats ours, separating into shuddering bunches of sound until it seems a dance beat. The cup, getting bent, is more effective used against the bars. A perfectly attuned engine, bang bang bang bang bang, metal on metal, ringing after the blow, then the aftersound wha-a-a-ang, caught up and cut off by the next clash of blows. The elation of children and savages.

1:45. In the middle of the noise, the Judas-hole opens again. "We want to see our lawyer!"

"Your lawyer's in jail." It's the deputy again.

Suppressing the reaction he seeks: "We have others." "We want to make a phone call." "It's a Constitutional right."

"We ain't got a phone."

"Then what is it we hear ringing all the time?" "We're being illegally detained."

"What y'all think you in here for?"

"You tell us, we haven't been charged."

He doesn't answer. The men in civvies are there behind him, though not the FBI type. They nudge each other, whisper, look us up and down. The small door shuts. A moment later they appear again, this time around the side, staring at us, animals in our cage, pointing, chewing their cigars. The local lynch mob, come to measure up some necks for nooses. They get nothing back but the sullen looks of children—almost women, almost feminine petulance.

When they are no longer amused, they sidle out. We continue the noise.

2:00. At last, the lawyers arrive at the peephole. They are unfamiliar, new lawyers, come to Greenwood for the occasion. Brought around to the side, they introduce themselves and push retainers through the bars—seven mimeographed sheets for seven signatures. We are numb with the effort of getting them there and can only gaze at them with incredulity, forgetting all our questions. They answer some gratuitously anyway. The bail is two hundred dollars each for us, one hundred dollars for the local people. There are 111 of us altogether, distributed among three jails. The boys downstairs are fasting too. They would try to get us out today or tomorrow. "Be good girls," they say nervously. "Don't make noise, or they'll shut the windows."

"We know how to open the windows."

"Well, try and behave yourselves. These men are only doing their jobs. We think you're marvelous." They're gone, and we realize we've neglected to ask them everything, but most of all for matches. Although we know quite well the sacrifice involved in each lawyer's coming to Mississippi, all our sense of charity is suspended. "Whose side are they on?" " 'Be good girls!' Where've they been for twenty-four hours?" "Wherever it was, they haven't been south of Foley Square in their lives." " 'These men are only doing their jobs.' " "Nuts."

2:30. Bambi Brown is summoned to the door. She leaves the cell and we eavesdrop on the mumbling going on outside. Anxiety. Are they taking her somewhere to set an example? Fingerprinting? Separating us? "I'm Hardy Lott," a jovial voice is heard. "We got a telegram heah this mornin' from a judge in Des Moines. Now I want to write him a letter tellin' him they're treatin' you all right. Otherwise with all them Northern newspapers they might think y'all are bleedin' to death." Bambi's answers are subdued. She reappears a moment later. The judge, she explains, is a friend of her father's. A small chink: they care about Northern judges, perhaps it will help.

3:00. A groan from a corner: "God, I wish I had a gin and tonic. All I can think of is gin and tonics." In a pool of feverish moisture, we doze off again. The new mattresses are beginning to smell too, though not of sweat exactly—it's as if the sweat is a catalyst liberating collections of meaty, horrid straw and packing odors.

What happened to the time? The day passed, and the next, coming together with each other and their successors in a somnolent haze of light and darkness. The meals—two a day, at seven and noon—were never eaten, and began to consist of the same steadily shrinking piece of bologna cooked and fried and reheated; they were left for longer than an hour to tempt our weakness. But a note from the boys downstairs propped up what resolution was still failing after views and reviews of the shriveled bologna.

> Dear Freedom Fighters,
>   We have decided not to eat till we get out. This was decided for the same reason we picketed. We are protesting, as best we can, the system. It's fine if you eat, but we will not.
>   Love,
>   Eli, Peter, Ray, Bob, Adam, Rick, Dave, Paul, Ed
> P.S. We are weak but O.K.

Though time as a whole was a blur, the hours themselves were being measured for us; the most constant irritation became the chimes which rang out every quarter of an hour from the clock tower in the courthouse roof above our heads. Ding dong ding dong, dong dong *ding* dong (repeat). "The chimes"—I read in a guidebook later—"are pitched to duplicate the tones of the Westminster chimes in London. On the hour, they peal forth the air to which has been set these words:

> Lord through this hour
> Be Thou our Guide
> So by Thy power
> No foot shall slide."

Somebody's foot, however, had slid; the bells were fifteen minutes off. On the hour, when they were supposed to serve up the whole thing, they made a single "Ding dong ding dong," saving the final blast for quarter to. Greenwood was probably used to it.

At night we washed our clothes and spun them in the air to dry, or hung them on the unused upper bunks and slept in our underwear. Sometimes jailer or deputy blundered in unannounced to provoke the only spurts of energy of which we were still capable, a rush to dress. The checker pieces got lost and the board dissolved on the floor. There was a growing, common gin-and-tonic hallucination. In a fit of creativity we started drawing our own cave art on the wall, one word, FREEDOM, and Erin struggled over the SNCC emblem—an interlocking pair of black and white hands—on the bottom of a broken bunk. In the dark late at night Patterson and another trusty, William, came with cigarettes and talk. They had no knowledge of or involvement with the movement, but it was the first chance they had ever had to talk as equals to white girls, if only on the other side of bars. The singing that punctuated the day raised morale and closed windows, reopened the instant we were alone. Honey Styles, coming in to shut them once again, unaware of our increasing skill in thwarting him, asked no one in particular, "Which one o' you went with a nigger thirty-two times?"

In the middle of one of the days we heard that two of the Negro girls had been released for being under fifteen. In the middle of another, four unarrested friends from the office were allowed about thirty seconds at the peephole to give us our accumulated mail; among the letters and clippings, a book for Bambi, *Siddhartha.* Also for Bambi a badged man appeared, to say, "I've wired your judge you all right and in jail of your own choice. And that we're movin' you to Parchman."

The lawyers, perspiring in their suits, had turned up late Friday evening with the news that the bail documents had been filled out wrong: they had been headed "*State of Mississippi v. _____,*" instead of "*City of Greenwood v. _____,*" and the local U.S. Commissioner refused to honor them. Therefore they would have to be retyped and we would be in until Monday morning. "We feel awful," one lawyer said. "Believe me, if we could serve your time for you, we would." Our debility from not eating made this offer almost excruciatingly irritating. We lay on our mattresses in a stupor of hunger and anger. "They'll come back on Monday," Iris muttered, "and say they're terribly sorry, but they put the carbon paper in the wrong way."

We took turns reading *Siddhartha* aloud to an audience that was half asleep and draped about the floor, bunks, and bars. "I can do three things," the Indian mystic says. "I can think, I can wait, I can fast." This seemed grandiosely funny, and choked laughter cut into our sloth for hours at its repetition. In the middle of the reading, in the dingy twilight, we were interrupted by a call from below. Dotty Zellner, George Johnson, and some other allies were outside holding up huge parcels of what looked like potato chips. It was too much to hope: food? In order not to hope, we continued reading. Then the door opened.

It was the jailer and some deputies bearing a large tin basin and a paper bag. "Here. From your friends." The basin was filled with barbecued chicken and pink hot dogs, and the bag with apples and oranges, candy bars and cigarettes. There was bread and half a pound cake. From a deputy, a quantity of newspapers, paperbacks, magazines: *Look, True Romance, Jet.* Inside a book of matches, FREE-DOM was inscribed in Zellnerish handwriting. Gravy, crumbs, and newsprint littered the floor. Carol wouldn't touch anything but a peppermint stick, but no one else hesitated over theoretical consider-ations—it was our chicken, after all, not theirs, and implied no coop-eration, or something like that—and we bloated ourselves with the feast of food and print. "I like it here," Margaret said when it was done. But after we were finished we learned to our cost a virtue of hunger: the heat, even at night, was overpowering. Hunger makes you cool.

Sunday, 8 a.m. Patterson and William come to sweep out the cell, and allow us a brief freedom in the hallway outside. Finally we can see what we have only heard before. The girls, thirteen in a cell, have four mattresses (none of them new). They cluster round their bars and tell us about the day before: their shower worked even less well than ours, they flooded the floor in a mass attempt to wash, and the deputies entertained themselves by lining the girls up naked in the hall while the cell drained. But they are relatively cheerful from the meal the night before, as are the boys, whom we can finally see across the way. Their cell is more cagelike than any, bars within bars, and the boys with their black skins almost indistinguishable in the gloom. They were fingerprinted, they complain—and are about to go on when we are rushed back to our cage, clank.

9:30. The hunger pains start up again as they take away the break-fast, whose moldering company we have had for two hours this time. Left behind is the daily ration of soap and toilet paper. Sounds of hymns merge into a dream I'm having. The girls down the hall are holding a Sunday service. They don't need Bibles and tracts. "God hath not given us the spirit of fear; but of power, and of love, and of a sound mind. Be not thou therefore ashamed of the testimony of our Lord, nor of me his prisoner. . . ." The voices ring, as each participates: a sermon, a psalm, a long, low, troubled hymn. We are a silent congregation. At the end they shout to us to join them in the Lord's Prayer.

10:00. A wave of sudden peace. We are clean, our clothes are washed, the cell is scrubbed and the air fresh through the windows; a bluebird is singing "cher-weet cheer-e-o," and an electric mower "pu-u-ut, put put put"; the police are crude and their own worst enemies, but unlikely to kill us in here; we have books to read; and *we have a future*. At last we know, on Monday we'll be out of here. A leftover packet of salted peanuts is distributed—five and a half each —on squares of toilet paper, and we make a couch on the floor, propping one mattress behind another against the wall, so that for three, at least, there is finally somewhere to lean.

11:00. For no particular reason, everyone takes a shower. Naked bodies drip-drying, we discuss the state of our figures, each other's tendency to fat or lean, emerging bones. "Carol, when you get out you can pose for atrocity photographs." In a brief welling up of vitality, by-product of today's bliss, we try out exercises, modern dance positions. Our comfort feels complete when measured only by the days before; *we have a future*. Even the jailer seems adorable. He is willing to speak a few words at last at dinnertime, and among them is the revelation that he is the brother of baseball star Early Wynn.

2:00 p.m. Linda has cramps. Impossible to perform on the public hole they claim is a lavatory. "Mr. Wynn!" the shout goes up. "We need some medicine." Crouched in pain on the floor, Linda waits. No one comes. "Mr. Wynn!" "Hey, there's somebody sick in here!" "Mr. Wynn!" The cup-and-broom banging goes up again, but no one comes. After nearly half an hour, distant clinkings materialize in the face of Honey Styles at the Judas-hole. "We need some medicine, someone's sick."

"What's goin' on? You pregnant?" His smile is half a snarl.

"No."

"I wouldn't be surprised, all them niggers you livin' with down there."

"Look, the girl is sick. Will you get her some medicine or not?"

"You sick, Red?" Mock solicitude. "I can give you a good punch in the belly to fix you up."

Finally he agrees to send to the drugstore. We compile a list, milk of magnesia and suppositories, including on it Midol for someone else's menstrual pains.

"What's this?" Honey asks, scanning the list. "Mi-dol?"

"That's what proves you're not pregnant," Margaret says.

"Well, who *is* pregnant then? Somebody in there must be pregnant." Slam.

2:30. He returns with the bag of supplies. "Where y'all gonna put them suppositories?" He giggles. No one even looks at him. "When y'all goin' home?" he asks then.

"Tomorrow."

"I mean goin' *home*. Home to where you come from."

Shrugs. "When our work is done."

"What are you doin' down here anyway, messin' around with them niggers?" He points to Margaret. "I saw you huggin' a nigger. Another nigger was kissin' a white girl full on the mouth. What y'all gonna do when y'all go home with your little black baby?"

"Believe it or not, that really isn't part of our business down here." Slam.

10:30 p.m. All the talk has been of ice cream. The water, no longer tomato juice or cider or even gin and tonic, has been nothing all day but ice cream. Now Patterson appears in the dark outside with a package. "I has somethin' for you," he whispers, "but I don't know if it'll fit through the bars." *Raspberry sherbet*. Desperation squeezes the box through, and we eat it with the lid. "Oh, I'm so happy!" Linda laughs. "Oh, I love people!" She does a dance around the floor.

There is endless comfort in the idea that this is the final night. Shapeless time at last has limits. We're padded from any conceivable horrors: a certain numbness has set in, as if the sensibility had lost as much weight as the body, and we're suspended in an amniotic fluid.

Monday morning dragged along as though it didn't know what day it was. The lawyers were soundly cursed, tempers were edgy.

Breakfast, dinner, came and went. "I wouldn't mind waiting," someone said, "if I knew what to wait for." The books were read; we had played all imaginable match games. "I mean I forget. What's it all about? Does anyone remember?"

The first answer, though to an unasked question, came at one. The voices of the next-door girls were abruptly displaced, coming from the hall, the steps, and in a few minutes we saw them through the window being herded into the black bus. Release? But no one is released to a paddy wagon. There was no use asking why or where, just a glum silence as we were left where we were. An hour later they came for us—where to? "To be arraigned," they answered, and that was all. "But where are our lawyers?" "Git on, git on."

Maneuvering down the stairs, I felt as though I was constructed of elbows and hollow tubing held together with loose nuts and bolts. My stomach was flattened against my spine, everything rattled and had a new relation to the force of gravity. At the bottom of the first flight, with no one in sight but Mr. Wynn, I sneaked onto the scales in the hall to discover a loss of ten pounds. For years I had been trying to lose ten pounds: it took only four days. Down more stairs to the bus in a breathless, weightless weakness which seemed to be mine but couldn't be, really. The boys were coming out as we took our seats and, seeing them, we quickly rearranged ourselves singly so that each of us could have one to talk to. It seemed essential to communicate with anyone else at all. But the cop at the back of the bus forced us forward in pairs again, prodded our friends into places behind us, and we drove off.

The boys looked strangely gaunt, with merry eyes like buttons in their furry faces. Eli, Ray, and Paul were almost svelte; those who had had less to lose had lost it anyway with not such glamorous results. They had refused the meal of chicken, believing it a jailers' trick: since their windows faced the other way, they hadn't seen our friends deliver it. Pent-up chatter crowded out of everyone. Eli and the Reverend Hall told of being taken first to the city jail, then to the county farm, where they were thrown into an unsegregated compound. The prisoners there had no mattresses. One, a man of seventy-eight, was being denied the daily medicine he needed. He complained that all he had done was try to register, then somebody had stuck a picket sign in his hands and the next thing he knew he

was in jail. But it was all right with him, he had reassured Eli, because he was fighting for what was right. Back at the county jail, segregated again, Dave Hall had been roughed up by another white
prisoner in the open cell block. The man had had a knife. But after
the first day, they had been more or less ignored.

We thought we should plan strategy, but there was still no clue
what to plan it for. Whatever happens, stand mute, was the catch-all
theory. That would be equivalent to innocent, but imply non-
cooperation. The total disappearance of the lawyers was as baffling
as the destination, which turned out to be the beige brick city hall
(as usual, the side door marked POLICE DEPT.). I leaped off the bus
with the muscular spring of someone much heavier and crashed
lightly to the ground a few feet away. To move at all seemed the
nearest thing to flight. The cops in their helmeted lines ushered us
into the air-conditioned anteroom where I had so often stood before,
with the FBI poster face of Andy Goodman profaned with a mustache, the poem about St. Peter and the policeman, the citation for
Tiger, and the desk and doors and walls and faces so precisely
familiar—everything except what lay at the top of the stairs, where
we were now led.

Two cells up, two cells down—four being the minimum number
of cells in any Southern jail. Ours was a quarter the size of the one
we had left, just big enough for two camp beds, a broken sink and
a toilet. The door slammed us in, the afternoon sun poured in
oblongs through the bars, and we watched a group of cops and
white men across the road, armed and smoking, gossiping and giggling in the summer afternoon. Then Paul Klein appeared, being led
by a cop to the bus, which still stood at the door. Seated, he shouted
out at us through the wire mesh, "They tried me. A hundred dollars
and thirty days. They won't accept a stand-mute plea, just guilty or
not guilty." Eli's voice was heard, and we discovered that we could
talk to our friends via Paul—the Negro girls were in an adjoining
window, and the white boys directly underneath. In the bus, Paul
orchestrated the conversation, repeating each remark back to the
other windows. "What about pleading *nolo?*" someone shouted. "No,
that's like guilty." "We've got to stand mute, whatever they say."
"Where are the lawyers?" "I think they've absented themselves because they think this is illegal." "Of course it's illegal—haven't we

been removed to federal court?" "They ought at least to tell us what to do." "Stand mute, they can't do anything." "Thirty days at Parchman working on the roads is nothing?"

The men lounging across the street were highly amused at the split-level show being staged for them. Rick Miller was dragged out by a club-swinging, helmeted policeman. "There's nothing you can do," he shouted. "The whole thing's rigged." He was pushed in beside Paul. "What did you plead?" "I stood mute, they said that was not guilty, then they tried me and found me guilty." "Let's not go without a lawyer." "We've got to stick together, you can't start that now." "But it's *illegal.*" "Maybe they're seceding," said Eli.

Our cell door opened and Margaret was summoned. In the general confusion she refused to go until she had a lawyer. It was all the same to the redheaded policeman; he shrugged and left. By the time he was back, we had decided on the stand-mute policy; mine was the next name, and I followed him.

The crowd in the anteroom seemed an audience at a play as I appeared at the top of the stairs, and the eyes, quiet and hostile, watched me descend, intensely conscious of my body, trying to make it walk straight and move casually. I waited at the entrance to the courtroom for the policeman to open the door; there was a perceptible pause while he indicated his contempt, refused, and waited for me to pull it open myself. Inside, the seats were full, the refrigerator and the air-conditioners hummed, and I walked forward to face the American flag, Judge Kimbrough, and Chief Lary. It was the same scene as at the trials of Freddy Mangrum and Phil Moore, but there were no friends among the spectators. I felt myself trembling, and hoped it was the sudden air-cooled chill. But the hatred in faces packed together watching was enough. Lary and a long-faced policeman were sworn in; my sin was recited—I had picketed—and my plea requested. "I stand mute," I said, wondering briefly, since they had given me a chair, whether I was sitting mute instead. The policeman said I had blocked traffic. Lary agreed. "Where do you come from?" the judge asked. His manner was tired and devoid of sympathy. "New York," I said. "How long you here?" "I won't answer any more questions until I can see my lawyer," I answered, with an effort at composure.

He waved me off. "I already *found* you guilty, I just want to know how much to sentence you." As an afterthought, he now pronounced the guilt, entered in a book by the court clerk, then: "A hundred dollars and thirty days." I found myself reflecting the malevolent stare of the auburn-haired policewoman straight back at her, and with a start heard someone say, "All right. That's all." The same policeman led me back to the courtroom door, while whispering voices darted out of the hubbub; without thinking I paused for him to open it again, then did it myself. A third time I waited, in the anteroom by the door to the street—wondering if instead he intended to lead me back to the cell upstairs—confusedly began the climb, then felt him shove me at the door. I opened it and nearly fell into the heat. Above me through the bars were the faces of my friends.

The boys, all but Eli, were waiting in the bus. Ed Bauer suddenly appeared beyond the mesh, having driven past and stopped to investigate. "They wouldn't let us see you," he whispered. "We've been trying to get in all day." "Where are the lawyers?" "Oxford, to remove the case and arrange bail." "Did they *both* have to go?" He shrugged. The bus lurched off suddenly without the other girls, and I wondered if a special fate awaited me now, alone. But it sped us back to the county courthouse, pulled up at the jail, and spewed us out to Mr. Wynn again.

The cell seemed spacious, almost luxurious. The late sun dribbled thinly through the bars. Someone had cleaned up, piling the mattresses double thickness on the bunks. I pulled them to the floor again, paced around their edges, lay down, got up, took a shower, dressed, looked for a book I hadn't read, gazed out the window, walked around some more, and suddenly felt like shrieking. The girls next door had not returned yet either, and everything was still. The pleasure of being alone for the first time all summer was gradually transformed into the fear of being compulsorily alone, all symptoms very soon their opposites. I found the *Jet* magazine, a special issue on Mississippi, and flipping the pages came upon the most awful picture I had ever seen—the body of Emmett Till, gray and misshapen from the river, eyes eaten away, swollen neck stuffed into a dress shirt for the funeral. The criminals who did this were on the other side of the bars. I hid the magazine from myself under a mattress and paced the cell again, looking out at the neat, prosperous houses across the street.

Then in the town's sedate silence I heard singing. Steady and rhythmic, it seemed the music of a distant sea. Impossible to believe that all of Greenwood couldn't hear it, if not in their outer ears, then somewhere deeper, the sound of their insides, a constant without start or finish, the sound of the South. "O-oh free-dom. O-oh free-dom. O-oh free-dom over me, over me. And before I'll be a slave, I'll be buried in my grave, and go home to my Lord and be free." The bus turned the corner, pulled up below, and the song climbed the stairs outside. The prisoners were reunited.

We read aloud to each other again. Baldwin's experiences in a Paris jail. The end of *Siddhartha.* Quiet, a voice intoning Hesse's prose. In the last light I lay on half a bunk listening, feet on the bars and head hung down to ease a backache. The ceiling, whose every inch of paint I knew by now, seemed wobbly, flickering, and the greenish walls began to weave and sparkle in a haze of mescalin pinks and grays. Pimples of light burst, runny yellows merged with blues. The radiance of color seemed to inundate the walls and wash around me, watered silk, velvet shroud. I shut my eyes, afraid, and fell off into sleep again.

At eight that night the lawyers returned. They were different ones this time, but just as hot, harassed, unhappy. "We know you don't have faith in us any more." The two original lawyers hadn't returned yet from Oxford, they reported; they knew no more. Either, they theorized, the two would be arriving back with the writ which removed the case to federal courts, or, because of our "trial," they would be starting on an altogether *new* writ, maybe habeas corpus. In any case, we could anticipate another couple of days inside— though at any rate probably not thirty. You're brave girls, they said, and left.

"I'm not too crazy about that 'probably,'" someone said. We had listened with stupefaction, and now sagged into separate pockets of self-indulgent despair. There were moments when we might have used it to hate each other: already we shared several reasons for smothering one girl; but animosity proved astonishingly difficult to express in such an enclosed space. Instead, as the fifth night came we split up into disjointed conversations, pretending the cell made this possible—two talking college, two making revolution, two going over Patterson's bum rap with him for the hundredth time through the bars in a corner, and Linda energetically asleep in the center of the two floor mattresses, her limbs flung out and hands clutching at space as though fending off the most dreadful of dreams. Across her the talk extended itself through half the night, long after it had worn out every extension of its every theme. It was a game we had learned to play with time: the nights were to be prolonged, the nights held hope, if only because they definitely, inevitably, always end. The thought of any end at all gave peace; the day was only to be despised for its hot and wearying foreverness: better used to sleep.

The light began, and sleep, and breakfast came and went. Then a noise intruded on our muddled, smelly semi-consciousness. My watch said eleven. "All right, y'all!" Rude shouts. "Git up. Git dressed." It was Honey Styles leering at the nearly naked bodies from his favorite post, the Judas-hole.

"Where are we going?" I clambered down from the upper bunk; arms reached languidly for skirts and blouses.

"Parchman."

"Ha ha."

"Come on, come on."

Maybe, maybe it was over? Even Parchman would end the monotony. How would we look in stripes? Toothbrushes were retrieved, the comb passed swiftly around. Honey watched. Then he opened the door and we filed past him toward the stairs, still pulling pieces of clothing straight. "How're you, Red?" he greeted Linda. "Next time you come we're goin' to hang you."

They marched us left at the bottom of the stairs, down a corridor past waiting, watching cops and into a large courtroom. There at a table our lawyers sat. They were smiling. It was true, it was over. We approached the table one by one to sign the forms releasing us on two hundred dollars' bail. The print was long and blurred; I read only: "Date of Execution: 7/21/64," and signed. Our bearded men were seated in the first few aisles of benches. I found a place near David Hall, who was telling someone, ". . . they took us to the city jail first. Someone said, 'You're under arrest'; I asked, 'What for?' and he said, 'Shut up, you're a prisoner.' Then somebody else grabbed me from behind and emptied my pockets. I told him to stop roughing me up and he answered, 'I'm just doing my job.' I said, 'So was Eichmann.' But he didn't know who Eichmann was."

They were finished with their papers. We stood up, dizzy, and walked out free. The air smelled sweet.

10. The Riot King

Go, Mississippi, continue to roll,
Grow, Mississippi, the top *is the goal!*

—State Song

"Oooh, it make me sick when you all is in jail. Jus' *sick!*"

Mrs. Amos seemed to have spent the entire time we were away cooking the meal she set out when we came back. There were chicken and greens, stew meat and frogstools (mushrooms), fish and salad and freshly baked rolls, pie, cake, and two kinds of cookies, iced tea and Kool-Aid. Dorothy Higgins helped eat it, and talked about her time on the county farm—laughing half with the triumph of it and half from its simply being over.

"We broke all the windows, the chairs, two benches; then we took a piece of a chair and we beat on that old door till we busted it down too. Then we was ready to get out. We couldn't think of nothin' else to tear *up*, only the air cooler, but we figured we might be back. The jailer, he was so scared he got hisself a dog—a mean old dog, big as a cow. Waitin' for us every time we went to eat. Mm-mmm! But you know, we had to do all that, we just didn't have no choice. They was real *rough* people in our cell, you couldn't control 'em unless you kep' up with 'em."

And George Johnson explained what had gone wrong with the lawyers and bail documents. Judge Clayton had signed the papers which transferred the case to federal jurisdiction, despite the wording "*State of Mississippi v. Stokely Carmichael, et al.*" instead of "*City of Greenwood v. . . .*" And we should have been released the day after our arrest. The lawyers had brought the documents to the U.S. Commissioner in Greenwood, whose signature would have ended the matter. In the courtroom, however, was Hardy Lott; the Commissioner let him look at the papers, and he was the one who objected to the phraseology. The Commissioner, the agent of the federal court, sustained him, though no one had ever questioned this point in all the hundreds of removal petitions previously produced. Even if it was an error, it is a rule of federal procedure that insignificant mistakes should not prejudice the spirit of such documents; and this one could have been changed with a stroke of a pen. The Commissioner went further: he refused to give the lawyers Judge Clayton's phone number, which would have enabled them to clear up the misunderstanding before the weekend. As it was, the new petitions could not be filed with Clayton until Monday in Oxford, where the lawyers proceeded and where they were held up until after office hours. Unable to return to Greenwood, they were in touch with the office by phone all day and had been told of the city trial to begin at 1 p.m. They had then requested the District Clerk at Oxford to phone the City Prosecutor of Greenwood informing him that our case was already under federal jurisdiction and the trial, illegal, must be stopped. The City Prosecutor said "okay." But the trial, obviously, was not stopped, simply "barred to the public" (George, who had tried to see and reassure us). The afternoon of our release the *Greenwood Commonwealth* reported that "defense attorneys for the group failed to show up at the trial. City Prosecuting Attorney, Gray Evans, said notice of the time and place of the trial had been given to the defendants' attorneys. . . . Evans said [the attorneys] did not request a continuance nor did any of [them] attempt to appear in court." The story went on to report that "all of the defendants stood mute when asked how they pleaded to the charge of unlawful picketing. One Negro woman said she 'stood brute' and several 'stood mutual.' "

After the meal, still somewhat shaky but containing a solid ballast, I went to see about the library. Outside there was a distraction, however—an invasion was going on. Members of the press, dozens of them, scores of them, rushing up in trucks and cars, carrying clipboards, pads, and tape recorders, setting up television cameras and unwinding cables, speeding around with questions and purpose. For an absurd second I thought they were there because of our release from jail.

"Hell no," one of them said. "Martin Luther King is coming. Martin Luther King is a *symbol.*"

There wasn't anywhere to sit because the press had taken all the surfaces. I asked this one if he could edge over on his table a little, adding self-indulgently that I was weak from a five-day hunger strike.

"Oh," he said. "Sure." He moved over.

"You're not going to do a story on that at all?" I said.

"Hell, hunger strikes are old hat," he answered. "All that stuff is a habit around here."

"Even with a hundred and eleven people in jail?"

"A hundred and eleven? Hell, eighteen hundred people were arrested in Jackson last year. What's happened to King?" he muttered, looking at his watch.

"So if two people are killed this month it won't be news, because three were killed last month?"

Dr. King arrived accompanied by four cars of FBI men, whose function was unclear since they were not, of course, a police force and could not, of course, protect anyone. Symbolic protection, perhaps, for a symbol. Greenwood, white and black, had been alerted by an "edition of the *Klansman* brought about by the eminent visit of the Right Rev. Riot Inciter, Martin Luther King, Jr.," and delivered by air.

The noise of a plane had wakened me early the morning before Freedom Day; outside I had seen it, a crop-duster, small and buzzing like an annoying mosquito, swooping, circling the office for more than an hour as though the pilot were getting his bombsights lined up. He had gone on practicing, though nothing was dropped until these paper missiles a week later, announcing that "it will now behoove each individual citizen to remain calm . . . completely lay aside their normal activity and do not go to work, but stay at home with their families."

Should King's credentials be in question, the *Klansman* reminded its readers that "his thirty three affiliations with known communist organizations clearly identify him as a conscientious communist." The purpose of "the eminent visit" was "to bring riot, strife and turmoil to . . . Greenwood, Mississippi, a citadel of endeavor . . . a tower of achievement," and "to milk all available cash from the local niggers, [who] have failed thus far to realize that the Riot King, and themselves collectively, are today just very black, very ignorant, very dumb and ill-smelling niggers right out of the cotton patch." The leaflet urged all husbands and fathers to be on the alert, for "if the agitators should overrun the law, and a violent dis-order erupts, it will then be the right, the duty, and the moral obligation of the white man in Leflore County to restore law and order and replace it into the hands of the duly elected and appointed officials." Then "peace and tranquility will return to Greenwood. The local niggers will go back to the cotton fields to make back the money Martin Luther King took from them." The people should not be "dismayed, diccouraged or deceived. If we face up to this responsibilities as American Mississippians, then our victory over the most awful disease of our time will be assured."

Mrs. Amos took great exception to this document. Later on I heard her talk about it with a friend. "If we smell so much," she said, "I'm goin' over there and stench them all out."

"You supposed to go back to the cotton patch," her friend said.

"What am I goin' to do there? And they say he wants our money. I never *had* no money till the movement come."

"Well my name's in the paper and I don't care," said the friend, who had taken the test that week, " 'cause I've cooked up cornmeal and grease and we sat down and put molasses on it and ate it like it was a meal, and now we got some food, and we gettin' other things, so it's not goin' to worry *me.*"

There was no way to tell how many whites had stayed home to protect their families, but as for the Negroes there hardly seemed to be anyone who wasn't rushing around looking for King, cooking for King, talking of King if they couldn't find him, and thinking of him if there was no one to talk to. There had to be two mass meetings that night to accommodate them, one in the largest church we were able to use, the other in the Elks' Hall, a gym-sized auditorium. In the latter, people sat on anything horizontal they could find, including each other, on ledges and table tops, in layers up to the ceiling, in the aisle on the floor to the front, packed. It was also the night scheduled for the FDP precinct meetings, so the audience, as delegates, had to be sorted out according to area, given colored paper badges matching the placard of their precinct, and quieted to vote. They chose from among themselves delegates to the county convention, then they waited for King.

He arrived. They leaped to their feet, screamed and cried, rushed tearfully to touch him and surround him, while those too far away began to chant: "WE WANT FREEDOM! WE WANT FREEDOM! WE!

WANT! FREE-DOM!" A SNCC worker standing behind me said to a friend, "That nigger's God himself, boy." SNCC workers usually call him "De Lawd."

King's speech was Biblical and flowery, without a trace of demagoguery, delivered with an incongruous placid balance. "Sacred halls of congress . . . manifesto of justice . . . the cancer on the body politic . . . transform the dark yesterday into a bright tomorrow . . . and every valley shall be exalted. . . ." Then the King wind-up: "So I say to you tonight, if you can't fly, run! If you can't run, walk! If you can't walk, crawl! But keep on—keepin' on!" The Elks' Hall was a bedlam of pounding and shrieking, and when he drove off into "the long night of segregation" with his FBI escort and the world press in pursuit formation, the room was in motion from the front to the rear as the audience reacted, spoke, stood, and left, oblivious of the other speakers.

"He didn't say what they're supposed to keep on keepin' on *at*," said the same SNCC worker behind me.

Outside, the crowd refused to disperse, swarming around the hall and the streets nearby chanting and singing while patrol cars circled, watching; until a mob, brave in their numbers, descended on a police car, which just as untypically sped off in front of them. A hundred people chased it shouting. Jim Forman stepped in to calm them down, and late at night they finally went home.

I heard King again in Jackson the following night. Trips were frowned upon—there was work to be done, cars were needed badly, and the roads are where danger is in Mississippi. But I had hitched a ride with some others going to Meridian, where our lawyers needed some clerical help for a hearing to begin the next day—the suit against Sheriff Rainey *et al.*, in which COFO was asking for federal commissioners to protect Negroes and civil rights workers. We drove over the dirty brown bayous through roads lined with kudzu vine—a creeper imported in the thirties to halt erosion, and now growing thickly over every surface it encounters. Beginning at the side of the road, its fifty-foot runners cover and kill, choking the trees, none too tall for it, transforming them into hooded green-leaved giants protruding above the countryside just about to pounce, mocking carnival creatures, strange witches and humped animals.

The talk in the car was of death. A white SNCC staff member, Mike Sayer, spoke of the grass-roots quality of the movement, concerned at present with the limited object of the ballot—"yet they're willing to die for it. Why? You've got to start somewhere. . . . And they're doing it nonviolently, which is even more dangerous. Death is a part of the effort; a person who works here must understand death, assume it will happen, and accept it." Howard Moore, a Negro lawyer from Atlanta, resisted this view. "I don't want to die," he said. "To die at the hands of someone who doesn't understand the significance of my death is the worst possible end. Death is the most important thing about my life; it gives me my impetus, and I don't want to be robbed of it."

The headquarters of the Summer Project was a store-front office on Lynch Street. Outside, a large blackboard bore chalked messages of events and statistics of the day's toll of beatings and arrests. Inside, someone had cut out and tacked up a headline: EXTREMISM NO VICE IN THE CAUSE OF LIBERTY: GOLDWATER. Near the door, a sign saying only, TO MISSISSIPPI, WITH LOVE FROM MINNESOTA. The tiny cubicles that had been constructed to save space and the cost of desks were mostly deserted; we went directly to where the blackboard indicated they were: "Martin Luther King, Masonic Temple."

The hall was a slick, plush place compared to anything in Greenwood, and the contrast carried through to the audience. As we entered, Bob Moses was speaking at the other, distant end, behind microphone cords dangling tangled from the rostrum. Every member of the audience, except COFO workers and kids wearing Medgar Evers T-shirts, was dressed in a suit or a good dress. Moses was saying something about "sharecroppers and people who earn fifteen dollars a week," and sounding strangely remote from this dark middle-class audience. Iris Greenberg, who had shared the Greenwood cell and was now back at work in Jackson, said, "I went to one mass meeting which was all about 'if you go downtown, wear suits so they won't say we smell.'" This was the NAACP, she said. "It's an N double-A town. They only organize the professional types, and make no effort with the others. SNCC and the other groups can't afford to compete with them; we need their cooperation."

Moses stopped. Luke-cold applause. Chuck Neblett, one of the SNCC Freedom Singers who still wore a bandage on his head from a clubbing in Atlanta on the Fourth of July, stood and started a

song. "Keep your eyes on the prize, hold on, hold on." He sang
bravely into all the microphones while a bare tenth of the audience
joined in. A few more were clapping languidly in time. Their eyes
were unresponsive until they hit on the clothing of a SNCC worker,
whose sandals and shaggy hair could only confuse people with their
eyes on another prize, seeking other goals. I caught the glance of a
slim smooth woman in a yellow silk dress and matching tulle hat;
her look—disapproving eyes on my clothes, tracking down, up, to
the face—contained a coldness I had never experienced in Greenwood except from the whites.

Then King got up to speak, and their attention focused on him.
But unlike the searing love that Greenwood gave him with its untidy
pandemonium, they simply sat, waiting.

"Every man who hasn't found something to die for, isn't fit to
live." (Polite applause.) He talked about the thousands of Negroes
who had attempted to register in the state despite "violence, economic reprisals, and other forms of intimidation." (No reaction; in
Greenwood they had shouted "That's right!" "Look out!") "Yet in
1963 only 1,636 Negro persons were registered in the entire state.
This is an average of 192 a month." A white worker with his shirt torn
almost clear down the back edged through the crowd, momentarily
distracting it from the moral: "At this rate it will take 135 years for
half of the Negroes ever to become registered." A fair proportion of
the audience was probably registered already.

When he had finished they waited politely to be dismissed, then
filed out like an after-theater crowd to their waiting cars. I saw
Stokely, who frowned at me for being in Jackson, and Chuck Mc-
Dew, who was on his way to Meridian for the hearing, as were
many others. I asked him if he could give me a lift there and he
offered to ride me around the Bronx River Parkway any time I
wanted. The cars, as it happened, were all Negro-driven, and no one
needed any white passengers. I took the bus with Mike Sayer, sitting
as near to the back as we could.

After a brief hearing, the COFO case was postponed on a tech-
nicality. The cars in Meridian turned around again, the colors in
them haphazardly mixed by now: in ours, pairs of black, white,
male, female. There was time to see only one more of the ubiquitous FBI posters—MISSING, with the portraits of the three boys
underneath; a house in the white neighborhood decorated with

inverted Army helmets used for flowerpots; and the community center which Mickey and Rita Schwerner had painfully put together the
previous winter. Blue curtains waving at the windows, the walls
lined with books, a shipment of more in a heap on the floor, and a
numberless crowd of volunteers. Paul Klein had driven a carload of
witnesses from Greenwood; with his glasses and the beard he had
begun in jail he resembled, to the people in Meridian, Mickey
Schwerner. "Just the way you say 'dammit!'" a local girl observed
sadly. "When I saw you, I would have sworn . . ." Maybe, she
thought, Paul could come to the hearing when it finally happened
—or better yet the murder trial, if there was ever to be one: it
would be curious to see Rainey's and Price's reactions. "Maybe they
would think . . . maybe they would say something, then."

Rita had returned to the state for the hearing. She spoke to a mass
meeting in Greenwood two days later. Standing on the stage, alone
and frail, she said, "I know what fear is, and I know it makes you
think, 'I'm not going to do this, I'm not going to do that,' because
the risk is too great. But I know that you can risk much more by
doing nothing. It's not unnatural to be afraid, but you're cheating
your children if your being afraid stops them from having something." A quiet, composed girl with a smile, and very pale, very thin,
dressed in black.

11. The Peacemakers

No one wants to deny the negro economic opportunity or economic equality. It is a historic fact that Southern white people are the best friends he has ever had.

—Senator James O. Eastland

It was the policy of the Summer Project to limit its activities this side of the Civil Rights Act, and not to engage in testing the law or desegregating public facilities. The reasoning behind this, on which agreement was by no means unanimous, was that the danger was too great—it might be worth risking lives for the vote, but not for a hamburger; voter registration was theoretically protected by the federal authorities, while at the time sit-ins were not; testing might increase police brutality, and make it harder for "moderates" to sympathize. There were people in Greenwood, however, particularly young admirers of Silas McGhee, who were quite unmoved by the idea of registering voters. The bill had been passed, and they wanted to see it work. Without COFO help or supervision, teenagers began to make forays over the tracks on their own. As the weeks passed, their frustration fed on itself, white outrage increased, and violence rose nearer to the surface daily.

Meanwhile Silas and Jake kept going to the movies. On July 25 their house was shot into; on July 26 they went to the Leflore Theater. They had been joined near the end of the month by their elder half-brother Clarence Robinson, a six-foot-six paratrooper (again on furlough and still out on bail). Clarence had a thirty-six-inch reach and a 136 I.Q., and his Army hat was reinforced with a silver dollar sewn under the emblem: picked on in a bar once, he had swung the hat and downed two men. He walked down the street in his uniform like Wild Bill Hickok on the way to a duel, cool, tough, infinitely menacing.

He spoke at a mass meeting one night, using his voice as he used his body, with precision and power. "When I went in the Army in April of 1952, I raised my right hand and they told me that I was fighting for my country and my brothers, my sisters, my mother, and my fellow man. And after approximately four months of basic training to teach me how to fight, they sent me to Korea. Now when I come back here and try to go to the Leflore Theater, me and my two brothers, when I got ready to leave, there was a whole *mob* out there. Well now, I've seen mobs before. I've seen mobs when there was fifteen of us, September 1952, at a little place called Sunchon about three miles from the demilitarized zone, which is commonly known as the Thirty-eighth Parallel, in Korea. We got orders to hold, with approximately fifteen hundred people attacking us. We held. We stayed. Fourteen of us was Negroes and one white man. We stayed.

"So . . . when I got ready to leave that theater, I told my two brothers, I said, 'Now look. We've got two points. This is a theater. There sits a car. We're going to walk from point one to point two. We're not going to run. We stick together.'

"There were three of us. My brother Jake, my brother Silas. We walked to this car. I opened the rear door, let my two brothers in, and I stood outside for approximately thirty seconds looking around. Nobody threw a brick at me. They could have, they could have knocked my brains out. I'm the same as anybody else, I can be killed, very easy. But they didn't do it. Why? Because I showed that I didn't mind being hit. That if I could get the man that wants to hit me within my thirty-six-inch *reach* [he demonstrated], I'll prove to him that I'm a better man than he is. We left from the theater, because there were incidents. When you go to that theater you've got to expect incidents. Why? Because the white man is scared of you!"

The "incidents" had been reported to the national SNCC office as they occurred, and most of the mass meeting audience already knew what had happened. The brothers had seen the movie in peace that night—largely because those who objected to their presence inside were on the picket line outside. But when the movie finished there were nearly two hundred whites waiting for them in the street. The McGhees tried to call for a taxi but none would come. The manager ordered them to leave: the theater was closing. They couldn't risk walking. There was one alternative, to call the SNCC office. Two of our cars volunteered to go down to get them while the office phoned the FBI, relating the facts to local agent Schaum. Schaum, responding that the FBI would not give protection, was told that the purpose of the call was to request FBI witnesses on the scene. Schaum refused to commit himself. The Memphis FBI was no more helpful: they implied that there was nothing to worry about, were asked if that meant FBI witnesses were in fact on the scene, and said, "We cannot give that information."

When the cars arrived at the Leflore from the office, the McGhees, inside in the lobby, asked two policemen on duty to escort them through the mob. The policemen took them outside; then one of them had a look at the crowd and said, "You got yourself into this, you can get yourself out." The brothers were abandoned between point one and point two.

They made their way toward the car. As they reached it, the whites began to scream at them. They managed to get inside, but the mob, cheated, closed in then. A bottle was thrown at the rear window with such force that it broke through and sprayed the brothers with glass. Jake was hit by particles in the eye. Instead of returning to the office, they drove to the hospital, where Jake was admitted to the emergency ward.

In the office calls came in on every phone, and the staff, like synchronized parts of a machine, answered them and phoned out again. One of the two cars returned, its occupants reporting that they had been followed by a car of whites and that those at the hospital were in danger. The office sent another car to the hospital. When it arrived, Judy Richardson called in to say that they had been shot at from a roadhouse on the way, a white teen-agers' hangout. Two cars had followed them at first, then sped ahead to reach the roadhouse ahead of the COFO car and point it out to some people who were parked and waiting: then the shot. At the hospital they found a throng of white youths milling around, of whom at least five were seen (by Clarence, who knew such things) to be armed with .22 rifles and .38 pistols. After Jake was treated and discharged, a group trying to drive away was threatened with bricks and sticks and blocked at the exit by a car full of white men. They returned to the hospital.

Judy was on the phone reporting each event as it happened, while other phones were busy with calls to John Doar and the Washington FBI, and giving a continuing relay of events to the AP, UPI, and the

Jackson office. Judy said that Clarence wanted to shoot his way out —or she implied it, since the line was tapped. Jim Forman, who had arrived in town the day before, grabbed the phone and implied back again that anyone interested in using his "Army equipment" had better think again. The next bulletin was that Police Commissioner Buff Hammond had arrived at the hospital to announce that they could expect no protection from the police on leaving. Well then, they wouldn't leave, Judy told him. The office started calling congressmen.

The hospital was closing; it was past midnight. Finally, at one, with the doors locked and the mob continuing to seethe outside, the sheriff turned up, wondering, "Why don't you go home?" "We don't have protection," Judy answered. There were several identifiable FBI men there by now; Judy asked one of them to speak to the sheriff about protection, but the FBI man walked away.

Something happened then which was never revealed to us but caused the sheriff to change his mind: he suddenly reappeared, amenable to escorting the cars out. As intense as the pressure had become, it suddenly fell away to nothing. Evidently one of the calls to Washington had succeeded. The cars came home.

The next night there was shooting again. Some Negro teen-agers had decided to go to a white restaurant, the Charmain. After midnight, a young boy came to the office and gave this statement:

At 11:30 I left the 82 Grill with about twenty-five guys, walking. When we got to McGehee and Main we saw about five carloads of whites with sticks, about three of our group got sticks. A police car was near the Charmain, and it pulled out toward where we were. One of the guys said, "Here they come," and we started to run through the alley by the hotel. We all scattered and I jumped a fence on E and Stone and stayed in the alley until I thought it was clear. I then found about fifteen of the original group. Two whites in a car drove by and said, "We'll get y'all later." J_____ hollered out, "Come on back" to the whites. The whites then turned and came back down Avenue G. When they passed by again they threw a bottle. One of our guys then threw a bottle back. More of us probably would have thrown bottles but only one of us had one. After they threw the bottle they started to turn down Stone and shot once over the heads

of about three people. When the shot was fired, those who had
not scattered after the bottle was thrown began to scatter. . . .
We got bricks and bottles to protect ourselves on the way home.
By that time we saw a car coming. It was the police. We hid
behind the school and the police shone lights all over so we began
to run to the other side of the school. Another police car came
by and slowed up in front but went on by. I then ran across
Stone Street with two other boys. We jumped fences, hid in
ditches and behind chicken fences. We came out on Avenue I.
Another police car was coming down I. I crossed the street and
yelled they were coming and started running, and caught up with
two others who were running also. We turned on Broad and
[saw] a load of white guys coming. They stopped their car and
told us "Halt!" They then shot up in the air once and then shot
near enough not to hit us but near enough to scare us. Then the
guys ran and I started hiding to get away from the whites who
were still trailing us. Finally I got here and reached the office.
I don't know what happened to the other guys or if the police
got any of them.

Something had to be done to avert a shooting war. The people in
COFO were anxious for peace in which to conduct their work, but
events were no longer in their control. The teen-agers were mes-
merized by the brothers McGhee, and felt more and more uninter-
ested in the tameness of the Freedom School, the Freedom Party:
they wanted direct action. The Freedom School teachers, sensing
this, invited Clarence Robinson to come to the Friendship Church to
debate with Bob Zellner. The audience had defined the confrontation as "Nonviolence against Violence"; but Bob began by mention-
ing that he and Clarence would "just have a little discussion on the
different approaches to social change." The students sat quietly in
their pews, eyes flicking back and forth from one speaker to the other.

"It has been proven time and time again," Clarence said, "that
when a man fights back, he is not attacked. Now, I've never been
the one to start a fight. But if someone is pushing me, I have to defend myself. You got to learn to stay flexible, to fight when you have
to, but *only* when you have to."

Bob's respect for Clarence was immediately apparent; he clearly
didn't want to argue with him publicly. He began by quoting
Gandhi: "If you can't be nonviolent, be violent rather than a cow-
ard." Then: "Because we're organized, we have to be nonviolent.

We don't have the strength, even if we wanted to, to carry guns and fight back. We're facing organizations with more resources, more money, and with unlimited access to weapons."

Clarence: "I'm not talking about carrying guns. If everybody did that, pretty soon you'd have a revolution on your hands. And I'm not saying we should go out there and *start* a lot of violence. I'm saying that you only resort to violence after you have done everything possible to avoid it." Speaking to the children, and pointing to Bob: "This man can't go to the Leflore Theater and integrate it for you, because he's white." Then indicating me, a pair of teachers standing nearby, and Staughton Lynd, the COFO Freedom School coordinator, who had dropped in on us that day: "She can't, he can't, she can't, he can't—it's something you got to do for *yourself.* But you've also got to be prepared for the resistance you'll meet."

Bob: "There's more guts per person in the McGhees than in any other family you'll ever meet. They're trying to desegregate the Leflore and they're doing a great job. But we feel that our concentration has to be on voter registration now. Integrating all the movies in the South won't achieve anything basic."

Clarence: "You got to act in areas that people understand, not just a nebulous political argument beyond them all. This house-to-house activity is fine, but people are afraid of what they can't grasp. They never *have* voted, they don't know what it's all about. But they know they can't go to that movie. I remember when the Walthall [the Negro theater] opened—the teacher let us out of school at two in the afternoon. But I never sat on a foam rubber seat till I got in the Army. You have to *get* them. How? Show them you're with them in what they want and what they understand, and you can have them on your side. You also got to demonstrate once and for all where the federal government stands."

The children broke in then. A solemn, composed girl of about sixteen raised her hand and spoke. "You say," she addressed Bob, "that we have to wait until we get the vote. But you know, by the time that happens the younger people are going to be too old to enjoy the bowling alley and the swimming pool. And the Civil Rights Act was passed this month." A little girl added, "Yeah, and do you mean we jus' s'pose to let The Man beat on our head?"

Bob: "Look, I try to be a disciplined man. That means I try to do what I say I'm goin' to do. When I joined with SNCC I said I'd behave nonviolently. I didn't say how I'd think, how I'd feel. But the reason I know I can do this, that I *can* behave nonviolently, is that I've done it. I was in McComb, Mississippi, in sixty-one. McComb is not a Freedom School or a playpen. I had eighteen men beatin' me, stompin' on me while the cops held my arms. They tried to pull my eyes out by the roots. And I was nonviolent, not only because I said I'd be, but because there were about five hundred people watching, and what am I goin' to do with five hundred people?"

Clarence: "If anyone has the guts to raise their right hand and say they'll be nonviolent, I respect that. I haven't got the guts to do that. If he's able to do this and maintain it, that's a fine thing."

Staughton Lynd stood then and asked if he could add something. All the eyes turned sideways. In his quiet, considered voice, he presented the problem: "The first week down here this summer, the teachers in Carthage had some trouble. The whites were saying that the deed to the land was invalid, and they were talking about getting their guns and setting fire to the schoolhouse. In a situation like this, what do we do? It's necessary to ask other people to protect you, and this is something we are trying to avoid. I have an uneasy feeling about getting someone else to do my dirty work for me. It seems to me that some time we are going to have to go one way or the other—either asking all the people in the movement to drop their guns, or picking them up ourselves."

It was all there, but the debaters narrowed it again. Clarence said that actual weapons were not the issue: "they bring trouble with the law, violations of the Sullivan Act. The point is you *got* a weapon—you got two hands and two feet, and I don't mean using them to run on. Only four people can get on a man at one time. If you bring certain death to the first *two,* then you won't have much trouble with the others. I'm just talking about if you're attacked, and you can do some damage, the next time they'll be a little more *cautious.* . . .

"Then there's this argument they're always having in the movement, you know, about what are you supposed to do if you're non-violent and you're in a house where the man has a gun, and 'letting him do the dirty work' if you're attacked, and should he have that gun at all if you're involved. Well, all I'm saying is that in a case like that, I'm not doing your dirty work for you; I'm defending *my* right to have whom *I* want in *my* house."

Bob: "I agree. I don't see where you get off tellin' somebody else to be nonviolent because you are." And he wanted to clear a few things up. "The way I am, I'd flatten anybody who came at me on the street. But when you're pledged to the discipline of a mass movement, you got to behave as you promised."

The children sat digesting it all for a while, then the same girl who had spoken before raised her hand and Bob recognized her. "How is it," she asked, "that SNCC has moved from a militant position to a rather subdued one?"

There was a little coughing. Bob said, "It depends on your definition of the word 'militant.' This is a policy worked out by the most militant people in the South today. As far as we're concerned, we're doing one of the most militant things anybody could be doing: building a new political structure." Returning to what she had asked before, he said he knew what she meant, that "a bowling alley is something you can see. It's much harder to see power."

Clarence, with a smile and a shake of his head as he lifted his vast khaki length, just said, "You people are in a heck of a position."

Clarence and his brothers had endured two days of chiding from COFO about having involved them in the case of *McGhee v. Leflore*. But it was gradually recognized that the McGhees stood for something that had to be faced—the kids were moving, with or without us. A meeting was called. From the pool hall and the streets, Blood's and all the cafés, the teen-agers came to the chapel beneath the office. The man who took over was Jesse Harrison.

Jesse was a small, dark, thoughtful man in his late twenties with a deep, well-directed anger. He was the one who had come from Atlanta to put the SNCC national office together—because he was willing to do anything and to stay up four nights in a row without complaint doing it, and whatever he did was efficiently, quickly over with. The Atlanta office collected signatures and petitioned to get him back, but by then he was singlehandedly keeping Greenwood from an outburst of war.

The kids called themselves "The Peacemakers" and elected Silas McGhee president. They wanted something to do, and they weren't interested in canvassing with freedom forms. They discussed the possibilities, and Jesse seized on the least violent alternative which might meet the teen-agers' challenge. He brought out a copy of the

Student Voice, SNCC's newspaper, on whose front page was a photograph of a policeman dragging a pregnant Negro woman down
Market Street on Freedom Day. Everyone knew the policeman: he
was Slim Henderson, who besides his law enforcement activities
owned and ran a grocery store in the Negro neighborhood. They
would organize a boycott of his store.

After that, "One Man, One Vote" began to lose out as Greenwood's slogan. The kids, aged seven to twenty-five, roamed the
streets with a chant that became the pulse of the town: "HEY, HEY,
WHADDAYA KNOW! SLIM HENDERSON MUST GO!" Arming
themselves with copies of the *Student Voice* with the incriminating
photograph, and stopping in the library to ask me to write "SNCC"
and "FREEDOM NOW!" with a felt pen on their T-shirts, they
spread out down every street, knocking on doors and intercepting
passersby to insist that no one buy from Slim. At night they came
back to the office for meetings.

Jesse said, "If your parents tell you not to come, you just tell them
that they been hangin' around for a hundred years not doin' anythin', and this is what we got to do, *now*."

Clarence said, "Now there's a policeman here who owns a store."
Leaning a thirty-six-inch arm over the speaker's dais, he picked up a
small boy by the scruff of his shirt and stood him on top of the lec-
tern; the boy was still not as tall as Clarence. "That store's been
there since I was the size of this boy. . . ."

Bob said, "I think we better have us a little role-playin'. Now, I'm
a seventy-six-year-old woman, and I'm gonna buy me a five-pound
sack o' flour at Slim's. Why shouldn't I go into that store? Will one o'
you please tell me why I shouldn't go in there?"

A fierce young voice called out, "Don't go in that store!"

"Why?"

" 'Cause I saw that man drag a pregnant woman down the
street—"

A girl cut in, " 'Cause we don't want'm in *biz*ness!"

Bob said, "Uh-uh, you ain't convinced me. I'm still goin' in there."

"*Well, don't come out then!*" a new boy shouted, and the meeting
broke up in nonviolent laughter.

Before they adjourned, Silas made an announcement. "We want
people to go to the Leflore tomorrow. People who'll keep *cool*. No

fighting, 'cause the FBI will be up there watchin', and we want you to just remember everybody's face real well, and remember everything they say to you, so we'll have a case."

There were a few volunteers, no one looking very sure about it. It was 10 p.m.; they agreed to meet at 8 the next morning to start on Slim again.

John Doar's had become a familiar voice in the national office. There was hardly a day when he wasn't called about a crisis somewhere in the state, usually involving the reluctance or the refusal of Washington's local agents to help. The argument about protection was too tedious to begin with a mob about to attack or a particularly severe threat on the verge of materializing; but it was necessary to have federal awareness, if possible a federal presence at the scene. Though passive, an agent was important as a witness; there was little hope of court action without one, in any case. It was a pity to wake up Mr. Doar so often at 2 a.m., but if his agents would not cooperate there was no alternative. "Keep it down, Doar's on the line." After a few weeks, he seemed to be there in the room. One day he was.

He and another J.D. man were traveling through, and dropped in to see Jim Forman. Jim had left for Jackson, but by the time they found out, Doar and his man were trapped by people and questions.

"Why have there been no further arrests [after the one in Itta Bena in June] of people violating federal laws by interfering with voter registration?"

"We can arrest only if an assailant's motives can be proven to a fair-minded jury," Doar said.

"You mean a *Southern* jury?"

"No."

"A Southern judge, then?"

"No. A fair-minded jury, that's all."

Where were you supposed to find one of those in Mississippi? No one bothered to ask that question. Doar was soon exhibiting the signs of strain that the similar situation had provoked in Ohio. Observing a Negro doctor with a tape recorder, he snapped at him to turn it off. Someone else was asking why it was that local FBI and Justice Department agents refused to indicate to us in any way whether they intended to act on a complaint. (Almost all conversations with them ended: "Well, can you tell us if you'll send someone or not?" "We can't give that information.")

"They're subject to orders as to what they can or can't do," Doar answered tersely.

Judy Richardson wanted to know if their orders included not showing their credentials, as agents had declined to do for her. He said he didn't know anything about that.

"What's the proportion of outside agents in the state now?" questioned a voice in the back. And, "How many Negro agents do you have?" another asked immediately.

"I don't know how you make that distinction," said Mr. Doar, in answer to one or both. "All the FBI agents I know of here are hard-working men." His eyes, traveling to the edge of the crowd in search of his questioners, hit on a sign someone had taped on a phone:

TO ALL PERSONS TALKING TO FBI OR JD: MARTIN LUTHER KING WAS PROTECTED BY 4 CARLOADS OF FBI MEN.

He smiled slightly, turned, and walked away.

On August 4 the bodies of the three young men were found near Philadelphia. The press came back to ask the volunteers "how you feel about it." Everyone had had to resolve how he felt about it long ago to be able to continue to work, and there was no new way to feel about it. Relief, perhaps, that the world would believe it now. After the news was exchanged, few people mentioned it—they just let it sink and add to the sediment of anger and pain that was growing under everything they did.

For the local people the news, and world reaction to it, was a confirmation. First, that no one was immune, white or black. Second, that because two of the boys were white, there *was* a world reaction. James Chaney was usually given credit too, if only for the company he kept, but the values of the situation were plain. At its most blatant it produced such references as on a Northern network news program recapitulating "the murders of Andrew Goodman"—cut to picture of Andrew, long pause; "Michael Schwerner"—picture of Mickey, pause; "and a Mississippi Negro youth." For James, no picture, no name. His mother's grief was recognized, but it had a she-

ought-to-be-used-to-it note beside that of the white parents, decent
martyrs to gratuitous Southern savagery. Nathan Schwerner, Mickey's
father, understood and equated his son's death with that of Emmett
Till, and the Goodmans mourned for more than their son, but the
media didn't see the story quite that way.

Such phenomena added strength to the argument about violence,
which was far from over. Arguments like "the Indians fought back,
and look what happened to them" made less and less impact on
people who were coming to understand the systematic violence with
which their rights had always been denied. Washington was far
away and had done little for them; and discussions about the orderly
processes of government, the guarantees of the Constitution, the
rule of law, influencing public opinion, or justice through the fran-
chise seemed a good deal less significant than the gun in your back.
To some it was a question of recklessness, allied to the general reaction of a generation born with the nuclear bomb; except specific, because here you could see the whites of the enemies' eyes and
through the muzzles of their weapons. When your life becomes
cheap enough, or when you realize how cheap it has always been,
you're inclined to try to raise its price. Negroes had been giving their
lives for nothing for three hundred years; it wasn't the life that
counted so much as the nothing. It was James Chaney's dismissal as
"a Mississippi Negro youth." If theories of justice and history made
no impact on the man with the gun, it would be reasonable to assume they made even less on his victim. This was not in fact the case
with the majority, but there seemed to be a time limit. If force is
what maintains the monolith, and if the federal government cannot
be prevailed upon to answer the force, someone else may have to.
That was the argument. On its lowest level, it meant at least *action*
—desegregate Mississippi, make the new law a reality. The conse-
quences of action, they felt, were no more disastrous than those of
continuing passivity.

Touches and variations of this mood seemed to intrude on the
gentlest souls. At the mass meeting the night the bodies were discovered, Brother Williams reserved his scoldings for other matters
than this or that failure to go down to the courthouse. Of the Peacemakers and all the young people who were forging out justice with
the only tools they had, he said, "Let me tell you, these chillun doin'
what you scared to do. These chillun ain't scared o' the white folks.

You ought to be *shamed!*" And then, from him, a new note: "If the white man ain't scared to die wrong, he oughtn' t'be scared to die right. If they ain't scared to go to hell, they oughtn' t'be scared to go to heaven!"

People at the meeting were getting angry at each other. A woman stood and berated those who still bought from the Snow Frost stand in Johnson Street. Negroes always had to buy at an outside counter; but just after the passage of the Civil Rights Act a man who didn't even try to go inside had had a cup of hot coffee thrown in his face. Now the woman shouted furiously, "I seen you all at the Snow Frost, standin' out there lappin' cream like a crowd o' hungry cats. You *buy*in' segregation! You got to have some race pride!"

Another woman announced that, because the minister of the Negro Methodist Church refused to open its doors to the movement, she was starting up a petition to the bishop threatening withdrawal of the congregation's financial support.

A man of about thirty called Little George, a taxi driver, asked to be recognized. He came to the front and, as though it were part of the agenda, said that he had started a committee to test the Civil Rights Act. They had held a meeting already and tomorrow two groups would go to a white cafeteria. "What we gonna do, we gonna go to the place to be served. If we're not served, we leave. We ain't havin' any violent." Anybody interested could meet him in the park at noon. "We ain't goin' to have a big menu," he added, "just a hamburger and milk."

Then Stokely got up to speak. It was expected that he would explain or complain about Little George's announcement. But Stokely was a leader; he grabbed the mood and ran ahead with it. He lashed out at them: "From now on we're gonna check on niggers who ain't doin' right! There's a lady named Beulah Brown. We heard a rumor that Mrs. Beulah Brown went down to the police and was telling them where the white volunteers are living.

"Well you tell Mrs. Beulah Brown that if she likes white people so much, she'd better go live with them!" He was very worked up, though hardly more than his audience. "I talk a lot of nonviolence to the white folks, but let me catch a black man doin' us wrong . . . You tell them to keep their mouths shut. 'Cause just as soon as I'd tell a white man to go to hell, I'd shoot a black man. I'm goin' to loudmouth everyone in this town ain't doin' right!" They were very quiet. "Another thing. We're not goin' to stick with this nonviolence forever. We don't go shooting up *their* houses. It's not *us* who does that. . . ."

There was a late staff meeting afterwards. Everyone knew that it made no difference what we told Little George; the demonstration tomorrow would go ahead. If it was followed up and greater numbers participated, there would be repercussive violence. Stokely sat hunched on the floor, still—though a stillness only this side of turmoil. "Our lives are on the line now," he said finally, then lapsed back into the argument he was conducting with himself. "*I* can't prevent their carrying guns. Negroes have always carried guns in Mississippi. Not only that, it's legal." Quiet again.

George Johnson said, "Well, what is it that they really want?"

Albert Garner answered quietly, "The first thing they want is to kill white people."

Mary Lane and Jesse nodded. The Negroes in the room were together; there was an instant, uncommunicated electric current running from one to the other. It was suddenly understood by all the whites how little they had ever understood.

"We can only control them by joining them," Stokely said finally. He was still on the floor; the silence was intense. Then he explained, "I'm not thinking how to justify it to the community; I'm thinking how to justify it to COFO." In the end he got up to telephone Jackson, "to get the mandate from Bob."

We waited a long time for him. He came back a different man. As calm and thoughtful as Moses himself, Stokely said, "What I think we ought to do is work harder on freedom registration forms."

The next day Stokely was arrested. Little George's group, which included the McGhees, didn't get inside the white café. The proprietress was on the phone and told them to wait at the door; they walked around the block to avoid attracting attention. On their return, they found a mob of more than a hundred whites waiting; they left, determined to try again the following day. That night, the lights went out in our office and in all the houses and streets surrounding it. We sat outside and looked at the stars, prepared for war, while sentries paced the roof and nearby alleys. On the phone the authorities said that all their equipment was in use and they couldn't do anything. The equipment could have continued to be in use for days. We had to call Washington to have our lights turned on.

Early the next afternoon the McGhees and Little George put on their neat clothes and went to the café for their milk and hamburger again. We waited, suspended. They returned to say a lawyer had been blocking the door and had told them they would not be served. The FBI had been informed before the attempt, as on the previous day—to answer any doubts about how the café proprietress had been prepared. They went again the day after that, armed with a copy of the Civil Rights Act that I gave Silas from the library. The proprietress herself was waiting in the door this time, and screamed at them hysterically, "I don't care about no Civil Rights Act! Get out, get out, get out!" The door was impassable as long as she blocked it; they couldn't push her away. They would go somewhere else next time, they said.

The Charmain, which had been closed since the shooting incidents ten days before, hung out a new sign: CHARMAIN CLUB, INC. The white swimming pool had been leased to the Greenwood Kiwanis and reopened privately. Other places were closing briefly to have new signs made and to arrange membership organizations circumventing the Civil Rights Act. The dues were usually a dollar a year; you only had to be white. Byron de La Beckwith's haunt, the Travel Inn, was the only one that didn't bother. So the desegregators went there. As they drove up (again, having notified the FBI), a curtain was being drawn across the door with a freshly painted sign pinned to it: CLOSED. Two white reporters went there for breakfast next morning and were told that the restaurant was closed but would reopen tomorrow as a club. "Why?" they asked, and were told: "Because of the *situation*."

Every day Jesse Harrison held a meeting for the kids to organize shifts for the boycott of Slim Henderson's. Slim got nicer and nicer; he started paying calls on his old customers, dropping in for a chat and taking them groceries. There were people who continued to shop there despite the boycott: a man called up the office one night and explained the problem.

"I got a account there," he said, "and I guess I owes about eighty dollars. I had a account there since it been in business. Now you know, I don't have no money, and I'm not able to buy my groceries cash. See, I need money to buy some food, or I got to go to Henderson's. Can you all give me some money?" We asked him about going to a Negro store. "We got more than a few colored grocers in town," he said. "But if you comes in there with less than even a penny you got to go home for it. They ain't gonna give you no credit, not even a penny. What am I gonna do? My children's hungry."

There was nothing we could tell him to do. The kids were not going to stop, on the other hand. More and more of them were involved each day, feeling powerful in Slim's evident anxiety. He would be standing around his empty store for long hours, strolling inside, then out again, failing completely to look casual. The Peacemakers started talking about boycotting other white-owned stores in the Negro neighborhood. A three-year-old girl who lived across the street from Slim's and heard their chant joined in one day with a version of her own: "Hey, hey, whaddaya know? Slim Henderson ain't got no sto'!"

12. Politics and Battle Fatigue

Deltans are rich; they live well. . . . Deltans have access to money, and they do not hesitate to spend it. Social life in the Delta tends to be gay; Deltans lack few of the good things of life. The cultural element is not forgotten, either. Delta folk spend considerable money getting educated. They dance and frolic, but they also read books and write them.

Generally Deltans are inclined toward conservatism in politics, a condition which befits the Delta's aristocratic background.

—John K. Bettersworth, MISSISSIPPI: A HISTORY
Mississippi State University, 1960

After Freedom Day the emphasis of the voter registration campaign had shifted: from getting people down to the courthouse to take Martha Lamb's test, to the massive effort of organization needed for the Mississippi Freedom Democratic Party's challenge at Atlantic City. Eight state delegations to the Democratic Convention had committed themselves to support the FDP—or at least not to support the "regulars"—but there was a stronger case to be built to reach others. We needed freedom forms by the thousands, which meant constant canvassing and tighter block-captain systems, with each captain responsible for the people on his street; and a party organization to parallel the regular party structure, with the election of representatives on the precinct, county, congressional-district, and finally state level.

Reaching greater numbers of people to fill out forms meant working longer, odder hours. The number of Negroes in circulation in the civilized daylight was limited; we had to find the others before and after work. Voter registration workers started getting up at sunrise and sleeping in midday, then making the rounds again at night. This still left the cotton workers; volunteers had to take their clipboards out at 3 a.m. to catch the plantation buses and sign up

186

riders. The buses, hideous ramshackle affairs, started their rounds at 3:30 or 4 in the morning collecting the cotton-choppers from various pickup points around the town; the workers had fifty cents deducted from their three-dollar daily wage for this transportation. If the volunteers could find a bus on one of its first stops, the Negro driver would let them stay on as it filled and get off just before it left for the fields.

The Freedom School students were recruited to register neighbors and relatives, and their teachers, the community center people, and the federal programs researchers worked in spare time. Everyone who could was out at dawn and again at dusk, or sitting at tables outside mass meetings to intercept those left unsigned.

There were constant frustrations in canvassing. People were afraid, and didn't want to listen. The active and courageous had joined up long ago and came to the mass meetings, became block captains, worked on getting their friends' signatures too. The distinction between registering in the FDP and registering at the courthouse was hard for some to grasp; others refused to try.

"Have you freedom-registered, sir?" you asked.

"Yes ma'am," they said, "I filled out one o' them las' week." And you knew they hadn't. Or "I got to aks my husband," women said, or "I got to think about it," their husbands said. And you knew they wouldn't, that they just wanted you to go away. They were always courteous, often warm, they never shut the door in your face, but they made it clear that you could talk all summer and they weren't listening.

"*Every*body's signing up!" I'd say cheerfully, my smile-muscles aching more than my feet, "and there's no danger, nothing in the papers, nothing to do with Martha Lamb, the police won't find out . . ." Their return smiles were taut, blank, anxious with fear. "Yes ma'am," they'd say, "but I don't b'lieve I will this evenin'." "I'm too old to fool with it." "I sure appreciates y'all comin' to fight for us, but I jus' can't take no chances right now." "Not me. I'm the only one my children's *got*. I'm all they *have*."

Then someone asked a question, and you knew it would be all right. The simple act of asking a question—"Now, what *is* that thing?"—established a by-pass to fear, a willingness to consider the facts, the first step before acting on them. Somehow the forms piled up.

On Sunday mornings all the volunteers were assigned to churches. White shirts and ties, the boys were told, and stockings and hats (if any), the girls: "It's a great insult to them if you dress down. They think you don't wash because you think they don't." Walking nearly a mile to church in the dreadful heat in stockings was bad enough; but maneuvering high heels through the ruts in the road was impossible without generations of experience. There were compromises all over.

The services were up to two hours long, most of it sermon. The preacher began on a regular Biblical theme and deserted it soon; his voice would start a throaty chant, the words fulfilling a powerful rhythm, and if the phrase he spoke was not the length of the rhythm's design, he interspersed an "er" here, an "mmm" there. Soon the two-note song overpowered the words, and the message was conveyed almost entirely by the music and his emotions. "Wait and pray, mmm, that's all you got to do, oh, wait and pray, er, and in due time, mmah, the Holy Ghost will come. Wait and pray, er, and when it come, mmm, tell the world. . . ." Then a shriek from the audience; a woman had got the spirit. Groaning, writhing, oblivious of everyone, she built it into a frenzied climax—until the ushers, ready for this, came to her and carried her out. The preacher continued, but winding up now, and behind his last words the throttled moans of the woman could still be heard outside.

At some point in the middle of the service would be a moment for announcements; one of the volunteers would stand and plead, exhort, or simply announce. When the congregation emerged at the end, we'd be waiting with our forms.

On Saturdays we went to Johnson Street. The tracks of the now unused railway line ran down the center of the street, which was Greenwood's uneven dividing line of black from white, and filled with second-rate hardware, dry-goods, five-and-dime, grocery, and department stores—mostly white-owned, Negro-patronized. Straddling the tracks were a garage, a frozen custard stand, the old station; traffic ran in both directions on both sides, so that it was really two parallel streets, with the width and aspect of a no man's land.

Farm workers came in from "the rural" to shop there on Saturdays, and COFO workers spent the day in shifts intercepting passersby to explain about the Freedom Party. The first Saturday more than 150 forms were filled out, and groups of white citizenry, maddened like bulls before picadors, began to collect near the garage, glaring and shouting threats at canvassers; others circled the area in their cars. Policemen warned volunteers not to block the sidewalks unless they wanted to be arrested. A man offered to crack Bill Hodes' head open against a car: "I don't care who you're protected by!" Adam Kline was beaten to the ground by a young white man whom the police, passing a few moments later, refused to arrest without a warrant. A Negro minister who also ran a Johnson Street barbershop allowed it to be used as a polling place; the window was shattered with a brick, and he was evicted on Monday. Clearly it would be worse the following week; but we had 150 forms, and we had to go back.

Stokely opened the county convention with a reference to a speech of Senator Eastland's. "Eastland made a statement yesterday about everyone in the movement being a communist. All we want is the right to vote. If that's being communist, then we're communist."

"That's right!" shouted several voices. "Amen!" pitched in an old woman.

"Eastland also says that Negroes are happy, Negroes love to pick cotton, Negroes love to eat watermelon, Negroes love making three dollars a day, being illiterate, not voting. Eastland is a liar, and that's all there is to it."

"Look out!" bellowed Brother Williams.

They nominated seventeen candidates from among themselves, then voted for four delegates, four alternates. Nominations were made and seconded; the chairman, a local minister, recognized motions from the floor; resolutions were introduced; each candidate was allowed a few minutes to speak his case; they voted; and with dizzying speed and confidence they grasped the meaning and technique of democracy. "In some ways," Eli said at the end, "this is the most important thing to happen in the country in a hundred years." In some ways it was.

A worn, thin board of a woman said, "I'm wrapped up in this like a mess, and I must say it's the best mess that ever I saw in my life." "I'm a baby," another woman said, "I'm just trying to learn to walk, but if you elect me . . ." A withered grandfather in clean, faded overalls promised to take his people's demands to the top, if they trusted him to send him along with the word. A young attractive woman with an educated accent said, "My husband is a bricklayer, so I know about building—and we are building something. We've got the foundation and the walls and we're starting on the roof. And this building's going to *stand*."

There were a good many bricks to go: the building was of people, and still deficient of materials. The district convention was just ahead; there were new forms and new failures and new efforts daily, and white Greenwood's outrage by which to measure our gains. Fear mounted with the stacks of registrations, and so did the reasons for it. The next Saturday, they were waiting for us on Johnson Street.

Besides some local toughs milling around the garage and the white side of the tracks, there was traffic on the level of a holiday weekend—whites circling to see what new evil we were up to. Word had spread about the Slim Henderson boycott and the attempts to test the Civil Rights Act, provoking the fiercest feeling. There was a new quality in the hatred the faces wore, a change from passive to active. We took our stations along the storefronts and tried to do the job, ignoring them.

On one corner the cars were being directed by Officer Logan. As Bob Masters and Mark Winter crossed his street, Logan greeted them, "Hey, you sons of bitches!" Two men standing with Logan had been seen by Bob and Mark to pursue Phil Moore and me, so they had followed along. The men turned and approached Bob instead, took his clipboard and the eyeglasses from his pocket, and, when Bob shouted to Logan for protection, one said, "Won't do no good to yell at *him*." Clearly not; nor at Police Commissioner Buff Hammond, whom Bob came across some fifteen minutes later, to be told, "Get out of here, God damn it! Get out of here fast!" Bob left (fast) to continue working a few blocks down, where a cripple stepped on his foot and hit him. (Two days later the cripple had Bob arrested for assault and battery.)

Events of this kind took place up and down the street while, in the hours from two to four, policemen and deputies drove past twenty-six times. I was standing on a corner counting, compiling information for an affidavit relating to the number of cars without license plates. Twenty-five such cars or pickup trucks went past in the same two hours. They were often directly in front of the police cars that only slightly outnumbered them; yet the day before, three of our people (among them Silas) had been arrested for driving two new SNCC Plymouths with temporary Tennessee tags—which had, in fact, five days to run before their expiration. It was probably hopeless to expect an affidavit of this kind to accomplish anything, but worth a couple of hours' work to try.

Halfway through the afternoon someone came from a COFO radio car with the news that a volunteer in the Holly Springs project, Wayne Yancey, had been killed in a car accident. The young man with him, Charlie Scales, had suffered a broken jaw and internal injuries, been refused treatment at the Holly Springs hospital, and been charged with manslaughter. None of us knew them; and few of us, in our general state of apprehension, could fully believe it had been an accident. In a short while the news had passed along the street, and it was as though the day had turned a different color. There was no further information; I kept counting cars, becoming almost resistant to the stares of the passengers, the heads swiveling round on their red necks, the same cars returning to stare again, and the pale, redheaded cripple doing a malevolent, misshapen dance of rage at me across the street.

The Peacemakers not at Slim's were down on Johnson Street too, milling around in a large parking lot at one end. Opposite, next to the defunct railway station, a COFO car had come to pick up a shift of canvassers. Cars which had been circling careened down the street now, aimed at anyone holding freedom forms; it took more than fifteen minutes for a few of us to cross over to the waiting car. It was a search not just for a gap in the traffic, but for a gap so wide that it would be impossible for the next car to speed up in time to maim you. I waited for my chance at the edge of the parking lot, into which drew a particularly vicious driver who tried to run down Bill Hodes. The Peacemakers, less peaceful by the minute, took offense and began to taunt the white man, "Come on out, we dare you!" The man got out of his car with a knife. Then from the midst of the kids stepped Clarence Robinson. He faced the man head on and said, "You've got the knife. Come on and get me." One sight of Clarence's towering confidence was enough: the man backed off with a few tired obscenities, and Bill continued canvassing. Half a block down a patrol car pulled up opposite him and a policeman stepped out, shouting, "You better watch out, or we're

gonna run you in." That instant came another shout: a white man
ran out of a store as if on cue and called to the policeman, "That's
the one, he's the agitatah! He's been makin' trouble all day!" Bill was
grabbed by the cops and frisked, then pulled with his arm twisted
behind his back to the patrol car while the police continued their
dialogue with the white man: "Will you testify?" " 'Course I will."
Halfway to the car Bill was clubbed in the ribs and fell to the street;
he was dragged the rest of the way, thrown into the patrol car, and
driven off.

Meanwhile, two local youths were picked up near Slim Henderson's (who was offering free beer to entice his customers back).
Three dozen Peacemakers had crowded onto a porch around the
corner from the store to avoid trespassing, and were singing and
chanting their "HEY, HEY, WHADDAYA KNOW!" from there.
Two had been arrested anyway. One of them, John Handy, a handsome light-skinned boy with a goatee, had been standing on a sidewalk at a distance when Chief Lary picked him up for disorderly
conduct, giving him over to a patrol car that had been following behind. News of the arrest was phoned to the office by a sympathizer
who saw Handy being roughed up in the patrol car on the way to
the station.

The day continued on this level of harassment and confusion, with
our radio cars out-patrolling the cops between Johnson Street and
Slim's and back again, sending in news for the office to have a cohe-
sive enough idea of events to organize bail and legal attention for
the arrested, medical help for the beaten, news for the press, factual
protest material for the FBI and the J.D.

George Johnson called the police station and was told that all
three who had been arrested, Bill, John, and Peacemaker Freddy
Harris, were charged with disorderly conduct, and that the bail was
one hundred dollars for Bill and fifty dollars each for the other two.
The desk sergeant was asked if he had change for a five-hundred-
dollar cashier's check, and answered that he had. George and Betty
Garman left to bail the three out—particularly important as Saturday night the jails are often packed with drunks likely to beat up
civil rights workers. The rest is from George's affidavit:

> When we walked into the police station, the place was swarm-
> ing with cops. On the way in they called us vile names like

"fucking nigger." When I asked Desk Sergeant Simpson to let me pay the bail, he replied that bail had not yet been set. He disappeared into Chief Lary's office. While he was in there, I checked the arrest book. The bail for the summer volunteer was penciled in as one hundred dollars, but after the other two names, it had been erased. I could tell that there had been an erasure, but couldn't be sure the figure had been fifty dollars. Desk Sergeant Simpson reappeared and said that bail on each arrestee was two hundred dollars. I told him that I had been informed by whoever was on the desk at 6 p.m. that bail was one hundred dollars and two fifties. I asked to see Chief Lary. Simpson glared at me and told me that if I wasn't prepared to pay six hundred dollars on the spot to get out of the station. I repeated my request to be permitted to see Chief Lary, and asked to be informed of the name of the man on the desk at 6 p.m. who had told me the original bail. At that point, a voice behind me asked Simpson, "Do you want him out?" Simpson said, "Yes." About four of the cops grabbed my arms and legs and threw me out the door and into the alley. When I regained my balance, I looked around and saw Miss Garman being pushed out the door by a tall thin man, who was not in uniform, and who was holding a baby in his other arm.

Back at the office, George phoned the local and Memphis FBI offices and the Justice Department, and then Chief Lary, who said the bail was "one one-hundred dollars and two fifty dollars." George related what had happened and asked the Chief to be present when he returned. He made ready to leave again, and the volunteers at the office all asked to go along. It was settled by a one-two-three-shoot of the fingers, and the rest of us waited.

People milled about the national office, sat on free desks, and found things to eat in the kitchen. Bunches of tense conversations about events of the day: whose feet had been trodden on, who had a Coke thrown in his face, who was threatened, sworn at, pushed, slugged, beaten. Some of them had been at Slim's, where a near riot had developed when a car of whites had thrown bricks and bottles at the kids—who retaliated, throwing them back. One of the bricks had gone through the car's rear window. There would be more arrests. Phone calls came in about a severe beating in Carthage, the arrest "for investigation" of six summer volunteers in Canton, a shooting in Batesville. Other calls went out for bail money and a thousand dollars for the hospital care of Charlie Scales. The nurse was looking around for the misplaced bag of the doctor, who had to fly to Memphis to see that Scales, who had been taken there in a hired ambulance, was properly treated. A bag of cheeseburgers appeared from Blood's. Ed Rudd wandered in vague from bed; he had the night shift. All the stories were brought up to date for him. A local girl wearing a T-shirt crayoned FREEDOM NOW! on the front and BLACK AND WHITE TOGETHER on the back dashed in. "They're breakin' windows on Broad!" She was taken off into a corner for her account. Stokely shouted, "Keep the noise down! I can't take any more!" A few volunteers moved outside, where they sat on the bench and on a car to wait—to see what had happened to Bill and John, and just to wait, because there was nothing else to do. I went upstairs to my desk, unable to bear the strain any more.

Samuel T. Mills and two more children his size followed me to the library wanting coloring books and crayons; it was too late and they should have been sent home, but I gave them what they wanted and they sat in the back quarreling over whether rabbits are ever pink. June and Willie James came up with bowls of potato salad, punch, and cold-cuts; they had arranged a party for the medical team, which had been due to leave that day—and now was leaving too early for a party. No one felt like it any more; but June and Willie James set things up laconically, since it had all been prepared already. Then they left and went back downstairs, drawn irresistibly to the tension. I turned the fan on to High and tried to work out where my exhaustion began and ended, realizing as I thought of it that it was the first time in five weeks that there had been time for such self-indulgence, or that *I* had occurred to me at all. The best thing to do seemed to be to write a letter to a friend.

> Probably I'm suffering from battle fatigue, which is why, among other things, I haven't been able to write letters lately. Just ride along with what comes, and it always comes. Something to account for every second, but at the end of it I can't remember how it worked out into anything. All I have to do is sit still and the world piles in on me. I would like something simple, to go swimming once, or see a movie, or walk in a field, or go for a drive without having to look out the back window, or just to sit somewhere cool and quiet with a friend. Only once might work. Tired. The *crowds,* life squeezed together as it always is in heat and poverty, a dozen people a family, but everyone is everyone's

family. God eases them and the pressures they exert on each other; the common battle against The Man gives them a solidarity I've only heard about in wartime London; evil has confronted them all their lives and provided a set of clear alternatives—many such things that can't work for me as on them, and I'm simply exhausted. I yell at everybody. No, I don't yell at anyone at all, I only think I do, but I can't. Madness, a constant agitation, unrest. It could all be explained by fatigue, but that is simply cured, and this contains another element that bars the view of causes and cures. Having to get up around dawn, sensibly you'd go to bed when they do, at ten or earlier. But there's a strange mechanism at work on us at night preventing it—when the children are gone, the chicken eaten, the mass meeting over, then there are still all of us left to egg each other on, everyone full and fed up with it but somehow longing for the next disaster. Then suddenly there is news of an arrest, someone has been beaten up, and the competition starts to see who can go down to the jail, who can get beaten up too, who can pick up the next phone call from the bomb crank: something, anything, to *do*. Standing around, waiting far into the night, exploring all the recesses of fear, stunned by the danger like a deer by the headlights of an oncoming car. When I first arrived I often wondered about the people who had been working here for years—why they sometimes walked around like zombies, never ate or slept, and fell off into some great depth in the middle of a sentence, so that you'd have to wait for them to come back from hell or the middle distance; and how it was that though they had the sense to be here and to run an intricate, methodical campaign, they failed to see that such a sacrifice of themselves was a loss to the very effort they were making. There are incipient nervous breakdowns walking all over Greenwood. One of the best left yesterday. He'd been wandering around in a trance, deteriorating every day, and had forgotten by now what he ought to be doing about it—some synaptic connection in him had worn out in his year here, and the only choice was sink or flee. I haven't had time enough for the full array of symptoms to immobilize me completely—I still *tell* myself to go to bed, though am far too tangled up to do it, while the negative feedback operating on the veterans has tired them out too disastrously for them even to know how tired they are any more. It has something to do with fear. Fear *can't* become a habit. But there is something extra every minute from having that minute dangerous, and if you can't convert the extra into something you have nowhere to *put* it. You can't assimilate it; you can't subtract from it (since the tension is necessary, the fear reasonable); so that leaves addition: aggravate it, bite on the sore, collide with it head on, and in that way at least stay awake on nerves when you might otherwise fall into a walking sleep. The final extension of this necessity is the stance of the mighty daredevil—but that comes years later. All I've got is a fabulous depression, split in two—I can't bear another moment of it but it's impossible to believe that it can end in three weeks. How can I leave? How can I leave people I love so much? What made me think I could accomplish anything in this length of time? There's nowhere else I want to be. I'm only beginning to build a few things with people, and none of it is strong enough to stand yet.

I heard a shout, "They're back!" and went downstairs. In the center of a crowd, George was collecting affidavits from Bill and John, both of whom had been beaten. John had been first—at the station they grabbed his arms, twisted them behind his back, and set about kicking him. "Then they threw me up against a concrete wall so that my head hit the concrete—three times," John said in a dull, deadened voice. His face was puffed and his shirt bloody, and he slumped to one side in the chair. He no longer had his little beard. "Then they opened the iron door against my head. . . . They slammed me up against the desk. . . . One cop smashed me in the mouth with his fists. . . . Then they pulled out my goatee. They pulled it out with their hands. Then they shoved me up against the door, and opened it, and shoved me against the bars . . . opened the barred door, and kicked me several times so that I fell through the door into the cell. Then they started kicking me while I was down. I asked them to get me a doctor, but that made them kick me some more." He was treated by the doctor for severe contusions and lacerations. His shoulder had been dislocated and they gave him a sling.

The last we had seen of Bill was in the patrol car after he had been dragged over and flung in. After that, he said now, he had sat upright quickly so they couldn't accuse him of resisting arrest; on the way to the station, the policeman in front had turned around suddenly and yanked some hair out of Bill's arm. Then the policeman pulled the SNCC button off Bill's shirt and stuck him with it in the leg. "*Kid* stuff. *Sense*less." At the jail, they had pulled him out of the car and pushed him against every door they came to, then against the desk. One policeman, shouting, "Git yer God damn feet out of the way," had stamped on Bill's offending feet. Then they threw him into the cell for white males, kicking him on the way.

He had spent three bad hours after that, anticipating the arrival of the Saturday night drunks, hoping the office would manage to bail him out. They hadn't allowed him a phone call, of course, or told him the charge. At one point the cell door had opened and two white men whom he recognized from Johnson Street were there. "I thought my time had come." All that happened was a question to the men: "Was he the one?" They looked at Bill a while and answered "no." Two other visitors showed up shortly afterwards: the FBI, wanting to know if Bill had been "brutally beaten." No, not brutally, he told them, and found out then the charge and the bail. Betty and George had come (for the second time) after that, and Bill had been released to them.

His story finished, Bill called his parents on the WATS line, and the others continued to stand around, to wait, to talk everything over once again as though its reiteration would make it understandable. Now that I had put it in writing, it seemed absurd that I couldn't go to bed: it was eleven o'clock, and the next day began early for the trip to the district convention. But it wasn't possible. I went upstairs.

June and Willie's "party" was still sitting on the desk, neglected, though someone had fed a little potato salad to Now, the kitten, who sat on a shelf eating it. June stood beyond among the library books with her back turned, and Willie and a white volunteer were talking. Then I realized that June was crying, and Willie almost crying too. He was saying, "Well it's true what she says, it's true!" June turned and brushed past me on her way out, tears in runnels down her face. "It's true!" Willie cried. "You don't know how they goin' to do us! It's goin' to be *hell* when you leave!" He ran off after her, the volunteer in pursuit.

I tried to eat something but failed, and then decided to go home. Outside I stopped in the dark for a moment, caught by the view through a window: John Handy was sitting in a chair while two FBI men interviewed him. One of them was prodding John in the arm, in the stomach, in the kidney, as if to say, "There? Does it hurt there?" John nodded his swollen head, or shook it.

None of the Amoses was asleep. It was more than two hours past their bedtime. The lights were on, and Mrs. Amos had taken all the boxes out from their places against the walls; their contents tumbled about on the floor. Just then she was rummaging in the bottom of a huge trunk. "Mrs. Amos, what's the matter? What are you doing?"

"Lookin' for the buckshot," she said, her voice muffled in the trunk. More clothes were tossed out behind her. On the table were four capsules of shot. Each was a different color, and all looked very old. Mr. Amos and the children were wandering in and out of the kitchen dazedly. "They been shootin' into windows on Broad," Cora Lou said.

Mrs. Amos found two more buckshot capsules, arranged them all in a row on the table by her husband's bed, where the shotgun leaned, and eventually put things away and turned out the lights. I went back to my room and tried to go to sleep. All the noises sounded abnormally loud, but I couldn't tell if the cars that sped past outside were driving oddly or if I was oversensitive. Then there was a sudden violent screeching of tires and brakes, and voices. I got up, put on a raincoat and crept into the kitchen. Mrs. Amos was already there, and the others emerged behind me; we hovered at the window, but there was nothing to see. I stepped out in the darkness and found someone nearby who said, "They tried to run over Silas, and he wouldn't move." It was a volunteer, in shock. The car had gone straight at Silas, he said, and at the last second had veered off. Silas hadn't even flinched.

I told the Amoses and we went back to bed. In the distance a dog was barking on and on hysterically. I kept peeking through the blinds as strange sounds came, then forced myself to stop. Suddenly, in another minute—or maybe it was half an hour—five shots were fired in quick succession. Near and loud, but with a strange spongy sound. I went out into the kitchen again; Mrs. Amos was still there in the dark. Gloria Jean came out again from the other room, pulling a robe on and saying over and over, "It had a silencer on it. It had a silencer on it."

Through the window we could see Bob Zellner crouching around a corner. A woman who lived across the street came rushing over, tugging something over her nightgown. "I seen it! Carroll County! The tags was Carroll County!" In the kitchen Mrs. Amos stood tight-faced by the window, pushing her children back out of the way. We waited there endlessly. Across at the office they had started their phone calls again; the FBI, unfortunately, had left before the shots. "We'll have to shoot back," Mrs. Amos was muttering, almost to herself. "With these people, ain't nothin' else you can do. You got to make 'em scared, or they ain't never goin' to stop."

We stood there silently. Nothing more happened. I forced myself to bed, but had hardly got there when the noises seemed to start again in the kitchen. An FBI man was climbing up a ladder across the way with a flashlight, looking for holes. He had a penknife and started poking about in the side of a telephone pole. Couldn't find anything. Zellner and a small group from the office stood by. The FBI man, teetering on his ladder, kept turning around nervously and asking Bob, "You're watching for cars, aren't you? You'll tell us if you see any cars, won't you?" Mrs. Amos, watching the man with the penknife, became impatient. "Ain't nothin' to do with that *pole*," she muttered, leaning out and calling, "They hit on that roof over there. I heard where they went."

"You were standing there?" the FBI man inquired.

"Right here," she said.

Little Earl Henry, hopping about bright-eyed, contributed, "Wait till I tell my children 'bout this! They ain't never gonna believe it!"

"Hush up, Earl Henry," said Gloria Jean, peeking out anxiously. "Will they come back?" she whispered.

"No, they ain't comin' back," Mrs. Amos said. "Some others might come, but they won't. They scared. They might think they hit somebody. And they'd change the car. Then they might come back. Or some others." She shook her head, looking up at the man on the trembling ladder who was feeling around on the roof. "The polices know who done it. They'll call 'em and warn 'em not to come back. They know who done it." The police had come and gone again just before the FBI arrived, she said. "They looked around and lef' again." She had never moved from the window, and had seen everything.

The FBI man put away his penknife and flashlight and gingerly made his way down the ladder. He said he'd come back the next day, and drove off quickly. Gradually we all went back to bed. The dog was still barking in the distance, but otherwise it was quiet.

The Greenwood delegates, and as many other spectators as could find the cars to take them, made the trip to Greenville the next morning for the Second Congressional District Freedom Democratic Party Convention. In a church annex, a vast metallic quonset hut like an oven, they sat in sections marked off with placards: LEFLORE, PANOLA, HOLMES, COAHOMA, WASHINGTON, SUNFLOWER—and TALLAHATCHIE, the toughest county of them all, whose delegation of ten received an ovation from some, the dazed open mouths of others. (For the next week everyone was saying, ". . . and *ten people* came from *Tallahatchie!*") Mrs. Hamer stood at the front of the hall as the delegates assembled, greeting them, hugging friends, laughing. Volunteers who had never seen her before met her now and were instantly cowed with admiration.

Stokely opened the meeting again, but this time with an announcement: news had just been phoned in from the Greenwood office that ten carloads of deputies and highway patrolmen had come and arrested Carol Kornfield for assault with a deadly weapon —a felony. The Zellners and others immediately left their places in the audience and met in the lobby while the meeting continued. Bob decided to take one car back, picking out some tough male volunteers to fill its seats. A mob surrounded him with questions and irrelevant suggestions until he suddenly snapped, "Be quiet!" Zellner losing his temper made one realize the origin of the phrase. His "temper," the slow Southern charm, was a tangible *thing* which, under extreme tension, got lost, was misplaced momentarily, though found again as quickly, in time to be taken back to Greenwood. The rest of us returned to the meeting in great anxiety: What assault? What weapon? were still unanswered, and there was fear that they had pinned a gun on Carol.

Only four delegates were to be chosen from the mass, and each county wanted itself represented. They vied for the attention of the floor:

"Mr. Chairman!"

"I want to say—"

"That would have to be a motion."

"I move—"

"That motion's out of order."

While speeches went on in the interminable style of every candidate in history, complete with finicky disagreements about procedure and exaggerated declarations—though with a sincerity and truth unique for such gatherings—representatives of various counties and factions were furiously politicking behind the scenes. "We'll support your man if you vote for ours." "Did we commit ourselves to Holly Springs?" "Don't vote for ———, he's a Tom: pass it around." "Let's make a deal with Coahoma, Aaron Henry's sure anyway." People straight out of tarpaper shacks, many illiterate, some wearing a (borrowed) suit for the first time, disenfranchised for three generations, without a living memory of political power, yet caught on with some extraordinary inner sense to how the process worked, down to its smallest nuance and finagle. And yet when all the wheeling and dealing was done, they had chosen the four best people among them.

The speeches continued into the afternoon.

"Ladies and gentlemen, I am J. W. Wright from Clarksdale, Coahoma County, Mississippi. Just a few years after the Proclamation of Emancipation was signed, a few Negroes was admitted into the government of the State of Mississippi and to the United States, and after a little while they were banished. What we need today are men that are going to be able to stand on their feet and do the things that they conscientiously believe are the best things for *all* the people. You know some of us want to hate the white folks and the white folks want to hate us, but there's no time for that. We must love everybody. We must do unto all men as we would be done by. Thank you."

"I am William Douglas Scott, Sunflower County, Indianola, Mississippi. When I was growing up on the plantation a lot of things went on that didn't quite ring a bell with me, and I would ask my mother about it and she say, 'Well, you'll understand this better bye and bye.' What I understood, that every time I saw Mr. Charlie it was time for me to get *fast*er, you know, *run*. And I thought like that in high school, fact I got kicked out of high school 'cause of political agitation, as they call it. But I deeply convicted in my heart, in my mind, that it's time for a change in Mississippi, it's time for a change in the United States. . . . We're going to have to send delegates who's going to take your problems to that Convention, who's going to say, when that lily-white delegation get up and say 'We represent the people of Mississippi,' who'll say, 'You're *wrong*, brother,' who'll say, '*I* represent the people of Mississippi,' and then we're going to present all these freedom registration forms. We're not going to be talking all this wishy-washy that Stennis and Whitten talking for the last fourteen or fifteen years. We're going to say, 'We want the school buildings. We want some paved roads. We want some street lights. We want the right to *vote*. . . .'"

"This is Hartman Turnbow from Holmes County, and I'm an active worker in the movemint. I b'lieve it and all of its works is right. I b'lieves Negroes everywhere in the U.S.A. needs freedom and wants freedom. For that reason I've stuck my neck out in many places and took many chances workin' to try to help get Negroes free, tryin' to help them be first-class citizens, tryin' to help them get they feet out o' the mire. And in Holmes County where I live in sixty-three in March a little movemint started there, and I was one of the first men that ventured out into the county to spread this movemint, 'cause I felt like just we few peoples who went to the courthouse to redish wasn't enough. I felt like it took every lady and every gentleman in Holmes County to help with this burthen, to help fight for freedom. And, too, in that I got involved in many things, my house was fire-bombed, it was shot in, I was 'cused of arsonin' it, I was throwed in jail and I was bombed out. I had a federal trial in Jackson and they dropped it. So in that I got a chance to go to Washington, D.C., to represent Mississippi. And when I went there all of you peoples who I never seed till today, I was representin' you too, simply because I knew that you was a Negro as I am and I felt like you had been long 'pressed, I felt like you done endured long sufferin', and for that reason I tried my very best to make a good talk in Washington with the Congressmans and the Senators. . . ."

"Mr. Chairman. I'm Dewey Greene from Greenwood, Mississippi. I'm the father of Dewey Greene who applied for admission to Ole Miss. His application to the University of Mississippi caused them to shoot in my home. But when they shot in my home they didn't dampen nothing. Dewey was the only one then active in civil rights work. I have seven children. When you shot in there you got seven more. The white people of this state pushed me into politics, *shot* me into politics, and to get me out, they'll have to shoot me out."

Dewey Greene, a white-haired, distinguished-looking man with horn-rimmed glasses and a dignified manner, got eighty-eight votes, the most received by anyone. William Douglas Scott was elected chairman of the District's delegation. The one about whom the word

"Tom" had gone around, supported with treacherous anecdotes, received no votes at all.

Mrs. Hamer, who had controlled her delegation's vote with the smallest shift of an eyebrow, suggestion of a hand, was elected the Second District's representative on the State Executive Committee. She stood and in her booming voice spoke briefly on the Mrs. Hamer theme: "We are sick and tired of being sick and tired!" She told of the time they had shot at her, and "my house was so full of holes it wouldn't hold water." And comforted: "You shouldn't be afraid. Some people stay in their homes, won't move out. I walk right around, 'cause you ain't safe in the house either." She led them in the national anthem and in "We Shall Overcome," and they sang with fight in their voices. The white students, sophisticated graduates of Ivy League political science courses, exchanged looks as they sang with the rest: they had received their first object lesson in politics, and not where they had expected to find it. A journalist from New York stood in something of a daze, saying, "Maybe politics is an instinct."

Everyone left by four, to get home before dark. All the cars were full, so I was assigned to ride with six Negroes, spending most of the fifty-mile drive crouched low in the back seat between Sue Taylor and Willie James Earl—though none of them even implied concern for the danger I represented if we were seen together. Freedom Smith, another passenger, was an old man who had been in Ohio during orientation week and was often around the office, but I'd never had the chance to ask him how he got his name.

"Well, I used to be *Henry*," he explained, "but I said *Freedom* so much that my friends jus' said it back to me." After a moment, he added, "Don' matter what people call you, nohow. In my life, I been called everythin' but human."

There was carefully no mention of what had happened to Carol. From Stokely's announcement, it had sounded like a minor siege, and there might have been all manner of disasters, with the authorities using our exodus to the convention as an excuse. But when we arrived, Carol was there: released, charges dropped. The "deadly weapon" with which she had been accused of assault was a brick: someone had decided to pin on her the incident outside Slim's the day before, when the white car window had been smashed. Not only had Carol been with us on Johnson Street, not at Slim's, she was hardly large enough to wield a brick. Before the lawyers had gone to work, she had spent a sentimental couple of hours back in Mr. Wynn's cell in the county jail under one thousand dollars' bail. Four local people who had been arrested during the day were less lucky—they were still in. A blockade had been set up outside Slim's for two and a half hours, with a riot car and tear-gas equipment, and the four had been picked up elsewhere and singly on John Doe warrants. One of them, a fifteen-year-old girl, had had nothing to do with the boycott. (After they released her she did.)

Mrs. Amos had a big meal waiting for me. After I had eaten, she quietly presented me with four freedom forms; she had registered some friends. This was the first time she had done anything for COFO but feed and house it; but she didn't elaborate on what she had done, or refer to the previous night. She was still thinking about something else. "That leaflet they dropped about us smellin'," she said. "Everybody stink if they don't take a bath. Everybody got a odor. Even a cat got a odor."

13. Yoknapatawpha for John Handy

Saturday, August 8, 5 p.m.

In the late afternoon sunshine on Avenue I, three dozen children are standing in rows on the corner diagonally opposite Slim's. From a radio car we listen to them sing:

> I'm gonna sit at the welcome ta-able, oh Lordy,
> I'm gonna sit at the welcome table one o' these days, Hallelujah!

A squad car is parked near the gas pumps outside the store, and four or five of fat Slim's colleagues are lounging around near the door with him gossiping. One of them breaks from the talk for a second to make an obscene gesture to the children, who start on the next verse:

> I'm gonna tell God how you tre-eat me, oh Lordy,
> I'm gonna tell God how you treat me one o' these—

Suddenly and simultaneously they interrupt the song to burst into cheers, whistles, and screams, leaping into the air and clapping their hands, then take off running in four directions. Only then can I see the cause—the big black paddy wagon is bearing down on us; Jesse Harrison has spotted it and given the signal. The black bus pulls to a halt in the street and the doors swing open, spewing out two dozen more policemen in helmets, with guns at the ready and kits containing gas masks strapped to their backs. The kids have completely vanished, all but John Handy, his arm still in a sling from the

205

beating last week, who inexplicably walks past the cops and is caught—by his injured arm—handcuffed, and thrown into the bus. The car I'm in takes off toward the office. In the front seat someone picks up the two-way radio microphone: "This is K-U-Y-one-one-oh-six mobile unit Sweets [for Stokely] calling Greenwood base, come in Greenwood base." Click. "This is Greenwood base, we hear you mobile unit Sweets, come in please, over." Click. "Cops got John Handy outside Slim's. Everyone else okay. Returning to base. Over and out." Click.

Zellner and the boys are pitching horseshoes outside the office. We pull in and call the jail, which obliges us with instant answers: Handy is being held for inciting to riot; the bail is five hundred dollars. Jesse Harrison is mad at him for standing around long enough to get caught; he wasn't following discipline. But what matters now is to get him out before he's beaten again, and no one has the five hundred dollars. We'll have to go to see a man who once offered us a property bond. I get back in the car with Nan Grogan, a Southern white girl who works in the Atlanta SNCC office and is spending her two-week "vacation" in Greenwood. She starts the motor, Jesse comes from asking this week's doctor to visit John in jail, and we're off—except that two Negro boys now say they need the car for something far more urgent, and give Nan an argument before Jesse tells them to forget it. Nobody talks back to Jesse. We're off—but then Albert Garner and a white boy want to come along too, and direct Nan to move to the back seat. "Oh my," Nan says, climbing in behind with me. "You really are at the bottom of the heap around here. 'You females get in the back.' 'You white folks let us have the car.'" Well, we're off.

We drive past Slim's to find it relatively quiet—neither customers nor demonstrators. Albert says, "Let's go on over there and park." "What for?" Jesse asks. "Agitate, man, agitate." Jesse doesn't credit this with an answer. We drive on to the property-bond man, who isn't home, and then the radio speaks to us: "Mobile unit Sweets, return to base." At the office, a new crisis. Adam Kline is missing; he had mentioned to someone that he was going to Johnson Street, unaware that the decision was made late in the afternoon that tensions were too high to risk it today—and a local person had seen him there and overheard some whites nearby discussing means to "git 'im."

Mobile unit Sweets pulls out again immediately, with time only for Jesse to leave to work on the bond, June Johnson to get in, and Phil Moore to take the wheel. Phil is edgy, scared. "Adam alone on Johnson Street!" We can't hurry, the speed limit is twenty-five and we must stop at all the signs. Johnson Street is full of shopping crowds. It's almost dark. No sign of Adam. We drive the length of the tracks and back again: nothing. "What about trying where he lives?" Phil drives there, knocks, nobody home. Maybe he's with that girl, someone suggests. There's a girl he's apparently interested in. Maybe she'll know where he is, anyway. But where does she live? June thinks of a way to find out. Phil drives on at her direction, stops at another house. June goes in and returns with a girl who knows the girl who knows Adam. She gets in with us and directs us further. Stop at a third house: no one there. All we can do is return to Johnson Street.

Halfway down, we see Adam. He is standing outside a store with his clipboard registering someone. Phil is furious and calls to him to come on. Adam finishes what he is doing, then crosses calmly to the car, gets in. "What's going on?" he says.

There it is, all that loose adrenalin with nowhere to go. "Adam, we thought you were dead." He hadn't noticed, he says, that nobody else came to Johnson Street today. All he can talk about is how many people he has registered.

We drop his girlfriend's girlfriend off and June insists we wait while she goes in for a tuna fish sandwich. We wait. It's very quiet; the only sound is the hum of the cicadas in the trees. June strolls back gulping down the sandwich and we return to the office, where the car empties and fills again with customers for Blood's. On the way there someone reports that the doctor has succeeded in seeing John Handy at the jail, though with twenty policemen looking on. John had been clubbed in the back and his arm wrenched out again. The doctor gave him a new sling. He will have to stay in now till Monday—Jesse hasn't been able to raise the five hundred dollars. He was arrested, it evolves, because he was trying to retrieve from the street two cases of empty pop bottles which were his responsibility to return for refund.

At Blood's there are pork chops, French fries, and salad on the menu. The jukebox is bombing away, people are throwing quarter after quarter into pinball, and we order a quart of beer. The meal arrives finally, but we've hardly begun when a volunteer—not from Greenwood, a sort of mobile volunteer, often traveling around the state on COFO business—appears and says, "All right! Everybody out of Blood's!" He is an annoying young man who constantly inflicts his paranoia on others, so no one pays him a great deal of attention. Someone, actually, does ask, "Why?" He says he's been listening to some redneck conversations on the citizens' band and has figured out that *we* are what they mean when they refer to "Blackbird"; furthermore, they have been having a sinister exchange: he has just overheard, "You gonna visit your sick aunt tonight?" "Yup." "How long you gonna stay?" He just stands there—that speaks for itself—until someone asks, "Well, how long *is* he going to stay with his sick aunt?" "I got interference after that," says the boy.

In any case, it all indicates to him that there is trouble afoot, and we had better leave. He stands there. He wears a big cowboy hat and a tooled Western belt, a red bandanna thrust casually in his pocket, and very tight cowboy jeans slung low. Everybody just looks at him. It's cool in here, and we haven't finished our pork chops. "Well," he says, "I'm not leaving till you're all out."

He stands beyond the window like a guard. We feel guilty and leave without coffee. Maybe, I think on the hot drive back, he is entirely right and there is danger tonight. Maybe we have all become callous, in the true sense—you have to have calluses on your sensitivities in Mississippi as surely as a ditch digger needs them on his palms.

Monday, August 10, 8 a.m.

Our lawyer this week, Jack Wysoker from New Jersey, has to drive 130 miles to Tupelo to see Judge Clayton to file a removal petition for John Handy, and needs a passenger who can also serve as witness to John's arrest and nonriotous behavior. So I go along, for a lesson in the confusion of dealing with each of these cases—not least our own three weeks before. We start out early, planning to stop on the way for coffee. Eupora is an hour out and more than halfway, and we come upon a likely roadside dairy bar. Only after parking do we notice the sign on the door: PRIVATE CLUB, MEMBERS ADMITTED ON CARDS. There is a window for outside service, though, and we knock and ask the woman for a coffee and a milkshake to go. As we wait a truck pulls in labeled MISSISSIPPI HIGHWAY DEPT. Two men swing out and, gossiping casually, mosey over to the door. One of them spots the sign and pulls up short. "Hey, looka that! We cain't even go *in* there." They stand there scratching themselves and discussing the situation. The woman produces our order and, when we're sitting in the car again, I can see her beckon to the two men to come inside.

Judge Claude Clayton sits in the middle of a paneled roomful of lawbooks: carpeted, leathery, cool, a room of great dignity. The only ornaments are an American flag and another one, red fringed with gold, and a tinted portrait of the judge's daughter. He is an ex-general, very military. A portly, spectacled, kindly looking man with jowls and a receding crewcut, neat to his shiny buffed fingernails. He reminds you of all the prosperously retired American tourists who climb around the Acropolis or the Eiffel Tower in lightweight speckled suits.

Neither he nor Wysoker can locate the statute citation under which John is being held. This is the first time they've used "inciting to riot," and the lawmen don't know if it's a city or a state charge. They thumb through stacks of books. Then each one has an idea. Clayton's is to phone the Greenwood judge, after which he reports mystifyingly, "He says he doesn't know, and can't tell till one o'clock this afternoon." Wysoker's is a pamphlet put out by the Lawyers' Guild with sample charges in it, which he finds in his briefcase, and locates inciting to riot listed as number 8576. They look that up. The judge, the military in him contradicting the Southern, uses a studied severity of manner to deal with this perplexity, lots of pauses and telling inflections to let us know who's important around here. "Number eight-five-seven-six," he says pregnantly, "has to do with the National Guard." More discussion, then somehow or other they figure out what to do, and I have to sign a paper as affiant. The judge doesn't look at me then or at any point. He listens benevolently while Wysoker requests a bail reduction. Five hundred dollars is clearly excessive for a Mississippi kid who has never been near a riot, much less knows how to incite one, and considering that previous bails for local people have been set at around fifty dollars or at most a hundred. The judge considers the case, patting his manicured fingertips together, and decides, now that the case is federal, to grant a reduction to three hundred dollars. Now, he says, the two of us will have to proceed to Oxford to give the documents to a deputy marshal who will go to Greenwood and inform the authorities there that John Handy has become a federal concern. (Why all this can't be done with phone calls I can't understand, but the same procedure has had to be observed in all arrests in Greenwood.)

There is a time problem, apparently: we have to get there by one and the drive will take that long. The judge offers to help by calling Chief Deputy Marshal Ticer Young in Oxford to tell him we're coming. "Is Ticer there?" Pause. "Hi, Charlie, Bill around?" and so forth, until he gets his man and has it set.

We phone the office about the new bail and speed to Oxford. Lafayette County, Faulkner's Yoknapatawpha, is only a few miles from the start of the Delta, yet another kind of country altogether. The road is straight but bucks up little hills and down, a washboard, between trees and fields with wooden fences, corn and grazing cows. After the alluvial plain around Greenwood, with its levels shifting no more than the heights of the different varieties of cotton, there are dimensions to the land for the eye to rest upon, but fewer man-made distinctions: the poor little houses of the whites are often little better than the Negro huts nearby, without a sign of the ante-bellum opulence available to the few in plantation country.

All places seem to think they are the center of the world. China's name in Chinese means "center country"; I once had a Chilean atlas that somehow managed to get Chile into the middle of a world Mercator projection. Oxford, Mississippi, has its own pre-eminence. Not "home of William Faulkner" or even "home of Ole Miss," but WELCOME TO OXFORD, the sign says, THE REFORESTATION CAPITAL OF THE WORLD. A little town: the map gives its population as 5,283. After a short, pretty residential section, we ride beneath a banner announcing the PUSH CAR AND BICYCLE DERBY into Courthouse Square, which looks entirely fake, like a Hollywood set. In a ring around the white stucco courthouse are shopfronts that can't conceivably have anything behind them, with names like Shaw & Sneed Hardware, Fred's Dollar Store, Bill Crockett's Dry Goods, and the Toxey T. Fortenberry Auction & Realty Co.; and there are quaint ads painted on walls like one for QJ's BEAUTY LOTION, THE QUICK AND EASY WAY TO BEAUTY SINCE 1903.

We go in search of Chief Deputy Marshal Ticer Young, and find him lolling behind a counter in a large-check sports shirt, a home-spun type who fits with his setting. He is in his late sixties, with a small paunch and a sort of vagueness and gentle charm to him: no connection whatever with the Honey Styleses and Officer Logans of the world. He and a Mrs. Lumpkin, a comfortable woman rather like her name, receive our documents as though they're computer programs, stand around peering at them and discussing what on earth to do. "Everything we get," sighs Mrs. Lumpkin, "seems different than what we got before." She goes off holding the papers at arm's length.

While we're waiting a man sitting nearby asks me in a friendly voice, "Been here long?" "No," I answer. After a while he asks again, "Goin' to Ole Miss?" I say in a Southern accent, "No, I'm one o' them outside agitatahs." He looks at me, nods neutrally, goes back to his musing; then in a minute or two fumbles in his pocket. "Have a cigarette?" he offers.

Ticer Young, chewing on something, has been listening. "Well," he says to me after a bit, "you-all're blazin' a lot o' new trails, ain't you?"

It's all so astonishing that I decide to ask about Faulkner. "Could you tell me how to find the house where Faulkner lived?" seems a possible beginning, though I know we haven't the time to go there. Assisted by the other man, Ticer Young gives me elaborate directions. He is slow-speaking, even for a land of drawlers. "Old Bill," he says then, "yup. Sure was a character."

"Did you know him?" I ask.

"Nobody *knew* him," says Ticer. " 'Course my boy used to go sailin' with him quite a lot. And I worked for his first cousin, U.S. Marshal Faulkner for—what was it? Guess about eleven years. Eleven years, that's right." He pauses a minute, then goes on, "You know, once you got old Bill to talkin', it sure was hard to make him stop. He'd just talk your head off, standin' there for two, three hours. Then the next day you'd meet him on the street and he wouldn't say a word." He shakes his head, then leans on the counter toward me. "Bill had to stay inside himself, you understand," he says, "or else he'd a been bothered to death."

Mrs. Lumpkin comes back in and over to Ticer. "You want this certified?" she asks, holding out a document. Ticer looks absently at it and says, "Oh well, I don't see any use of it." He thinks a second.

" 'Less Bill wants it. Why don't you show it to Bill." She leaves, and Ticer falls back into our conversation. "People used to say when I grunted and Bill grunted you'd have to look twice to see who 'twas." He laughs. "Tell you a story. My daughter-in-law one day comes and says how she saw these two real *trampy*-lookin' fellas cuttin' crosst the field, and how they come over to her to get a drink o' water. She didn't recognize 'em till they got up close, then she saw 'twas Bill and that other fella, on TV all the time, you know"—he snaps his fingers—"Bennett Cerf. Said they stayed around about a hour and a half, just chattin'." He chuckles at this and other things he is remembering. "Oh, if you could stay a while," he says, "I could tell you a lot about Bill."

"Have you read many of his books?" I ask. He looks at me with a shy smile. "Well, I *tried* to read 'em all," he says. "We had a deputy marshal here who used to say the only way to read Bill's books was to get yourself a bottle of Old Crow, sit yourself down by the fireplace, and by around eleven o'clock when you was halfway through the bottle that book would get as clear as day. 'Course you forgot it all the next mornin'."

The papers are just about ready, and we are taken downstairs to another office, where we are introduced to a Mr. Williams, who is referred to as a deputy. Ticer leaves us there, inviting me back any time for a good long talk about Bill, and Williams leads us to a third office where we meet *his* deputy, a Mr. Phillips. Since Ticer is a deputy, Phillips must be a deputy's deputy's deputy. He is the one who must come to Greenwood to let John Handy go. We are to set out in two cars, but Wysoker suggests that he and I stop for a second to get a sandwich, since we missed lunch.

There is a rustic place across the sleepy square with WINTER'S 5–10–25¢ STORE AND SANDWICH SHOP painted on the glass in a crude hand. Inside are rows of tables laden with every sort of household necessity from mops to rings with royal-blue brilliants. In the very back is a dingy eatery lit by one bare bulb and a menu offering Dr. Pepper soda (no other brand) and eggburgers (no other food). It is full of flies and grease, and the mercury in the thermometer on the wall is lodged at ninety degrees. The lawyer leaves me at the counter to order for us while he goes to tend to something.

"What's an eggburger?"

"I invented it," answers a woman as grubby as her surroundings.

"But could you tell me what it is?"

"You ain't gotta have a egg on it."

"But what else is there?"

"Burger. 'T says 'burger' don't it?"

"Okay, two eggburgers, and two Dr. Peppers."

There are three other customers sitting at separate tables below me. (The counter is weirdly high, with tall, teetering stools.) No one is eating anything or talking. The woman squishes two bits of fatty ground meat on the grill and fries two eggs beside them, sending up clouds of rancid smoke. None of it looks very promising, but you never know.

"Could you tell me," I ask anyone who might be listening, "how I'd find Faulkner's house?"

Silence—but less hostile than thoughtful, I find in a moment. With her back to me and squeezing the juice out of my burger, the cook/owner eventually answers, "Well now . . . I don't know." She turns the eggs over, frying them into compact little disks no longer resembling eggs in color or consistency. After another pensive silence, she brushes a fly from our meal and says in a slightly raised voice (her back still turned), "You know how to get to the Faulkner house?" This has caught the attention of an oldish woman fanning herself at one of the tables. "Well," this one says lethargically, "I guess you take a left . . ." she thinks a minute, ". . . then you take your second right . . . and a left again . . ." Long pause. "I'm not sure where you take that left . . ."

My eggburger is served to me between two slices of white bread. I ask for the ketchup. "Oh, we don't serve ketchup," says the proprietress. Some arduous chewing. The woman with the fan is still at it. She has turned to another old woman sitting at the next table. "You know how to get to the Faulkner place, Agnes?" Agnes turns it over in her mind until I've nearly finished my eggburger. Then she says, "I don't know that." The first woman faces to me again and shrugs. "Well," she says, "you just take your first left and your second right, and then you can ask somebody."

A new, male voice enters the conversation now, a worn-out-looking man of fifty or so at the third table. He says, "I reckon yer talkin' of John's house."

"John?" I say. Everyone else has turned on him in the only abrupt movement they've made.

"John's his brother," says the man. "Bill's brother."

"Oh," I say, "*that* John. He was a writer too, wasn't he?"

The woman with the fan speaks up sharply. "A sight cleaner and better than his brother, too, if you ask *me*."

Jack Wysoker comes back then, eats his eggburger doubtfully, and no one says another word.

We leave for Greenwood, and soon, on the road, spot the deputy's deputy's deputy behind us in a black car. The day seems different from any in Mississippi before. Even the trees that, dressed in kudzu vine, usually loom up like ferocious predators, now have the aspect of rather nice green dinosaurs. Perky little farms, a cow slopping around neck-deep in a mudhole, a sign saying ATTEND WATER VALLEY METHODIST CHURCH, WHERE YOU CAN MEET THE MASTER. Another on a drive-in: ELVIS KISSIN COUSINS RIGHT NOW! Beside the road: LOOSE STOCK ILLEGAL. Then for half an hour the only sign says READ THE SIGNS. But at Grenada I remember everything: another sign, FIRST AND LAST COLORED CAFE. Right after that the radio, which has been playing jolly music, switches to Robert Abernathy, NBC News, with a commentary on the Mississippi Summer Project. "Now that the project is drawing to a close . . ." he says, we can look at it objectively and see that "like a mediocre play, it got mixed reviews." I stew over that for a while, until we stop behind a school bus letting out Negro children (August!) and there is time for the realities to intrude again: in the field beside us, a band of a dozen cotton-choppers, men and women and three children too small to have been on the bus. It is two-thirty, and the sun is sizzling. They are bent over their hoes silently weeding in Millet postures, except their skins are black.

Greenwood. Somehow we lose the deputy's deputy's deputy; "somehow" because the lawyer is new in town and I have the illusion that I know the way to the office. We pass a creek with old cars dumped down its bank, overgrown and rusted hulks like rocks. I've never seen that before, so we must be going wrong. I've been down Robert E. Lee Drive and Jeff Davis Avenue—but here is a new one, Hemingway Street. (There is none named Faulkner; but it may be another Hemingway, for that matter.) Finally, back to Main, the Confederate States Savings and Loan Assoc., Inc., the Greenwood Primitive Baptist Church, home. It's nearly four o'clock. And all of it for two cases of pop bottles.

We pick up George Johnson and Jesse Harrison, who have the bail money now, and head back toward City Hall. In the anteroom of the jail they have stripped the bulletin board of its WANTED posters—probably in removing the MISSING notice for Mickey, James, and Andy. Deputy Phillips from Oxford has already delivered the writ removing John to federal jurisdiction, and gone back. George deals with the bail and the key to the door of the cell is produced; John is before us. His arm is still in a sling but better; he only looks bored, as if he is used to it and, though glad to be released, expects to be back soon. On his T-shirt—I hadn't noticed in the confusion of the arrest—he has painted SNCC BLACKMAN.

Jesse is still angry with him over the bottle question, which has resulted in two days of work for everyone concerned. In the car John further endears himself by his first remark: "Hey, Jesse, did anybody pick up those bottles?" Jesse turns on him. "Do you realize your bottles cost us three hundred dollars? How much you think you'd o' got for a refund, man?" John doesn't answer. Instead, the noises on the citizens' band radio remind him of something: "You know, they listen to that thing in the fire station right behind the jail. They'd turn it up real loud so I could hear it from the cell. 'K-U-Y one-one-oh-six mobile unit three calling Greenwood base,'" he mimics. "It made me feel real good."

I see him later at Blood's. He's shaved, changed, and sprightly, and has spruced up his sling with SNCC buttons. Greeting me, he announces his score for arrests is eleven now, starting at age fourteen. (He's just twenty, he says, though he looks younger.) "But you know, jail's the only place I can sleep. Nothin' to worry about in jail. If they gonna beat you, they beat you first, but once you in that cell, you can sleep. I jus' *sleep!*" I ask him what his family thinks of it all, if they support him; he says they live in another town and don't concern themselves, and his wife and son of two are in Florida. A wife? "She did me wrong," he explains. "And ain't nobody gonna do that to me again, either. Now I'm real tough. With women you gotta be, you know? That's the only way you get anywhere. I don't *hate* women, but I swear we got damn little in common."

The next morning at eight Jesse was downstairs in the chapel with twenty rapt children deciding on the battle tactics of the day. Outside, Mr. Sanders, an old man who owned the building and acted as caretaker, was catching hold of stragglers. "Which one o' you pulled this screen out?" he demanded of three small boys. "The rain did it," one of them said. Mr. Sanders got very angry. "Now don't you tell no tales on God's rain!" he said. "Tell me who did it. And you got to *prove* who did it, you got to have a *witness.*" The boys slithered away from him and went inside. Mr. Sanders looked after them, grumbling.

When the Peacemakers had been assigned stations, Jesse directed them to pick up any paper and butts under their chairs. They bent and did so. Before they left, he had another word. "You people have got to use your heads for something besides hatracks. Anybody who's getting violent isn't going down there. We have SNCC support but not COFO support. There's nobody to call on for your bail. You got to follow SNCC discipline. We can't have people who won't follow orders: when I say disperse, I mean get *out* of there, leave your shirt, your shoes, your pants, just get out of there. I don't want no more foolin' with Coke bottles!"

John Handy was sitting in the second row, trying to look as though he weren't listening. But he followed discipline that day, as they all did, and he was arrested anyway, with five others. On Wednesday, ten more were picked up. By Friday, the catch had risen to twenty-one. Their average age was sixteen, and by no means all of them had anything to do with boycotts—until they got out. They had been arrested singly on John Doe warrants—with which anyone can be arrested, guilty or not, near the scene of the "crime" or not, in their homes or on the street, at work or at school—and charged with disturbance in a public place.

14. The Resistance

[*The necessity of treating Negroes with rigor*] *gradually brings a numbness upon the heart, and renders most of those who are engaged in it too indifferent to the sufferings of their fellow creatures.*

—Captain John Newton, Eighteenth-century slaver

Five girls were led down the stairs from their cell. They huddled in a corner waiting to be summoned to the courtroom. The lawyer directed, "Don't say anything before they pronounce you guilty." I felt something being pressed into my hand, a note folded very small, but couldn't tell who had passed it—then saw Catherine looking at me. "It's from Nadine," she whispered. Nadine Delaney was at the county farm, from which the rest of them had been brought that morning for their trial. "She's been beaten," Catherine said. She had also been charged with destruction of public property for throwing a bar of soap at the man who had beaten her, missing him and breaking a window.

They were pushed forward and took their seats inside. The lawyer asked Judge Kimbrough for a continuance. Denied. "Catherine Edwards, you are charged with creating a disturbance in a public place. To that charge, how do you plead, guilty or not guilty?"

Silence. Unless you knew, you couldn't even tell which girl was Catherine Edwards.

"Enter a plea of not guilty."

Five times this routine was repeated. Then Mrs. A. M. Dorris was sworn in, a tinted blonde with metallic eyes, about forty-five. Mrs. Dorris testified she had seen the girls on the corner of Pelican and Young, "dancin' and hollerin' and singin' 'Dorris must go.' They was doin' vulgar dances."

"Were they threatening your customers, Mrs. Dorris?" asked the prosecutor.

217

"They'd meet 'em out there in the street and dare 'em to go in the store," she said indignantly. Her husband, seated beside her, nodded his pinched gray head at everything she said. The two of them looked like stock characters out of *Blues for Mister Charlie.* "They told 'em they couldn't trade in my store."

"And did it keep them away?"

"It did."

"How long has this been going on?"

"Since Friday."

In my lap I unfolded the note Catherine had given me. "When you all go see your lawyer today," it read, "tell him they got John wearing stripes and the boys are working. They told us if we do anything they was going to beat us so we can't sing. I saw you this morning when you went down to breakf"—here the pen ran out of ink.

The girls in the row in front of me sat so still they seemed to be holding their breaths. The judge's mechanical voice intoned their names again. "Mary Austin, seventeen, fine fifty dollars. Catherine Edwards, fifteen, fine twenty-five dollars. Barbara Edwards, seventeen, fine seventy-five dollars." There was no connection between the amounts of the fines and what the girls were or were not supposed to have done; none of them had been individually accused in any case. I thought the judge was determining punishment by age, until he got to "Mamie Parker, fifteen, fine seventy-five dollars. Ernestyne Pruitt, seventeen, fine fifty dollars." The lawyer, unsurprised, asked for appeal bonds to be set.

"Two hundred dollars," said the judge.

"For each case?"

"Each case."

"Even the twenty-five-dollar-fine case?"

"That's right!"

Judge Kimbrough was losing his cool. His face had stiffened over the summer into a kind of contained rage. The belligerent glare he gave the girls as they were led away was maintained for the boys, who took their places a few minutes later. The show was restaged, the same in every detail, but this time two of the fines were one hundred dollars. The children were returned to the county farm, and the lawyers went to see Judge Clayton.

On the radio once an hour came the voice of B. A. Ainsworth, owner of the third store the Peacemakers had chosen to boycott: ". . . I have this to say to all the citizens of Greenwood, both white and Nigra. What we are allowing to take place here is a shame and a disgrace. We are allowing a communist invasion of our city and not putting up one fragment of resistance. Our local Nigras are not resisting because they have been threatened and intimidated by these communist agitators and are fearful of their very lives and feel that our local law enforcement will not offer them protection which, of course, is not true." All over town, white and black heard rumors of the broadcast and were tuning in. "The entire South is the last absolute stronghold of freedom," said Mr. Ainsworth. "If the South falls to the communists, then the United States will fall and then the whole world."

"Well, well," said a young woman at the office later. "Ain't it easy? First you get Massa Ainsworth's store, then you get the world!"

". . . running true to form the communists will create something to exploit, as was the case of Henderson's Grocery on Avenue I. . . . Through trick photography and the distribution of such to the Nigras in Mr. Henderson's neighborhood trade area, these agitators have effected a picket and boycotted his grocery store that has virtually put him out of business. All the photograph shows was the back of an officer having to use moderate force in effecting an arrest. Their next target was Mr. Dorris's grocery in Baptist Town. . . ." And so forth, until he came to his own position. "Whether my business as such survives is relatively unimportant to me. It is now a matter of principle!" The "so-called students" were "here to take over, and if we allow it they will take over, and all of you who have hesitated to get involved in a resistance movement will be lost to the most formidable power on earth, the International Communist Party."

Mr. Ainsworth used less decorous language when it was not for broadcast. His store was located on a border street with whites living nearby who were arming and coming out in support of their neighbor. The grocer himself, with a rifle in one hand and a carbine slung over his shoulder, was shouting at the kids, "You ain't helpin' the other niggers none, you're hurtin' 'em! I got lots o' white friends.

I don't need any o' you black bastards." He continued similarly for ten or fifteen minutes, waving his rifle, while the kids stood nearby giggling at him until Jesse took them away. The next day they returned, and this time Ainsworth had supplemented his weaponry with a pistol in the free hand. "Okay! The next one o' you sons of bitches comes on my property, I'm gonna kill you!" The scene was observed by agents of the FBI.

Forty-three John Doe warrants were out now for more arrests. The Peacemakers began demonstrating at still another store which had victimized their families in the past. The woman who ran it reacted by stationing herself in the street with a shotgun, blasting off at her tormentors. The children skipped around the corner, but she stayed there cursing at them and brandishing the gun, now and then shooting it up at the sky as though heaven were responsible.

Jesse was arrested in mid-morning for disturbing the peace. Since he was the only one capable of keeping it, George had rushed to the jail with two hundred dollars to bail him out, and in the meantime cars left the office frequently to patrol the streets. With Paul Klein and a couple of other volunteers I rode out to view the latest Peacemaker boycott. There was a warrant out for Paul too on a charge of profanity. His innocence had nothing to do with it: there were cops ahead, and they knew his car, so we circled around the block to a parallel street, parked, and asked the children how it was going. Two women were shooting today, they said, standing well out of range around the church. There were at least a hundred of them; but few of their parents' generation were amused enough by such games to be out watching. We ducked down an alley leading to the grocery, and from a vantage point fifty yards along could see the police in formation opposite it. The two women were silhouetted against the shopfront, indistinguishably scrawny and dressed in baggy dresses, their heads thrown back in supplication, awkwardly grasping their shotguns. We stood suspended in our separate groups: the children, the police, the two women, and the four civil rights workers, squinting at each other, distracted by the number of rivals for our attention. Then down the middle of the block walked Willie Blue, a SNCC man. He walked backwards toward us, pointing a movie camera at the women on his right and the policemen on his left. The police, jarred from their confusion with something tangible to follow, started after him in a strange, almost motionless dance. Willie

Blue walked very casually, the camera at his face, taking pictures of the policemen approaching him. His pace quickened, then theirs; theirs, then his. The distance between them never diminished. Then one person broke into a sprint, followed by the others, too quickly to see who had started it. Willie Blue leaped into the alley where we stood and released us from our spell: the five of us tore madly back to Paul's car, never looking back until the end, when we saw we had won. They were far behind, too far to have spotted Paul. He gave the keys to someone else and fell to the floor in the back, our feet covering him, while the car raced back to the office. Jesse appeared a moment later, released on bond.

The weather was getting a little cooler, or maybe we had adjusted to it. At least the dazzling constant heat was broken after the middle of August with rain and a breeze now and then. As the sun set beyond the library window an edge of black cloud slid slowly over the hot pink and orange. Soon it had crept to meet the light and darkened the day, until there was nothing but a soft, still blanket covering the sky. Then the wind blew, churning it apart into racing masses of purple and inky El Greco colors. The cool was beautiful, dry and keen before the rain, and everyone stopped in it, just stood there alone while it washed away their summer's sweat and fever. Samuel ran calling up the stairs to show me, and took me out to the park across the road. We stood in the grass with our faces to the wind while the clouds tumbled chaotically past from horizon to horizon. Samuel said nothing, just laughed with it wildly. He did a handstand in the grass and I did one too, then somersaults, wheelbarrows, flying angels, and exhaustion, giggling on our backs. The first heavy drops of rain fell and we didn't move until we were *cold*.

In the "conference room" downstairs there was a staff meeting. Some of the volunteers had left already to lobby in the North for the Freedom Democratic Party, and others would be going in the next few days. Most of the chairs were broken, so the odd dozen people sprawled about on a couple of tables, on the floor, on each other's laps, or on an old mattress propped against the wall, a makeshift couch like the one we had in jail. It was a conversation more than a meeting; no one needed to chair the gatherings any more. We were smooth, affectionate, relaxed, quarrelsome, rundown, bored, all the things a family is. This was the meeting at which Mary Lane was chosen—by default, as far as she was concerned—to take over as Project director. The talk went on in the shorthand possible to brothers, and was over soon so everyone could go to Lula's, a restaurant whose owner was giving us a good-bye party with free tuna fish and punch. Cars began to leave, volunteers straggled about collecting things and each other, and I went upstairs to type some legal documents. The rain was pelting the windows by now and the library felt snug. "Private Harassment and Violence in Greenwood; Official Harassment and Violence in Greenwood; Arrest Record . . ."

A fantastic scream came up the stairs. "They've shot Silas!" Someone was crying. "They've shot Silas in the head!" I ran down.

Bambi was standing absolutely straight inside the door, with tears falling down her cheeks from open, catatonic eyes. KUY 1106 was speaking, and the telephones: to Lula's, the hospital, the FBI. The story was reported out of sequence and put together in the WATS report. Silas had driven a group to Lula's for the party, and when they arrived had waited behind in the car for the rain, now pouring, to let up. He was resting his head on the steering wheel. A white station wagon passed, slowed, shot once, and sped away. It had contained two men, one of them described—there were three witnesses. At first they had thought the car was one of ours, because it had an aerial long enough to bump the trees as it drove off. Then they saw what had happened, and called into Lula's: "Someone's been shot." Little George was the first to get to the car. When he opened the door, Silas fell into the gutter. Then the others came outside; Bob Zellner and Eli took off their shirts to bandage the wound, lifted Silas to another car, and drove him to the hospital. There they were not permitted to accompany him because they had no shirts on.

Something to do: in the library there were, for some reason, two new shirts. I sent them in the next car going to the hospital. Then someone handed me a phone—Linda at the hospital. We had to keep the line open. "I heard Logan talking to a white woman," she said. "He was laughing. He said, 'They finally got that nigger Silas.' The woman said something like 'Really?' and Logan answered, 'Yeah, ain't it wonderful?'" I relayed this to Judy Richardson, who added it to the WATS report she was typing while talking to Lula's on another phone. "The police have arrived at Lula's," she had just

written, "twenty minutes after the shooting." They had never been a
minute away from us before. The relay continued with Linda, who
added on the subject of Logan that when a volunteer had asked him
and another officer for their names, both had answered "Jones."

They were trying to talk to Eli and Mrs. McGhee on the citizens'
band. Our station was being so badly jammed that the voices were
scarcely audible, until a moment's pause when a woman said clearly,
"Did the nigger die yet?" Bambi hadn't moved. People were coming
from all over the neighborhood to see if we had any news, and a
phone rang each time it was free with tearful questions from strangers. "Don't let him be dead," a small boy was mumbling to himself
in the corner, the fingers of both his hands crossed.

Then, an hour later—how long?—Judy typed on the report:
"SILAS WILL BE ALL RIGHT." She was speaking to the hospital: the bul-
let hit him in the cheek, just below the temple, and was lodged in
the left side of his throat. They were going to move him to Jackson
for surgery.

Afterwards, the details, the responses were clear again. Before, it
was like hearing it and feeling it through a concrete wall. But still
there was a strange state of shock; it couldn't dissolve that easily. In
the office they did what they could, moved, spoke—surprised, in a
way, that the legs and voices performed as usual, that it looked down
there like a normal night. The calls to the FBI were going through,
then to Washington because of the local bureau's recalcitrance. An
hour after the shooting the FBI had still not gone to Lula's. The office
was pleading with them to investigate and take pictures so the damaged car could be moved. Their Jackson agent kept assuring us that
his men would "be on the job." When by ten o'clock no federal
agents had turned up at Lula's, the Jackson FBI suggested that the
reason they hadn't appeared might be that they were "making in-
quiries."

A volunteer rushed into the office soaking wet and carefully carrying a jacket out in front of him as though it might explode. One of
the people at Lula's had had a pistol, and he had taken it, afraid
that shooting might break out. The people were incensed and
anything could happen. I offered to hide it in my room, since the
office might be raided, and was given the jacket. The Amoses were
sitting in the kitchen, the whole family, quiet, shelling peas. I came
in with my bundle and showed Mrs. Amos what it was, a little uncer-

tain because of the danger it might mean to her. She nodded that it would be all right, and I put it under my bed. On the way out I saw another pistol on the sink.

I got a lift to Lula's. There were crowds outside, a hundred people standing silently in the rain. Some of them were crying. The downpour had flooded the street, which had no drains. The car stood opposite with its front window smashed, pieces of glass strewn among the puddles. Chief Lary drove up seeking witnesses: of the three, only one would admit anything except to SNCC. No one forgot what had happened to Louis Allen for testifying about the murder of Herbert Lee. The witness was a girl, her head covered with curlers, and recklessly, furiously angry; but Chief Lary had to ask her three times before she would reluctantly approach him. What did the car look like, he wanted to know, and the driver. "He had long hair," she said in a tone that indicated her awareness of how futile the conversation was: "and he flung it out of his face as he drove off. He looked like he had done somethin' *big*." Closed, hostile faces watched the Chief write down the details. He observed their look and cut the interview short, requesting the girl's name "so we can talk to you later when it's quieter." She shrugged and walked away without looking back.

Other policemen were taking pictures of the car across the street. Flashbulbs illumined the facets of glass still left in the window, on the front seat, and floating in the mud. Pictures of faces in the crowd were lit in jagged frames by the flashbulbs. Jake McGhee standing rigid, transfixed, tall among the other heads. A white civilian leaning out of a sheriff's car and shouting at me, "Nigger-lovin' bitch!" Jesse wandering among the crowd steering people to the office, trying to break their trance: we'd all decide together what to do. An old woman looking at me, looking. I returned her expressionless gaze and we stood for several seconds that seemed very long. Finally she said, "It's been a tired night . . ."

Back at the office, someone had just added to the WATS report: "10:15 p.m.—Sheriff has arrived, but ne'er a sign of the omnipotent, omniscient, omnipresent FBI." An hour later, after the police force, sheriff's department, highway patrol, and a Greenwood television unit had come and gone, and a report passed on that the car would be bombed if it wasn't moved, the FBI had still not arrived.

Outside, through the rain falling steadily and turning the roads into rivers, men arrived at the office from all directions carrying guns. They were new faces: a generation seldom seen at mass meetings, working men beyond participating in the Peacemakers, in their late twenties and thirties, Army vets, a fighting force. Albert Garner snapped at me and two other volunteers to get inside. "They goin' to kill white people tonight, and they may not look who it is." I saw Mrs. McGhee wandering among them, mumbling and asking everyone if they had seen Jake. I didn't know, I answered, and asked her where Clarence was. "Jail," she said, and moved on. A tall, powerful black man was standing in the streaming rain, his face crumpled, shouting, "They keep killin' our people! *When* are we goin' to stop them? *When?*"

I went home for a moment. The pistol still lay on the sink, and a young man, his clothes dripping on the floor as he gesticulated, was arguing that it would be deadlier in his hands. None of the Amoses answered him. They sat among basins of multicolored beans and peas, the pile of pods a foot high on the floor, each one shelling, picking up another, dropping beans one way, pods another, each withdrawn, concentrated on his hands as though their use this way prevented them from strangling someone. I passed through them to my room; the eyes were turned in, refusing to admit me any more than the man at the door.

Out again, I saw Jesse herding the newcomers into the chapel. He got them relatively quieted and sitting in rows, though they shouted out and interrupted sporadically. He was talking continually, molding their anger with his strained, controlled voice. "I'm nonviolent," he said, "but I can be as violent as the next man. You people want to go violent, don't even know what that mean. We can't go out shootin' innocent people. What's goin' to happen then? What's goin' to happen to the women and children over here? You want a riot? You *all* be dead by morning." There was a buzzing at the back as more men arrived and tried to push into the room; he split them into two groups and sent the other half into the conference room. The choice was careful, selective: he asked Albert and some others he trusted to sort out possible Toms, and get the crowd down to a manageable size. The rejects grumblingly left, tried to hang around the door, and were shut out. Finally a dozen or so remained. Jesse never stopped his steady, soothing monologue. "You got to cool down. You can't achieve a damn thing this way. How you think I feel? You think I like it any better than you? But you got to have a plan, man, a *plan*. You want retaliation you got to do it *right*. Any o' you mean business, that's fine with me, but you get here at seven-thirty tomorrow morning and we'll set up a *plan*."

"Now!" a man in the back interrupted. "We got to do somethin' *now!*" Others shouted out assent.

"What you want to do? What do any of you want to do? You jus' want to go out killin' anythin' white. You think they won't be back here in a minute, shootin' up our homes? We got to get out and protect the streets. They goin' to be drivin' around stirrin' up trouble. Ain't you got no *sense?*"

They quieted again. "Now," said Jesse, "who's got a car?" A few hands were raised. "We goin' to divide up and assign neighborhoods, and drive around to see nobody gets hurt." He picked out three or four men per car, and two groups left. "What do we do," a voice asked, "if we see a car circlin' around with white men and guns?"

"I'm not tellin' you what to do," said Jesse. "If I said shoot, one of you would start gettin' stupid and come back later sayin' 'Harrison told me to do it.' Now, who wants to stay and guard the office? Whoever guards the office can't be armed."

"That's me!" shouted an eager voice.

"I said *can't* be armed."

"Oh." The man wilted, sitting down again.

They gradually left for their stations; the office guards were the same as usual—two local men who stayed up every night patrolling Avenue N.

The rain was spattering, dripping, splashing down erratically. In the national office it had seeped in all the cracks, under the doors, down the walls. They were still trying to get the FBI. Mrs. McGhee had found Jake and they had taken Silas in an ambulance to Jackson. Dotty and Jesse conferred briefly; he went off to supervise the night's patrols. After he had gone, she said, "Sometimes I think Jesse stands between us and certain death." Someone appeared with large bowls of tuna fish and punch: the good-bye party from Lula's.

Jesse's talent lay in giving people something to do. There were no further outbursts that night, from either black or white. The most violently inclined were made patrolmen; after a full night awake, none of them showed up at seven-thirty. But Sunday had to be filled. For the first time, a mass meeting was organized for midday.

People packed into the Seventh Day Adventist Chapel, over-flowed into the waterlogged street, and sang. "This little light of mine, I'm gonna let it shine. This little light of mine, I'm gonna let it, let it shi-i-ine . . ." There were new verses that day, called out from all over the audience. "All around Slim Henderson's, I'm gonna let it shine. When they shoot at me, I'm gonna let it shine. Even if they kill me, I'm gonna let it shine. . . ."

Jesse announced that a larger church was available now, and everyone who wanted to could march there. Everyone did; the procession, two-by-two, singing, stretched for hundreds of yards. On some streets the rain had left pools two feet deep, but no one changed direction; they just got their feet wet. Curious faces looked out of windows as we passed, joined the song, and came out to follow the line. Cars of radio and television men sloshed slowly through the flood in parallel, arms out the windows holding microphones to record the singing. Patrol cars passed too; out of their windows hung uniformed arms dangling billy sticks. "It's that free-eedom train a-comin', comin', comin' . . ." We passed a house where a woman was sweeping her porch: "Get on bo-oard, get on board," we aimed the next line at her, and she dropped the broom and came.

Jake McGhee stood up front at the meeting, blinking at the lights of two TV cameras. "Silas told me to tell you, don't let one of those bullets turn you round. He said if you do, then freedom ain't worth fightin' for." Jesse got up then and, using the opportunity to speak to new people, appealed to them to give the movement property bonds for the kids who were, and would be, in jail. "If you ain't willin' to pay the price, Greenwood, we're fightin' a losin' battle." A very young, thin girl stood up spontaneously in the audience, and pitched in: "These people are goin' to do it again, and we got to fight harder and harder, they gonna arrest us, and let me tell you it's no *fun* in jail!" Her diminutive voice rang out over them angrily. "I think you should stand together as Negroes, and be proud of it! We got three classes o' people in Greenwood. The teachers, who say 'Well, we got ours.' And the middle-class in houses with brick fronts. And *us*—we say 'Wade in the water,' and we tellin' the truth! Every time it rain we wadin' in the water. Now you got to *help* us! If you got property, you put it up for bond! We ain't askin' you to go to jail, but you got to support us!"

Two rows in front of me sat Mrs. Delaney, mother of Nadine, the girl who was beaten on the county farm and for whom bail had not yet been raised. Her slender, small-boned face kept moving as the teeth clenched. She stood and said that she had just heard Nadine had been taken from the farm, no one knew where. "I'd like to see a lawyer after the meeting," she requested, and sat again. Another daughter, a girl of about ten, clutched her mother's arm with both hands and kept searching her face. The two sat pressed together for the rest of the meeting. Two days later they were evicted from their home.

Dewey Greene, just returned from Jackson where he had been chosen in the FDP state convention to be a delegate to Atlantic City, was the next speaker. "Whether we're seated in Atlantic City or not," he said, "we'll be there to tell the world that we are *dissatisfied* with what is happening in Mississippi."

They listened to him with respect, nodding and agreeing audibly. "For a hundred years we've done nothing. All you'll get for doing nothing is being called a 'good Nigra.' A good Nigra is the one who does what Mr. Charlie say do. Mr. Charlie tells you the things to do that's right for *him!* But look what's happening now. Five people were at the mass meeting the night in sixty-three when they thought they'd get them a nigger. They shot Jimmy Travis. They thought by doing that they could get rid of the movement. That was a Wednesday. But Saturday the whole town was here!" "That's right!" voices shouted. "Then they burned the office and shot at my house. Every time they did something, they just got more of us participating in the action. I think this is getting like their cancer. They start foolin' with it and it'll kill them!"

Outside there was suddenly the sound of sirens. *That's next: they're going to burn us down* was everyone's thought, and no one's words. Only in Mississippi could you hear sirens before the fire. The meeting dispersed; outside at the corner was a vast red firetruck. It had no visible purpose; nothing anywhere was burning, but it was a place for firemen to sit and jeer at the children. A group of girls stood looking at it, outraged, one of them shouting, "We got to *do* somethin'! And what we want you can't get marchin' and singin' 'God is on our side' *no more*. We got to *do* somethin'!"

Jesse again found a use for their energy: "To Slim's!" A black Pied Piper, he led the way. The kids began to chant, "We want Silas! We want Silas!" The sun was shining on the sheets of gleaming water that engulfed the houses up to their doors, as though they were boats. Some of the children marching through the water had no shoes; some wore ragged, flapping sneakers. "We want *Silas!* We want *Silas!*" A long black car passed and a white girl sitting in the front seat stuck her tongue out at the line.

At Slim's they stood on their favorite corner and sang a few verses of their new "Oh Freedom": "No more snipers, no more stitches, no Uncle Toms over me, over me . . ." But the store was closed and they wanted more. Jesse took the march on toward Ainsworth's. Halfway there the white volunteers were ordered back to the office: Ainsworth's was too dangerous for that sort of provocation. We straggled back. "I'm so damn sick of being white!" Evelyn said.

Police cars were parked or patrolling by Avenue N. At the corner we were overtaken by a pickup truck which slowed nearly to a halt, its two armed white occupants gazing at us malignantly before turning and driving slowly off. "It's Ainsworth!" someone shouted. "He's been circling," said someone else. Bob Zellner stopped Chief Lary, who had driven up that instant, and explained the Ainsworth situation. Lary thought about it a while, then his car inched around the corner after the truck, which was fifty yards down by now, and when it was safely out of sight, he picked up some half-hearted speed to pursue it. I got into a radio car going the same way. We passed Wing's and the playing fields of the high school, then saw the procession up ahead, a neat line of pairs, Jesse by their side with a walkie-talkie. The black paddy wagon was groaning along in low gear beside them. Chief Lary was nowhere to be seen. Our radio suddenly announced a message from another mobile unit near Ainsworth's: a mob of whites with shotguns was milling around the street there and the march must not proceed. Jesse heard the news on his walkie-talkie, and within a minute had the children walking back the other way. As they changed direction, the black bus turned and crept up behind them. Our car circled back toward the office.

We took the highway briefly, speeding down beside the cotton fields, a landscape at peace. The washed, growing green stretched out to touch the sky, a brilliant blue turning orange in the sunset. On Avenue N, the police. They had parked their cars cater-corner from the office, and blocked the roads with their prickly shapes, each one helmeted and sticking out all over with rifles, pistols, and machine guns, and one of them grasping a grotesque machine that someone identified as a tear-gas gun. Each had a satchel with gas mask strapped to his back. As we turned the corner again, I could see the kits were lettered USN. Then the crowds came into view: all our neighbors were out in front of their houses watching with sullen faces. Way up Broad Street they could see their children, and the big black bus.

Our car turned toward it. On the high-school field the children were standing in a straight, precise line, waiting for Jesse to finish communicating through the walkie-talkie. He signaled for them to come on then, and like a *corps de ballet* in the hands of an expert choreographer, they moved in a graceful bend to the sidewalk, to the street, toward the office. They were shouting as they marched, "Hey, Hey, whaddaya know? Chief Lary must go!" The black bus moved with them. In another fifty yards they would confront the police. Chief Lary stood among them, his flinty little face shrunken under its white dome. I had never seen him wear a helmet before.

In the national office, two FBI men were interviewing people about the shooting of Silas. They had finally appeared that morning. KUY 1106 was picking up constant bulletins from the two mobile units and the walkie-talkie, and the staff inside, anticipating a riot with tear gas and machine guns, were frantically broadcasting back while trying to persuade the FBI men to go outside. "Look, he was shot last *night,* there might be a riot outside *now.* We need you as *witnesses.*" The FBI men dawdled by the radio, listening to the reports of what was happening ten yards away. Finally someone opened the door and nearly pushed them out of it, whereupon the two men took off in a mighty sprint to their car, leaped in, and drove away.

"*Hey, hey, whaddaya know, Chief Lary must go!*" the shout kept coming, approached the corner, turned it; they passed Chief Lary without lowering their volume, hardly looking at him, and marched toward the office after Jesse. Lary was unmoved. Among the local people still lining the street there was an equal absence of audience reaction—the impassive masks of Negroes surviving. Then the Chief brought out his megaphone and in a bellow only just discernible over the sound of the chant, called, "I have to ask y'all to disperse, otherwise I can't be held responsible for what will happen." His cry was redundant. Jesse, wielding the children like a weapon, was splitting them neatly into two, half to the chapel, half to the national office. Inside he called on the best voices to lead them in freedom songs, which soon rang out in competition from the different rooms. The police just stood there with nothing left to do. Soon they got into their cars and drove away.

Jesse sent everyone home when it was quiet. A few of them lingered briefly outside, and in a sort of coda burst into hoots and catcalls at a car pulling a small yacht called *Mi Corazón*. Released from the law, the people joined in. A few of them picked up rocks and loose chunks of asphalt. Another car with a Goldwater sticker provoked a little boy to the chase, gathering stones to heave as he ran. His mother, rushing to stop him, was caught up in the action in spite of herself. She picked up a brick and threw it; they both missed.

The next day, with the children's case now federal, Jesse went to the police station to bail them out. Chief Lary called him aside and said: "I want to thank you for helping me out on Sunday." He didn't mention arresting him on Saturday.

The children were delivered back to the office in the big black bus. For minutes before, we could hear their approach: "FREEDOM! FREEDOM! FREEDOM!" The bus pulled up and they fell, tumbled, catapulted out, crying and hugging everyone they saw. Catherine Edwards was there, and John Handy, but not Nadine. They had come straight from the county farm, where they had been beaten and forced to work at hard labor. Soon they had thermometers in their mouths, bottles of stomach medicine in their hands, bandages on their limbs, and were off to Lula's to celebrate.

15. Sing It for Mississippi

We are waiting to hear from the American people. It's not the noise of the bad, but the thundering silence of the good people that causes so much trouble.

—Aaron Henry, Atlantic City

The Free Southern Theater, a traveling interracial band of performers loosely connected with COFO, put on *In White America* in a church one night. More than a play, it was a series of readings and dramatizations from Negro history—and the most exciting theater I had ever seen; it was about the people for whom it was performed, who had never seen a play before. They spoke back to it when they were moved, and joined the songs they knew: the drama went in two directions. The next day the audience communicated what had been communicated to them.

"Chile," old Mr. Hampton said to his daughter, "you should've seen that picture last night! They showed slavery, and all the way we come. 'Ladies and gentlemen,'" he mimicked, then his voice faded, and he began to act out the play for her. Mrs. Brown, a neighbor, had been there too, and nodded as the old man redramatized it. "That picture was so *good*," she said, "I wouldn't take *any-thin'* for it! It was just like TV," she explained to those who had stayed at home. "If you'd had a screen you'd a thought it was that. It was so lovely!" "But you know," Mr. Hampton said, "it's much easier to understand when they up there tellin' you about it, than jus' seein' a picture."

The group standing outside the office had grown to five or six. Mr. Hampton explained about John Brown on the gallows, and Sojourner Truth. An old woman on her way to Wing's stopped and listened. Mr. Hampton, now an impassioned W. E. B. DuBois rebuking Booker T. Washington, saw her and delivered an impromptu rebuke of his own. "You got to go to the mass meetin's!" he said to her, "or how you gonna learn anythin'?" Then to his audience: "Some old niggers around here jus' listen to what the others say about it, never go to see for themselves. Ought to be ashamed."

Mrs. Brown, sympathetic to the old woman, though a strong movement worker herself, said, "Sometimes you can be too afraid. You can be so afraid you can't do *nothin'*."

"Well I ain't scared," said Mr. Hampton. "Everybody scared in the dark, if they come at you in the dark, but ain't no need to be scared if they come in the light. That's what we doin' in the movement, makin' light. If we all join up in it, Miss'ippi goin' to be light as the sun!"

"That the truth!" said Mrs. Brown. "People say to me, 'How can you fool with it?' I just tell them, 'How come you *not* foolin' with it?' I marched down to the first Freedom Day at the courthouse, and everybody come to talk to me, sayin' I was crazy. Then the white folks come to see me—four o' them polices, they come to the door and they say 'Why you doin' all this?' I say I want my freedom. They say, 'Anybody payin' you to do it?' I say no, I didn't want nothin'. 'Well,' they say, real soft and sweet, 'Emma Bell, if you go tell all them people not to join the movement, we will do anythin' for you. Why,' they said, 'we'll go with you down to the bank and we'll draw up a note for all the money you want.' I said that sure was nice, I sure could use it, but no thanks."

Mrs. Brown and Mr. Hampton were both at the block captain meeting that night. The last voter registration workers had left for the North, and the meeting was run entirely by local people. This would be the FDP leadership in Greenwood. They elected a chairman and a secretary, and chose a delegation to see the mayor about police protection. Then they listened while Idell Kraft, a young girl who had just been released from the county farm, shouted at them. She wanted to tell them that the young people were fed up with their neatly businesslike discussion, that the boycotts were their job too, that they had been sitting around long enough. "This can be *our* Mississippi! If we stick together we can do it! And if it mean violent, we go violent!"

"You got to remember where we been a hundred years . . ." an old man faltered.

"Maybe on the next boycott," an old woman tried, "let's leave the children out and us old folks do it ourselves."

Anna Mae, the young woman who had worked for Miz McCaster, thought the block captains ought to be responsible at least for stopping Negroes from breaking the boycotts. "If you see people goin' in those stores, you beat those jokers up! You smash the food on the ground, and they not goin' back there again. If we make a law let's abide by it. When we come here and make our laws we must obey them, and stop dependin' on the white folks. They goin' now. The summer's over. We got to make plans and follow them through. That's what the block captain meetings are for. We come together to understand each other and decide what we goin' to do."

The complicated relationship of the McGhees to the law was not affected by the shooting of Silas. Mrs. McGhee and Jake were in and out of Jackson until he was removed from the critical list. After their return on Monday, Jake was arrested for (a) driving without a license and (b) showing a false license, convicted, and fined one hundred dollars. He had in fact lost his license; the second charge was concocted by the police when they found Silas's wallet among Jake's possessions handed in at the station. He applied for a copy of his license and was issued a certificate, good for thirty days, enabling him to drive until it came; however, he was rearrested on Tuesday for driving on the renewal certificate instead of a license. Mrs. McGhee went down to the police station to find out about the charges. The first policeman she asked directed her to another, who told her to return to the first. She hesitated and a third policeman hit her hard in the chest. She hauled back and socked him in the jaw; he fell, she left. A warrant was sent out for her arrest on the charge of assaulting an officer. She stayed in the office until some money was raised, and then, with a COFO lawyer, turned herself in, and was released immediately on bail. This procedure was necessary to prevent her being picked up unpredictably and beaten.

Meanwhile, Clarence was due for an Army court-martial for being AWOL; he hadn't returned to duty on time because he was in jail. He had been rearrested on the old charge of disturbing the peace, arising from the ditch-digging incident on the family farm. The sheriff informed him that his appeal had been heard the day before and that he had failed to appear. Clarence said he hadn't been notified of the hearing; the sheriff said he was under arrest; Clarence asked for a phone call; the sheriff said no.

He was released to the MPs after a week in jail; the Army dropped charges, but the other case was still unresolved. When I left Greenwood all McGhees were out on bail on at least one charge each; Silas remained in the hospital; and Mrs. McGhee was being sued for $150 she didn't have, and apprehensive about the possible confiscation of her property.

Some time after Lorna Smith left, Dick Frey asked me if I would move from the Amoses so that a couple could have my room. As it was, I had it to myself whenever there wasn't a stray traveling female in need of a bed, and it was selfish of me, but I couldn't leave the Amoses. I tried to explain to Dick. "I'm having a love affair with Mrs. Amos." "So is everyone else," he said.

Upset, I went to Mrs. Amos. She got angry. "Nobody goin' to move in here," she said. "That your room. You tell them one of the girls is sleepin' with you. Tell them my son is comin' back. Tell them what they want. Ain't nobody movin' in here." I thanked her. "Nothin' to do with *thanks*," she said. "We won't *let* you move out."

We were getting to be a family. I had been contributing a small rent, as did all the volunteers, though nothing like what the food cost, but at the moments when I felt most uselessly transient and white, I wished I had the means to do something for them. The son who was working for the summer in the North had gone to college the year before; it had cost eight hundred dollars and, though he had earned five hundred of it, she had had to borrow the rest and the family hadn't had much to eat that winter. This year there was no money for him to return, and he had done so well. He would probably stay up North.

"All my children want to go away," she said. "My baby want to go with my brother-in-law to Tennessee, and Glori-Jean want to go to California, and Cora Lou want to go to Chicago, they all want to leave me." She thought in the end she would have to take the family North, just to keep them together. She had never been there herself, and had only a faint idea what it could be like, mainly from Mr. Amos's short experience of Chicago. "He like it fine, only one thing he say, every time you go out you got to lock the door, and every time you come in you got to lock the door. And when somebody else come you got to peek at them first through a hole."

I hoped I could return to Greenwood to work, or at least to see her, and we talked about it sometimes. As I was packing to leave in the end she said, "When you come back I'm goin' to have the floor of your room painted and it all fix up."

"It's not *my* room," I said.

"Oh yes it is. Fact I'm namin' this room 'Sally.'" A while later I heard her muttering to herself, "Yes, that's what I'm gonna name that room. I'm gonna write on it, 'Sally.'"

Wednesday, 19th August

The silver-gray streamlined Greyhound sweeps out of the terminal, passing two other buses parked just opposite, much older, smaller, and identical except for their colors. One is a shiny yellow school bus decorated in black; the other, a negative of the first, painted opaque black with wired windows, and labeled in yellow: GREENWOOD POLICE DEPT.

Inside there is a certain amount of seat-shuffling. As an interstate bus it is theoretically integrated; I would rather sit in back to make the point, but that part is full: all Negro. In front then; and after I'm seated a middle-aged Negro woman crosses the color line and takes the place beside me. A white woman across the aisle gives us instant hate stares. When the seat beside her becomes vacant, she tells a Negro girl who moves forward to sit there, "It's taken." The girl stands still in the aisle for a moment. Then another white woman in the seat before them slides over, without looking back, to make room, and the girl sits down.

I feel afraid again as the bus leaves the town limits—a fear related to that in Ohio, of the unknown, unfaced, unpredictable. It's so much worse when you're not there. All day there has been a mounting panic about what will happen—after Saturday, when the last lawyer leaves, after the Convention, when most of the outside agitators are outside again and the state is free to shuck off its pretenses of legality—about what will happen to the McGhees, and Mary Lane, and Samuel (Nick fiel thectay), and Jesse, and Mrs. Amos.

The free people. It's too early to know if we have changed anything: others will judge that. But we have changed.

The woman beside me suddenly speaks. "You remember me?" I hadn't thought I knew her. "Ain't you the one who told me 'Get on board' on that march on Sunday?" she asks. "I was sweepin' my porch?" "Oh, of course, I remember." "Well I sure got on board!" she says.

A small plane trailed a streamer over the sea: BOBBY BAKER FOR VICE PRESIDENT. Pretty girls were dressed in LBJ advertisements, and a man as Santa Claus. Barry Goldwater beamed down at the crowded beach: IN YOUR HEART YOU KNOW HE'S RIGHT. The pop-art, circus quality of Atlantic City must seem unreal at the best of times, but during a convention and after a Mississippi summer it numbed nearly to the point of alienation. We had exhausted our supply of tensions in a confrontation with Southern reality, and now were flung with no transition into the world of deals and decisions, ulcers and dexedrine, funny hats and red, white, and blue—expected to participate, to be political. The set of our responses was wrong—a case of coming hungry to a meal that in the first chew turns to painted plaster, and lacking the manners to swallow it anyway. It was edible to our hosts, who were only dismayed at the size of our appetites.

We had two duties: to lobby among the delegates for support in seating the Freedom Democratic Party in place of the regulars; and to demonstrate in a silent vigil on the boardwalk in front of Convention Hall. The immediate object of FDP concern was the Credentials Committee, where we needed ten per cent of the members for a minority report with which the issue of seating the FDP could be raised on the convention floor. At that stage eight state delegations were necessary to request a roll-call vote. If anyone's optimism allowed for thought that far ahead, it could be assumed that in such a vote, with the delegates forced to stand and declare themselves instead of finding anonymity in a mass voice vote, a majority might side with us.

To accomplish these aims there were sixty-eight FDP delegates from Mississippi, equipped with courage and desperation more than what would have been more useful, power or a sense of "realism"; most of the COFO staff; and a crowd of volunteers making a detour on their way home. Operations were conducted from the Gem Hotel, where the delegates were staying, and a store-front SNCC-CORE office. In the latter, the first destination from the bus terminal, there were protest signs being painted, meetings and rallies planned, and a familiar set of voices singing the old song whose every verse began, "K-U-Y one-one-oh-six calling mobile unit Sweets, come in Sweets . . ." Sweets was presumably roaming the town, and all the walkie-talkies. Newcomers were told that if they needed a place to sleep we had a church with plenty of pews. Mary Lane was there, dressed up because she was a delegate, her limp worse in high heels. Eli, George, Phil, Evelyn, Iris from jail, and others— uncountable volunteers familiar from Ohio—rushed in and out, acting as salient points of subdued blue denim in the violently colored streets. There was the sensation again that you knew them, even if you'd never met, and we greeted one another as we passed, feeling anchored to the earth when the rest of the city seemed about to float crazily away, powered by its own hot air.

There was talk of the nationally televised Credentials Committee hearing the day before, when a series of witnesses, from Mrs. Hamer to Rita Schwerner, told what happens to black Mississippians who attempt to vote. Some of them spoke again at the two rallies that evening. Aaron Henry announced that the FDP had been assured of the support of twelve members of the Credentials Committee, one more than we needed: in the audience there was a brief sensation of hope. Everything suddenly looked possible, and when Henry said, "We can sit at home in Mississippi and watch things from the balcony, but we will not accept that here!" it sounded beyond the oratory like a battle cry. In the second rally, when Mrs. Hamer told of the inhumanities that had sent her and sixty-seven other delegates there, of the time they beat her in jail "till my hands were navy blue," and finished, "We are askin' the American people: Is *this* the land of the free and the home of the brave?" it seemed, just for that moment, that the question might not be merely rhetorical.

Later, Mrs. Hamer and other delegates sat on the porch of the Gem Hotel cooling off. The inside was beginning to look like the Greenwood SNCC office. Half a dozen phones rang in, rang out,

Betty Garman permanently attached to one of them and writing down the details, not of the latest beating in Selma, but the latest delegation to be won over. Above a debris of paper plates, pop bottles, and the heads of two legal researchers compiling a report, the others exchanged what they didn't know. "Is the Credentials Committee meeting tonight?" "They adjourned because we had enough support, and they have to figure how to screw us." "I heard they adjourned until after the convention. Then they won't have anything to figure." "What do you know about it?" "I know we have Guam." "*Guam?* Who needs *Guam?*" "A woman on the Credentials Committee just called up and said they told her she'll lose her place on the party ticket if she supports us." "What's she going to do?" "Fink." "Who wants to go to Minnesota?"

In the lobby of the Shelburne, delegates roamed between parties, milling and pushing, intercepting one another with pats and poundings on backs, politicking or waiting to politick, their eyes waning into the distance beyond your shoulder in order not to miss a more important passerby. Everyone was covered with buttons declaring allegiance, though nothing to indicate origins.

"Are you from Minnesota?" (To half of a pair emerging from a reception.)

"No, I'm from Nevada. Gosh, Harry, don't you wish you were from Minnesota?"

"Are you from Minnesota?" (Old uncle.)

"Sure thing. What can Minnesota do for you, honey?"

"I'm working for the Mississippi Freedom Democratic Party. We need your support in seating our delegation."

"Well, I don't know. . . . There're many questions to consider. That's one of those rump parties, isn't it?"

"That's just . . ."

"I'll give you an example of what I mean. In 1932 we had a sort of a mess over two delegations from Vermont . . ." After an interminable anecdote: "You see what I mean? You can't settle these things overnight."

There were many delegates and reactions, which ranged from one man who heard me out and vowed his full support, to another who listened vaguely and sardonically, and left with "Well, it's been swell talking to you, so long, good luck, and I know you're going to lose." Their sympathy was with us, they said, our cause touched their consciences: but political realities superseded moral claims, of course, of course, you understand. There were some who admitted it, and others who phrased their objections in terms of our questionable legality. Among them all was some degree of amazement that *I* should care about it; when, if asked, I said I'd spent the summer in Mississippi, there was an uncomfortable silence, then "But why? A nice girl like you, what do you want to get mixed up in that for? It's *dangerous* down there."

The following morning I joined the vigil. The sun rose to cooking heat, the surf made rhythms on the sand behind us, and the breeze smelled of popcorn and seaweed. My sign said:

FREEDOM'S NAME IS MIGHTY SWEET

SING IT FOR MISSISSIPPI

I held it straight, then learned to stick it in a crack of the boardwalk as the others did, and watched the lower half of the Democratic Party pass by. Smooth and mottled tans, thin and thickened ankles, weird footwear—the women's stiletto heels encased in tiny white rubbers to avoid catching in the same cracks of boardwalk, and the men knobby-kneed above their sandals or fluorescent plastic beach clogs. A woman stopped before me and said, "Were you here all night, dear?" At least a hundred had been. Some stayed there the entire five days of the vigil, sleeping on a nearby piece of boardwalk. They shaved and washed in the public lavatory, left the line to smoke, and ate mostly what passersby donated. That noon someone contributed a meal of hot dogs, beans, and milk. Later an old man thrust a bag of apples in my hands, saying simply, "I've had enough of these. Pass them around." A white woman brought us six boxes of saltwater taffy, and "I'm with y'all. I may be from Virginia, but I say, 'Civil rights is here to stay!'" Another Southern lady approached me asking, "Are you from Mississippi?" When I said, "No, not exactly," she explained, "Well I'm from just south of Jackson myself, and I thought we might know some friends in common?" She wandered off. I don't think she had read the signs beyond the letters that spelled her home.

Many who passed and looked at us seemed to change a little. They took in the pictures of Mickey, James, and Andy and the sign announcing WE ARE THE FREEDOM DELEGATES; some seemed moved, some looked around nervously, as though unsure whether the demonstrators could properly be acknowledged as members of a common race of human beings. Then the pauses—a man or a woman studying the crudely painted words AIN'T NO FREEDOM IN MISSISSIPPI. Eyes moving on: DEMOCRACY OR POLICE RULE? WHICH SIDE ARE YOU ON?—and faces reflecting the question, or frowning in the way of people who don't understand protest, much less what we were protesting, and as if the whole thing were vaguely unsavory, possibly dangerous.

Only a few were actively hostile, including some boys who kept trying to steal sticks from our pile of unused signs for their own demonstration. They said they were for Goldwater. There were others for the passersby to photograph. A Long Island group was taking a vociferous stand against zoning, taxation, the godless condition of their schools, Medicare, moon shots, foreign aid, or something else their signs failed to make quite clear. One morning a demonstration of Nazis was broken up by the crowd and its members arrested in a matter of minutes. There were gimmicks from horses to bagpipes, and a lonely man who sometimes wandered out of the mob with a sign saying BILL SOL ESTES FOR SECRETARY OF AGRICULTURE. The most natural enthusiasm was generated by The Best Party, composed of three young men and a girl, carrying signs reading MR. PRESIDENT! PICK MRS. YETTA BRONSTEIN FOR DEMOCRATIC V.P. SHE'S HONEST, SHREWD AND LIKEABLE. LBJ+YB=VICTORY. They shouted out their slogan a lot: "Vote for Yetta, and things will get betta."

During the brightly lit nights, delegates and visitors flocked around the police cordons outside Convention Hall, tired of trying to push through, and came to have a look at the vigil. The rows of demonstrators would re-form into a circle, and in the middle Mrs. Hamer would lead a song and the other delegates speak, while staff members conferred on policy—Stokely in his overalls huddled with Moses and Forman. Optimism continued—though "optimism" among Mississippi veterans is a quality so muted as to be barely discernible—that the Credentials Committee might still accept a plan proposed by Representative Edith Green of Oregon: to seat all Mississippians of both groups who would take an oath of loyalty to the national Democratic Party.

But pressures had been put on delegates, the rumors went, from the White House via Humphrey, whose nomination for the vice-presidency depended on a compromise solution which would not so

much satisfy both sides—since that was impossible—but perhaps dis-
satisfy them equally. Our support in the Credentials Committee was
whittled down, there was no minority report, and the final compromise was announced: to seat those regular Mississippi Democrats
who took the oath, and to give the FDP two seats at large, with a
vote each, for Aaron Henry and the Reverend Edwin King.

It was Tuesday afternoon. The lobbying stopped for a staff discussion in a Negro church like all the Negro churches in America
that become the movement's focal meeting places. Friendly delegates
from the Credentials Committee discussed the question of accept-
ance with the FDP people, and whether a minority report should
still be issued, as Representative Green had reserved the right to do,
while one movie and three network TV cameras, a dozen walkie-
talkies, and innumerable tape recorders awaited them in the late
afternoon shadows outside—the world press shoving and battering
at each other, trampling the lawn and knotting their cables around
each other's feet and equipment. Aaron Henry emerged with Bob
Moses to confront a series of microphones thrust through people's
legs, under arms, and over shoulders, and announce that the
delegates had unanimously rejected the proposal of the Credentials
Committee. The tune of a freedom song drifted out from the
church, where Henry and Moses returned; a group of staffers raced
across the lawn, off to resume the lobbying; and some little Negro
boys leaped up and down before the cameras, shouting, "Hey! Put
me on TV!"

The FDP's unanimity was in question. A few of the delegates felt
that the compromise was the most that could be expected, and Bob
Moses had actually raised his voice and interrupted their speeches,
declaring that there was no time to waste on discussing the compromise: they had all year to do that, and now must get the needed
signatures for the minority report. Nine of the eleven essential Credentials Committee members were present at the church, but with a
bare two hours to go before the deadline for the submission of the
report, another two names had still to be found.

The other two were not found. Several of us who had had a Mississippi summer sat among the chaos of a five-phoned hotel room,
from which we had tried to trace them. One man, exhausted,
slumped on a bed and said, "I've never had the really big ones
against me before." The Edith Green proposal was probably the

most we could have hoped for—by officially recognizing our delegates along with any Mississippi regulars who chose to join them,
more would have been achieved than a simple acknowledgment of
support within the Democratic Party; more than an assurance of the
Negro vote (certain anyway, with Goldwater the alternative); more
than a commitment to the party's stated principles: such a gesture
would have damaged irrevocably Mississippi's power structure as it
is presently constituted. This finally had proved an excessive measure for President Johnson and the party, whose concern apparently
was to keep the convention smooth and to hang on to what remained
of the solid South's doubtful solidity.

But the loss was not all ours. The Mississippi regulars, we later
heard, had also refused to accept the compromise. This implied that
they would no longer be able to ignore half their population, but
would have to come to some terms with the FDP, at least by 1968.
It was, in fact, the President's perfect solution: everyone was dissatisfied equally.

The vigil continued for two more days, though its focus was now
unclear and momentum dissipating as people began to leave at last
for home. In the middle of the next day I was discovered on the
boardwalk by a man I had met before in New York, and invited to a
party on a yacht. I left the line and dug out my slinky black dress
from the corner of the suitcase where it had spent the summer, and
followed him to the Atlantic City marina.

The *Blue Horizon II*, 118 feet long (the papers said the next day),
sat smugly, snugly moored at the end of several rows of lesser
yachts. A PA system was monotonously summoning one Mr. Cruik-
shank of the *Rosie Dawn* to the telephone. O. Roy Chalk, owner of
the *Horizon* and the Washington, D.C., transit system, met us at the
gangplank in a scarlet blazer. Behind him in the covered stern deck,
two or three dozen guests sat propped against leopard and zebra on
a built-in semicircular divan, or ranged around the carpeted space in
the middle saying things like "I had it done in Hong Kong for thirty-
five dollars. It's a copy of a Givenchy of course."

A man started speaking to me about a night club he had just built
in Palm Beach for three and a half million dollars and something
else he had also just built in Palm Beach for one and a half million
dollars. He drifted off somewhere, and while I gulped down cham-

pagne and hors d'oeuvres as though they were bread and water, the hostess told me and the mayoress of San Juan how hard it was to find parking places for the yacht in this country. "In Europe there's no problem. Every year we take her somewhere wonderful, and wherever else we go they always have facilities."

"How exciting," I said. "You cross the Atlantic in it?"

"Oh *no*," she said. "The crew takes her over."

Doña Felisa Rincón de Gautier, the mayoress, changed the subject to my mission in Atlantic City. "All my life I have been fighting for your cause," she said. "When I went to a hotel and they wouldn't let my Negro maid stay there, I moved to another hotel." There were no issues in Puerto Rico, she said: everyone is happy there. It would be wonderful if I could come down for a vacation from all my troubles. She would see to it that I had a lovely time.

I thanked her and moved on. A man wearing red, white, and blue trousers was explaining that he had had them made by President Kennedy's tailor, H. Harris of New York. A gleaming brocade woman approached and said she had just heard who I was, and she wanted me to know that "a perfectly divine freedom fighter gave me a lift to my hotel this morning when I couldn't get a cab." An alternate delegate from an unidentified state broke in: "You people are fine. You are really fine, fine human beings. It's just so moving to see you youngsters sitting out there."

"And all those *evil* people in Mississippi," added the brocade woman.

"We saw you there on the boardwalk the other night," the alternate said, "and I tell you the tears just came to my eyes. To think, those great, dedicated, *fine* young people, just sitting there in the hot sun all night long."

"Keep up the good work," said the woman.

At some point I began telling a couple of my admirers that SNCC's coffers had contained exactly six dollars the day I left Mississippi. One of them pressed a twenty-dollar bill into my hand; I didn't know how to explain that he had missed the point.

That night the vigil seemed to be victim to an itch. Its numbers swelled with inactive lobbyists and sympathizers from New York; friends and strangers, they wanted to demonstrate, to do something. Under the spotlights that shone on Convention Hall the white people looked green and the Negroes yellow. Mrs. Hamer spoke, then Aaron Henry, then Hartman Turnbow, and the crowd of spectators pressed in, heaving, as through the silence the vigil sang. The music grew huge, lost all restraint—the summer was over, the songs had to be sung with the most final volume and intensity. I sat with two friends from Greenwood, Bob Masters and George, while they bellowed out a summer's worth of frustration and tiredness, and at that moment their sense of what they were singing seemed almost to match that of the Negroes beside them. They were also tone-deaf, both of them—in Greenwood there had been enough voice to cover up. If that singing movement had room for the tone-deaf it had room for everyone.

"Freedom!" a shout rang out.

"Now!" a thousand voices answered.

The chant continued, and the crowd in one great crush rose and started forward. It moved for a moment, then stood still, a forest of signs thrust out as "Now!" they shouted, "Freedom!" *"Now!"* "Freedom!" "NOW!" and the spotlights blazed through bright as suns.

George and I found a bar television to see what was going on inside the hall. Twenty-three FDP delegates had occupied the empty seats of the regular Mississippi party—friendly delegates from other states had lent their badges, which Bob Moses was transporting in and out for more of our people to wear. Instructions had come from the White House to stop the sergeant-at-arms from attempting to dislodge them from their seats. Rita Schwerner, emotional and pale, was questioned by an interviewer outside. With Jim Forman, she was being prevented from entering the building. "The Democratic Party has endorsed murder in Mississippi," she said. No one else in the bar was particularly interested in this history via television. A pink old man came up and asked, "You got the sports news yet?" I shook my head. "Get the sports news," he said.

At the vigil again quite late we stood and sang "We Shall Overcome"—remembering all the impossible times, unlike any others, when we had sung it before. The only song that has no clapping, because the hands are holding all the other hands. A suspension from color, hate, recrimination, guilt, suffering—a kind of lesson in miniature of what it's all about. The song begins slowly and somehow without anticipation of these things: just a song, the last one, before we separate. You see the others, and the instant when it comes to each one to think what the words mean, when each nearly breaks, wondering: shall we overcome? The hands hold each other tighter. Mrs. Hamer is smiling, flinging out the words, and crying at once. "Black and white together," she leads the next verse, and a sort of joy begins to grow in every face; "We are not afraid"—and for just that second no one is afraid, because they are free.